ALSO BY ERICA WAGNER

*Chief Engineer: Washington Roebling, the Man Who Built
the Brooklyn Bridge*

First Light: A Celebration of Alan Garner (editor)

Seizure: A Novel

*Ariel's Gift: Ted Hughes, Sylvia Plath, and the Story of
"Birthday Letters"*

Gravity: Stories

MARY *and* MR. ELIOT

MARY *and* MR. ELIOT

———— *A Sort of Love Story* ————

MARY TREVELYAN
and ERICA WAGNER

FARRAR, STRAUS AND GIROUX

New York

Farrar, Straus and Giroux
120 Broadway, New York 10271

The Pope of Russell Square and additional material
copyright © 2022 by The Estate of Mary Trevelyan
Introduction, Editorial Commentary, Notes, and Compilation
copyright © 2022 by Erica Wagner
Quotations from the works and letters of T. S. Eliot
copyright © The Eliot Estate
All rights reserved
Printed in the United States of America
Originally published in 2022 by Faber & Faber Ltd, Great Britain
Published in the United States by Farrar, Straus and Giroux
First American edition, 2023

Photograph credits can be found on page 305.

Library of Congress Cataloging-in-Publication Data
Names: Trevelyan, Mary, 1897–1983, author. | Wagner, Erica, 1967– author.
Title: Mary and Mr. Eliot : a sort of love story / Mary Trevelyan and Erica Wagner.
Description: First American edition. | New York : Farrar, Straus and Giroux, 2023. |
    Includes bibliographical references and index.
Identifiers: LCCN 2022055045 | ISBN 9780374203184 (hardcover)
Subjects: LCSH: Eliot, T. S. (Thomas Stearns), 1888–1965—Friends and associates. |
    Trevelyan, Mary, 1897–1983. | LCGFT: Biographies. | Autobiographies.
Classification: LCC PS3509.L43 Z87236 2023 | DDC 821/.912 [B]—dc23/eng/20221130
LC record available at https://lccn.loc.gov/2022055045

Our books may be purchased in bulk for promotional, educational, or business use. Please
contact your local bookseller or the Macmillan Corporate and Premium Sales Department at
1-800-221-7945, extension 5442, or by email at MacmillanSpecialMarkets@macmillan.com.

www.fsgbooks.com
www.twitter.com/fsgbooks • www.facebook.com/fsgbooks

1 3 5 7 9 10 8 6 4 2

For Robin
with love

CONTENTS

Introduction 1

1938 15

1940 23

1941 26

1942 30

1943 40

1944 45

1945 57

1946 63

1947 70

1948 77

1949 87

1950 109

1951 124

1952 137

1953 153

CONTENTS

1954   174

1955   195

1956–1957   218

Postscript   246

Final Correspondence   255

Afterword   259

Abbreviations and Brief Bibliography   267

Notes   273

Acknowledgements   293

Index   295

MARY *and* MR. ELIOT

INTRODUCTION

One warm autumn evening in 1955 Mary Trevelyan met T. S. Eliot on the steps of Faber and Faber, the publishing house where Eliot worked as a director. By then the pair had been friends for seventeen years. He was the country's most famous literary figure – one of the most eminent literary figures in the world, having won the Nobel Prize seven years before. She was an energetic, passionate woman of fifty-eight, nine years younger than Eliot. She had devoted much of her life to the care of students who came to London from all over the world; her deepest wish was for her charges to feel safe and comfortable when they were far from home and for them to return to their native countries with only the very warmest feelings about Britain and the British. She was the kind of woman who knew she could make the world a better place, and whose clear thinking and vigour could shape the lives of those around her, even Nobel Prize-winning poets.

They climbed into her car. As a red September sun sank behind the cargo ships on the Thames, Mary and Tom went for a drive through London. Mary loved to drive and they cruised through the City, to the Tower and over Tower Bridge, Eliot quoting Shelley as they prowled about in by-ways – as Mary wrote in her extraordinary recollection of her two-decade-long friendship with the poet, a manuscript she called *The Pope of Russell Square*. Finally, in her account, they pulled up at a fine French restaurant where they ate and drank – and the head waiter bowed to Eliot and asked him to sign a copy of *Murder in the Cathedral*, which had been first performed in Canterbury Cathedral exactly twenty years before. The couple – and they must have looked like a couple – chatted happily, making plans for the arrival of Eliot's great-niece Priscilla in a few days' time.

'May I arrange your life for you?' Mary asked Eliot.

'That is exactly what I want you to do,' Eliot said, and the two went on to plot out Priscilla's visit. Eliot gave Mary a silver cigarette lighter. 'He feels very superior having given up smoking,' she recorded in recollection of that evening. It had been nearly two decades since their first meeting in 1936, when he had come to read, at her invitation, from his work at the Student Christian Movement (SCM) Conference in Swanwick, Derbyshire. That encounter was the foundation of their friendship.

Mary is one of four women who played a significant role in Eliot's life. The others are Vivien Haigh-Wood, his first wife; Emily Hale, a friend of his American youth with whom he had an enduring relationship which might have moved towards marriage; and Valerie Fletcher, his devoted secretary at Faber and Faber, many decades his junior, whom he married in 1957 and with whom he found great happiness at the end of his life. His relationship with Mary was a warm, strong bond for many years; it is not easy to categorise. But as it grew and strengthened, she came to believe it might lead to something more. This is a portrait of a romance as much as it is an account of a friendship.

And why should she not believe their relationship would develop into romance? Though they came from different worlds, they had much in common, the strongest link being their commitment to the Anglican faith. They were both from prominent families: Eliot's grandfather, William Greenleaf Eliot, had come to St Louis, Missouri – city of Eliot's birth – to found the Unitarian church there. Ralph Waldo Emerson called Greenleaf Eliot 'the Saint of the West'.

In an echo of his ancestor, T. S. Eliot too blended a religious zeal with practical qualities, especially in his work at Faber and Faber. There were links in his family to Noah Webster, Herman Melville, Nathaniel Hawthorne; he once told Mary: 'I know there are Eliots, non-Eliots and foreigners.' His father was a successful businessman, his mother Charlotte a poet herself; in 1926 her dramatic poem, *Savonarola*, was published with an introduction by her son. She was in some ways like Mary Trevelyan, a powerful figure whose power was often thwarted by the age in which she lived.

Mary also came from a distinguished family in which the ideals of faith and service ran strong. She had been born in 1897, the eldest of six children. (Eliot was the youngest of seven; and so they were at opposite ends of the sibling hierarchy in their respective families, a fact which may well have influenced the dynamic between them.) Her nephew, the biographer Humphrey Carpenter, wrote of the way in which his aunts – Mary and her three sisters – seemed to him to come from a different era:

> In their speech, though they had been born at the turn of the century, my aunts preserved the vowels of the 1880s or earlier. They never said 'girl' but 'gel', never 'cross' but 'crorse', and in the word 'golf' the 'l' was silent, so that the game was referred to as 'goff'. They belonged to a sublimely self-confident caste, an enclave of English society which has now entirely vanished, but which can be precisely defined – they were the daughters of a Victorian vicarage.

Throughout her life, Carpenter wrote, 'she retained the supreme social self-confidence of a child who is used to being given precedence over five strong-willed vociferous individuals'. Her confidence seemed expressed in her physique: her nephew wrote that she was 'not tall, but broadly built, with firm features dominated by the strong "Trevelyan" nose, which most members of the family possess'.

She was more than just the daughter of a Victorian vicarage: both of her grandfathers, her father and her brother-in-law were ordained in the Anglican church. Her brother Humphrey (later Baron Trevelyan) was a distinguished diplomat. She was second cousin to the historian George Macaulay Trevelyan, Master of Trinity College, Cambridge: his *History of England* (1926) was an important text in the interwar years. His long affiliation with both the National Trust and the Youth Hostel Association complemented the work which was to occupy Mary's life.

The Trevelyans were an influential family with a strong sense of their moral obligation to society. The historian A. L. Rowse noted that they were marked by 'integrity to the point of eccentricity, honesty to the point of rudeness, devoted public spirit, idiosyncrasy held in check by strong common sense; not much sense of humour. That distinguished family were apt to think there were Trevelyans – and then the rest of the human race.' It's a sentiment that reflects Eliot's own characterisation of his family. Mary's nephew Humphrey Carpenter's sketch of his youthful visits to her Chelsea flat shows both her energy and what one might call her forceful warmth. When a guest arrived on her threshold,

> The door would swing open, and there she was, generally with
> a cigarette in her mouth or hand, always with her opening
> sentence ready, so that one was immediately swept off on a tide
> of instructions: 'You're twenty minutes late, but it doesn't matter
> because it's only sausages, so I'm going to pour you a gin and tonic,
> and you will then play the piano to me while I go and cook the
> supper.'

He captured her perfectly: the feeling, her nephew wrote, was of being 'treated simultaneously as an adult and a very small boy'. Eliot, it is clear, received the same treatment.

Mary was not in Eliot's literary orbit – though she wrote all her life, and was an inveterate keeper of diaries. Music was her love: she was an excellent pianist and organist, and had studied conducting at the Royal College of Music under Sir Adrian Boult, the first conductor of Holst's *Planets*, and founding conductor of the BBC Symphony Orchestra. For a while she taught music at Radley College and Marlborough School, serving as a parish organist and a choir trainer at weekends. She would call herself an 'uneducated musician', but it remained a passion throughout her life; there was always a piano in her flat, and music played a significant role in her relationship with Eliot.

In the early 1930s, she had begun to venture abroad – journeys that would take her, as she wrote, to 'the ends of the earth'. She travelled to India and Ceylon – and, as so often happens, found that upon her return from these far-flung places she had a new vision of her native land. 'In London,' she would write,

I noticed groups of Indians on the streets looking lost in the wintry rain, snow and bitter winds. I had intended to return to the musical profession, but began to wonder if I might be able to do something to help these young men, since I had spent such a happy year in their country. One day I met a friend who offered me an appointment on the staff of Student Movement House – a centre for students of all countries. I accepted the offer for a trial period on both sides and, within a year, found myself appointed Warden. And this, though I did not know it at the time, was the beginning of the end as far as my own musical future was concerned. I have never regretted this change of direction.

Even this brief passage gives a sense of what a remarkable woman Mary Trevelyan was. Her character is wonderfully encapsulated by a story she tells of her adventures during the Second World War, published in 1946 as *I'll Walk Beside You*. On the last day of September 1944, Mary set off to Europe as part of a convoy of vehicles organised by the YMCA. The conflict was drawing to a close at last. Three and a half months earlier the Allies had landed in Normandy, and victory was now within reach. And so, as Mary wrote, a parade of twenty-two vehicles drove away from Great Russell Street in London, destined for Brussels – which had only just been liberated from the Nazis. Over the next six months the organisation would provide respite for front-line troops: by May 1945 nearly 50,000 had passed through the YMCA hostel – a requisitioned luxury hotel – on forty-eight-hour leave.

It was 9 a.m. when the convoy began to rumble through London's streets, still strewn with the rubble of the Blitz. There were, Mary wrote, 'mobile canteen trucks, stores vans, and one private car, a Ford V8, which I had the good fortune to drive. This car was the only vehicle able to put up a reasonable speed, and I was placed at the tail-end of the party so that, should accidents occur, I could immediately pass the convoy and inform the leader.' There were, in fact, three accidents as the train of vehicles lumbered through southern England – which, Mary confessed, she rather welcomed, 'as I found it rather tedious driving a high-powered car at fourteen miles an hour for a long distance and thoroughly enjoyed any opportunity of passing our convoy at forty miles an hour to catch up to the leader'.

She was herself a powerful engine: her greatest energies were directed towards her work with students from all over the world. She was able to make the connection between what she had seen in distant lands and what help she could bring to those closer to home. She worked hard to make that connection manifest. It was in 1932 that she became Warden of the SCM's Student Movement House, a hostel serving London University and based in Russell Square – yards from T. S. Eliot's office at Faber and Faber.

The SCM had its origins in missionary organisations founded at the end of the nineteenth century. In the twentieth century, SCM became a strong proponent of ecumenism, the belief in the global unity of all Christians, no matter what their denomination, nationality or race – an open-mindedness that was evident in Mary's work and her travels around the world on the organisation's behalf. Mary did cultivate the bonds of her own family, remaining devoted to her mother: Eliot was always punctilious in sending along his regards to her when he and Mary corresponded. She was not married.

When she took on the role with SCM, she found surrogate children through her work, and her care for them became a passion; it was a truly global family. As Humphrey Carpenter wrote, 'It became evident that her "family" was going to be this collection of rather lost young men and women, many of them from Africa, India and the Far East.'

She threw herself into the work, and she was willing to go to great lengths to understand the young people who landed on her doorstep. *From the Ends of the Earth*, published in 1942, is her remarkable account of a six-month journey undertaken in 1937 to the furthest reaches of the globe: Ceylon (as it was then), India, Burma, Hong Kong, Singapore, China and Japan, as well as the United States and Canada. The slim volume reveals a woman both passionately curious and absolutely fearless: she flew to Beijing – only the second flight she had ever made – on a tiny plane which 'appeared to be tied together with string'.

Her invitation to Eliot was part of her mission to make foreign students feel part of English cultural life. The students with whom she interacted truly came from all over the world: from the Gold Coast and from Nigeria; there were Germans, Scandinavians, Tamils from the south of India, men from Punjab and the North-West Frontier; there were Persians and Lithuanians. In her early days as Warden, Student Movement House was located at 32 Russell Square, one of the last remaining grand houses on the square. (The offices of Faber and Faber were at number 24, where the company would remain until 1971.) Although it was clear the house had seen better days, there were still white marble Adam fireplaces, a grand staircase, floor-to-ceiling mirrors. Characteristically Mary wrote that she liked to think that the house

was glad to give the last twenty years of its life to young people from all over the world . . . tramping up and down the beautiful staircase, crowding into the stately and spacious rooms, talking and smoking incessantly, making friends, laughing, playing, happy and unhappy, leaving at last for their homes in far-off countries with many memories and friendships which would last a lifetime.

A student membership cost twenty-six shillings a year – but many students, and especially refugees, would only pay what they could afford. That was one mark of Mary's care for her charges; by the standards of her day she had no regard for race or creed. Students of colour 'knew that here they need have no fear of the doors being closed to them, here they would be treated as ordinary members of society and would be accepted on exactly the same terms as anyone else'. Mary would write of her disgust at the racism often shown in England, noting when people got up on buses or trains so as not to sit by people of colour; she was aware that hotels, dance halls and restaurants, time and again, would not admit a man – or woman – of colour. 'Why? Just because he has been born under a tropical sun? What is there that is disgraceful in having a coloured skin?'

This forthrightness marked the very beginning of her friendship with Eliot (whose name, incidentally, she misspelled the very first time she wrote to him: 'Dear Mr Elliott'). Who would dare to mock T. S. Eliot upon first making his acquaintance? Mary would – as the opening of her manuscript shows with delightful plainness. *The Pope of Russell Square* is an account of an alliance that offers extraordinary and unusual insight into one of the greatest figures of the twentieth century. It is an account which, although it has been seen by scholars and biographers, has never been fully revealed until now. It is an astonishing document.

Her account of their friendship was assembled from their correspondence and from her diary. She put it together in the months after they ceased to meet, and the manuscript which forms the basis of this book is divided into halves. The first half, from 1938 to 1948, is composed of 'mainly letters', as she herself writes: exchanges back and forth between Mary and her new friend, the famous poet, as they grow closer. The second half, from 1949 onwards, is a diary account of their comings and goings over the next seven years, with Tom's experiences – always – in the foreground. It is a kind of mythologising of her relationship with Eliot: for any written account, any construction, must fictionalise a relationship. The reader gets Mary's version, not Tom's. I make an argument for her as a reliable witness, certainly as far as taking down her friend's opinions of his friends, enemies and world events is concerned. But hiding within her seeming objectivity is a story she kept secret, perhaps even from herself.

As for its somewhat awkward title, she doesn't claim credit. 'The Pope of Russell Square' was, she wrote, 'simply a phrase that, at one time, caught on in the literary world – indicating a certain restlessness among lesser lights. I think it was particularly prevalent about the time of the publication of *Notes Towards the Definition of Culture*.' Eliot's *Notes* appeared in book form in 1948, just the midpoint of their friendship: and around the time too when Mary's manuscript shifts from letter to journal form.

She preserved 170 of Eliot's letters, most of them written between 1944 and 1954. In the later years of their friendship they met so frequently, she noted, and telephoned so often, that letter writing was not necessary. Her wish to record their later meetings as a journal, she tells her imagined reader, had a two-fold purpose:

> I decided to write a diary of our many meetings; of his talk on many topics, of our church-going, concerts and theatres, of our many dinners and many evenings in my flat. I set myself this task because I have an unreliable memory and it seemed a waste to have so close a friendship with (as many would say) our greatest living poet and not to record some of his conversation.

Yet there is more to it than that. Mary directs all the powerful force of her vigour and attention towards Eliot. He is never not 'the Poet' –

she is given to capitalising that word – but he is too, as she perceives it, her intimate friend, and one in need of her protection and
care. Just as her charges at Student Movement House were like lost
sheep to be brought into a comforting fold, so was Tom Eliot. She
was the practical partner in their relationship, the fixer, the arranger.
He complained unceasingly about his health; she was – even when
she was actually ill – almost startlingly robust. But the force of her
gaze has in it also the intensity of the lover. As time goes on, no
detail – of his dress, his bearing, his behaviour – is too small for her
to notice. They had been drawn together by their shared interests:
their churchgoing, their love of music, their taste for good food and
a good glass of something strong. Mary imagined something more
than friendship in their future. The manuscript she left behind is, in
a very real sense, a romance.

She guarded the manuscript closely. It now resides in the Bodleian
Library at Oxford, and leafing through its pages one gets a powerful
sense of Mary's presence, for it is much more than a typescript. It
is a scrapbook as much as a collection of letters and a journal, with
postcards and photographs pasted in. Here is a windblown Eliot in
a soft windcheater, caught in a candid picture taken in front of the
Tennyson Memorial on the Isle of Wight. On 6 March 1950, Eliot
appeared on the cover of *Time* magazine ('T. S. Eliot: No middle
way out of the waste land?'): she carefully pasted the cover and its
accompanying article into her book.

The existence of *The Pope of Russell Square* has never been a secret;
Mary prepared it in hopes of publication and, towards the end of her
active life, showed it to her nephew Humphrey – or rather, allowed
him to 'glance at it', as he wrote; he was not impressed. 'It seemed
to me to consist chiefly of gossip about Church of England matters,
retailed in amusing but rather lightweight letters from Eliot himself.' But it was those letters that stood in the way of publication:
Eliot's widow, Valerie, was preparing her late husband's correspondence for publication in an official edition and did not wish for any

of the letters to appear outside of those volumes. Her nephew wrote that Mary 'felt this to be quite unfair; could not, indeed, easily be persuaded that the poet's widow had a legal, let alone moral, right to the copyright'. It was then that Carpenter understood that there might be something more to the manuscript: 'I began to glimpse the strength of feeling which lay beneath Mary's apparently light-weight, gossipy friendship with Eliot.'

At some point in the 1970s, when Mary had moved into a nurs-ing home, Carpenter was dispatched by one of his uncles to collect some piece of furniture from her flat in Chelsea, then being cleared out. It was not a task he was looking forward to; 'I went there in rather a bad temper,' he writes, and was dismayed to see 'a jumble of papers on the floor'. But he could not resist leafing through the pile, despite his ill temper, and found a version of Mary's manuscript very different from the one he had been shown. 'To the best of my belief many people – certainly my family and near friends – have often speculated on the real relationship between T. S. Eliot and myself in the course of our twenty years' friendship,' he read. 'Now, eighteen months after he has married again, I have tried to write what I can about the man I have known and loved for so many years, before time blurs the picture.'

As Eliot's biographer Lyndall Gordon has observed, '*The Pope of Russell Square* is the fullest record we shall have of what it was like to be Eliot's companion during his most invisible years of fame.' But until now that companion has never been given her full due. When Humphrey Carpenter saw the full text of his aunt's manuscript, he realised that what he had been shown in her lifetime was 'a severely bowdlerised text'; here, he understood, was 'the full story'.

My aim, in this book, is to reveal that story: the narrative of this friendship, the strength of this friendship, Mary's hopes for it. I wish to let Mary speak for herself, so that readers may come to know her as I have done in the course of preparing this book. I have worked with Mary's manuscript to show the closeness – as Mary perceived it – that existed between these two remarkable, forceful people, the dynamic between them. This is not a biography of Mary nor one of T. S. Eliot, though of course I have hoped to provide the context of their lives and of the events taking place in the world around them.

My commentary frames and centres Mary's account. For clarity's sake I have corrected Mary's erroneous spellings, when they occur, and dated letters instead of giving manuscript pages as references. Mary's account – quoted from her manuscript of *The Pope of Russell Square* – is rendered in regular type, while my contextual commentary on the events and meetings she describes are rendered in italic type. (There are occasional deviations from this rule for the sake of smooth transitions.) I have kept my focus tight: on Mary Trevelyan's experience of her friend, and her observations of him. But there was much about his life of which she was not aware. While the reader's experience will not completely mirror Mary's, the sense I wish to give is that of seeing Eliot through Mary's eyes. I refer to her throughout as 'Mary', and to Eliot by his surname. This seems to me to reflect the enduring formality of their relationship, even if that was a formality of which she herself was not entirely aware.

It is a truism, in the twenty-first century, to say that Eliot's legacy is complex. As Lyndall Gordon has written, he was at one time considered to be 'the moral spokesman of the twentieth century'. She noted, however, that 'as that century now recedes from view the question is rising whether the huge power of his voice to engage our souls can sustain sympathy for a man who was stranger and more intolerant than his disarming masks would have us believe'. That strangeness and intolerance pervades Mary's manuscript. One of the fascinations of reading it is the way in which those qualities are far more apparent to the reader than they were to the writer, who was, to a great extent, blinded by her own regard and affection. Eliot, perhaps, doesn't come out of it very well. But greatness and what is considered virtue – or at least good behaviour – do not necessarily go hand in hand.

In the years of his friendship with Mary – years in which she often arranged his life, and had intimate knowledge of that life – Eliot's was a cultural voice unparalleled in the Western canon of literature; he transformed the nature and form of that literature, and his influence is enduring and profound. Mary's direct voice has been largely unheard: she offers a clear portrait of a hitherto unseen T. S. Eliot. She wanted you to hear her story. Here it is.

Mary Trevelyan, portrait by Elliot & Fry, 1930s, held in
the National Portrait Gallery, London.

1938

T. S. Eliot was all the rage in the student world. Young men in corduroy trousers, floppy ties and long hair carried his poetry about with them and looked intense. In July of this year he was invited to give a Poetry Reading at a Student Christian Movement Conference at Swanwick, in Derbyshire. I had lately been travelling round the world and had therefore missed the tremendous excitement created by *Murder in the Cathedral*. The long run had just finished when I returned and I did not see it myself until 1947.

She begins her account of this transformative friendship with character-istic modesty. But it is worth describing something of Mary Trevelyan's travels in the years just before she met Eliot, for it gives a sense of her passion, her ambition – and her dauntless character. She had three aims for this round-the-world trip, she would write: to discover how Indian students had fared after returning to their home continent from London; to go to China and Japan to visit students she had come to know; but also to come to a greater understanding of their cultural, familial and edu-cational background, so as better to assist students from those countries when they arrived in Britain. She planned also to go to the United States, and study international student work there.

And so she left for Ceylon, on 1 December 1936, sailing aboard a Japanese ship, the Hakusan Maru. *While on board she heard the news of the abdication of Edward VIII. She felt 'as if the whole British Empire was crumbling', she wrote. For nearly four months she travelled all across Ceylon, then from Madras to Bombay and on to Karachi before flying to Delhi. Flying was still a novel form of transport, and it was Mary's first flight: the pilot invited her to come to the cockpit. To get there she had to crawl through a narrow passage full of luggage, on all fours, but 'once* there it was marvellous, though the noise was absolutely deafening and no conversation was possible between the pilot and myself'. From Delhi she went on to Lahore, Peshawar and finally to Calcutta. It had been five years since her last visit: she noted now 'a new confidence' in Indians; she remarked that 'even now the behaviour of some English people towards Indians is quite deplorable'.

At the end of March 1937 she left India for Burma, Penang and Singapore. Wherever she was, she pitched herself into the life of the place: she wrote of going to see a film at midnight in Rangoon – 'the "stalls" had no seats, so the audience squatted, closely packed, on the sandy floor'. She took another flight to China ('a completely new country to me', she wrote with energetic delight): this time in a plane which 'appeared to be tied together with string and only the force of the wind kept the door at my side closed'. She then departed for Japan, despite some misgivings – having spent a month in China, she was aware of the rising tensions between the two nations. Not long after she left for home the Sino-Japanese war broke out, provoked by Japanese territorial expansion into mainland China. Yet Mary remained open-minded about Japan: 'I could not fail to be charmed by the country and by the courtesy and hospitality of my Japanese friends.'

She travelled on a liner to San Francisco – her first trip to America – to see the International Houses for students built by John D. Rockefeller, in New York, Chicago and Berkeley. These were residential houses, far grander than anything Mary could offer her students in Bloomsbury, but she regarded these American efforts with a gimlet eye, thinking their grandeur was all on the surface: 'True international friendship does not gloss over difficulties and differences, but makes opportunities for discussion together.' She saw what she called too much 'vague sentiment' of goodwill.

In her six weeks in the United States she took in a great number of its famous sites: Hollywood, the Grand Canyon, the Rockies, Niagara Falls. She was also very much interested in what she called a 'particular problem' about which she was anxious to learn: that of the 'American Negro'. She *met Elmer Carter, editor of* Opportunity: Journal of Negro Life; *the magazine published writers such as Zora Neale Hurston and Langston Hughes and was a cornerstone of the Harlem Renaissance. Carter was a significant figure in the civil rights movement: Mary called him 'a man of great wisdom and balance'. 'He was emphatic that a vague enthusiasm for the Negro cause was no help, they wanted recognition and the rights of an American citizen.' She met with Bill Robinson, the famous tap-dancer; after strolling through Harlem, she was taken out to supper by Carter. She was the only white person in the restaurant and the other patrons stared at her. 'I thought of the many coloured students whom I had entertained in restaurants in London, when they, doubtless, shared my feelings.' After dinner they went to the Savoy Ballroom, where they listened to 'the hottest jazz'; it was midnight before she could tear herself away.*

This brief account of her trip gives a glimpse of the nature of her life, her boldness, her sense of adventure, the way in which she was open to experience, to cultures different from her own. She sailed back to England on 14 July 1937 as Europe was moving closer to war. Mary's concerns, upon her return, were more immediate: the lease of the house on Russell Square was due to expire and Student Movement House required a new home. Mary spearheaded an effort to raise funds to buy the freehold of 103 Gower Street, 'a very tall, thin house about one hundred years old, with a large studio built out behind it, all ready for conversion into the main clubroom'. That she managed this feat in increasingly anxious political circumstances is another testament to her vigour – but also to her vision. She saw that raising funds for Student Movement House could have a significance beyond her own individual aims: 'I suddenly realised that now, if ever, was the time to save the House. Now, if ever, the British Public might realise that we were talking sense; now, if ever they would be ready to put money into international friendship.' On 12 March 1938, German forces marched into Austria; in September, the British Prime Minister Neville Chamberlain met with Adolf Hitler to reach an agreement setting out a timetable and terms for the Nazi takeover of the German-speaking areas of Czechoslovakia, the Sudetenland. Mary

Students from India relax at Student Movement House.

*called this time 'the most difficult period I have ever known in the House,
not excepting the outbreak of war a year later'. At news of the Munich
Agreement the students were 'numb and speechless'.*

*As Mary saw it, the presence of T. S. Eliot in the midst of this was
an important distraction for her charges. It is difficult to overstate the
importance of his cultural cachet at the time, particularly for young people
– as Mary noted. E. M. Forster had written a decade before: 'Mr Eliot's
work, particularly "The Waste Land", has made a profound impression on
them, and given them precisely the food they needed. And by "the young"
I mean those men and women between the ages of eighteen and thirty
whose opinions one most respects, and whose reactions one most admires.
He is the most important author of their day.'*

*There could be little arguing with that sentiment. Eliot had begun his
working life as a schoolteacher, before joining Lloyd's Bank in 1917. He
spent eight years working there, beginning in the Colonial & Foreign*

Department – and his dress and manner could still reflect his former profession. But by the time he met Mary he was firmly established in the literary firmament. Eliot's seminal poem 'The Love Song of J. Alfred Prufrock' had been published nearly a quarter of a century earlier, in 1915; 'The Waste Land' appeared in 1922; that same year the influential quarterly magazine The Criterion was launched, with Eliot at the editorial helm, establishing him as both artist and critic. 'The Hollow Men' (1925) and 'Ash Wednesday' (1930) followed, cementing his stature at the centre of English-language literature. When Mary and Eliot first became acquainted, his play Murder in the Cathedral had been a sensation, despite what might have seemed unlikely or even unpromising beginnings. In the summer of 1934 Eliot had been invited by George Bell, the Bishop of Chichester, to write a religious drama to be staged in the Chapter House of Canterbury Cathedral. Eliot took as his subject the assassination of Thomas Becket, Archbishop of Canterbury under Henry II, murdered in 1170 after falling out with the king. The first performance took place on 15 June 1935, with the Roman Catholic actor Robert Speaight as Becket. Conrad Aiken wrote in the New Yorker that 'One's feeling was that here at last was the English language literally being used, itself becoming the stuff of drama, turning alive with its own natural poetry.' The play opened in London in November 1935; it was televised for the BBC in December 1936 and toured around Britain before crossing the Atlantic to Boston and New York.

But Mary's concerns were practical, not literary, and as her friendship with Eliot began, so it would continue. One of the most striking features of the way she writes about him, and the way that she perceives him, is that she is unfazed by his fame. She is outside his circle of literary admirers and is plain-spoken in her account.

His visit to the conference seemed to worry the organisers. He had a reputation for being remote and quite incomprehensible. My business there was to direct the music. Perhaps it was thought that I was freer than those who were organising lectures and discussion, and

perhaps because I was considered tough, at any rate I was detailed
to look after the Great Man. I soon discovered that this was quite an
undertaking. My first impression of my charge was that he looked
cold and miserable and as though he wished he hadn't come. I have
no doubt that I was right. It transpired that he had a cold in the
head and a stiff neck, which was very painful. But he was kind to
me and, I thought, sympathised with me in my difficult task and did
his best to help. He read 'The Waste Land' and 'The Hollow Men'
I remember, with his head on one side, a harsh voice and a face of
acute agony. As soon as he decently could, he disappeared to bed
and looked much brighter in the morning as he climbed into a taxi
and went off to catch his train back to London.

I well remember that first visit. He came with a lady who I took
to be (but wasn't) his wife. The students came in crowds to listen
to him and hero-worshipped him to their hearts' content. After
the Reading I asked a selected few to meet him. This was not an
unqualified success. The students were nervous and gauche. The Poet
looked terrified. Perhaps this was the only occasion on which I was
really thankful to see him go.

At the end of the conference it was the custom to produce a top-
ical entertainment. With the help of a friend I put on a parody of
'The Hollow Men', read by a natural mimic from the University
of Cambridge – harsh voice, stiff neck and all. Having suspected
T.S.E. of a sense of humour I boldly sent him a copy of the parody
and received in reply a kindly and amused letter of which I was
extremely proud.

Her parody begins a pattern of teasing:

> Here is Lady Proctor, the lady of the Week,
> The Lady of kind welcomes.
> Here is the man with Gumboots, and here is the Bugle,
> And here is the famous Poet, and this card,

Which is blank, is the stiffness which he carries
In his neck, which I am forbidden to see . . .

While her description of Eliot recalls one of Virginia Woolf's early impressions – 'Pale, marmoreal Eliot . . . like a chapped office boy on a high stool with a cold in his head' – it is too a no-nonsense account which calls to mind Humphrey Carpenter's sense of being treated, in her company, as both an adult and a very small boy.

This recounting holds in its shadows so much that would separate Mary from Tom Eliot. There was a great deal she did not know about him, and much that would be concealed as their friendship grew, though she would not perceive that concealment.

It was in this month of this year that Eliot's wife, Vivien, was found wandering the streets in Marylebone, talking 'in a very confused and unintelligible manner', as her brother Maurice wrote to Eliot; Eliot had left her five years before. By the following month she had been committed to Northumberland House, a private asylum in North London.

Nor did Mary know anything about the woman who she took to be Eliot's wife: that was, most likely, Emily Hale. Eliot and Emily Hale had met around 1912 at the Cambridge, Massachusetts house of his mother's sister; they were performing amateur dramatics devised by Eliot's younger cousin Eleanor Hinkley. Hinkley adapted scenes from novels, including Jane Austen's Emma; *in one of these her friend Emily played the snobbish Mrs Elton, and Eliot played Mr Woodhouse. Emily, three years younger than Eliot, had grown up in Boston. Her father was a Unitarian minister; an infant brother died when she was young, resulting in her mother's mental breakdown. She attended Miss Porter's School in Connecticut, founded in 1843 by Sarah Porter, who intended, as the school's website says today, to create 'an intentional community for young women to gain greater agency in their lives'. She would go on to teach speech and drama, and to become a dramatic figure in Eliot's life, an embodiment of the idea of romantic attraction but not its realisation. As Lyndall Gordon has written, Emily's 'attachment to [Eliot] – he was undoubtedly the love of her life – suggests the possibility of stronger feeling than he perhaps perceived'.*

Throughout the course of what Mary imagined to be her intimate friendship with Eliot, his connection to Emily Hale would remain almost completely hidden from Mary – though perhaps what looks like subterfuge to a twenty-first-century eye was, to Eliot, a kind of efficient separation. But in this first encounter the reader can see what Mary did not: and indeed, never could.

1940

The war came, and Mary did not see Eliot again until 1940. In early April 1939 Student Movement House departed Russell Square for Gower Street. War was declared on 3 September, and a few days later Mary would write that they had to close the restaurant in the house. There was a snack bar 'in the one room we can light properly. We all crowd in, eat, play shove ha'penny and chess unendingly and listen to the daily horrors from Poland.'

Eliot had been writing another play, The Family Reunion, *at the end of 1938; it opened at the Westminster Theatre in March 1939. In January 1939 the last edition of the* Criterion *appeared. In October 1939* Old Possum's Book of Practical Cats *was published by Faber and Faber, its cover drawn by Eliot himself. In February came '*The Waste Land' *and* Other Poems; *the second of* Four Quartets, *'East Coker', was published in March in the* New English Weekly. *Two reprints were made; Faber and Faber published the poem as a pamphlet in September and it sold nearly 12,000 copies.*

Throughout the Blitz, which started in the second week in September, we had a difficult time with the students, particularly the refugees. Tom was fire-watching (and writing 'Little Gidding') three nights a week in London. On one occasion, when the nervous strain was affecting the students to a despairing extent, I asked him to come and do an extra Reading. He saved the situation – calming the students simply by reading quietly, almost monotonously, to them. It was a memorable occasion. Only later did I learn that he had been on duty fire-watching both the night before and the night after the Reading, so it was a real act of heroism.

On 7 September, 'Black Saturday', German bombers attacked London, the first of fifty-seven nights of consecutive bombing. Eliot had signed on as an air-raid warden in Kensington, staying up two nights a week, looking out for fires caused by the attacks: exhausting work which found echo in the 'interminable night' of 'Little Gidding', the final section of Four Quartets, which would be published in 1942.

Mary kept close and anxious watch over the young people in her care, young people far from home. 'For the first time in its history, we had to give up keeping the House open until ten-thirty p.m. and took to closing down half an hour before black-out, for the shrapnel was too heavy to allow students to return to their lodgings in safety and our air-raid shelter was far too small for our numbers.' In late September, the Indian Students' Union, the House's opposite neighbour, took a direct hit, causing much damage to the House. 'We were windowless, doorless, ceiling-less, gas-less, and even water-less for long periods,' Mary wrote. She wondered if the House should be closed down, but felt it played too vital a role for the students still there. Her private war diaries, kept in 1940 and 1941, show her brisk attitude of realistic stoicism. 'A perfectly hellish night,' she wrote on 4 October 1940, 'with four high explosive bombs dropped within 150 feet of us at 10.30 pm. Rather to my surprise, however, I slept reasonably well.' Six days later she noted 'an awful day – traffic in rain hellish. A bomb on St Paul's which destroyed the High Altar – but no casualties. The Headmaster of Wellington killed walking out of his house!'

She was well aware, too, that some of her charges faced an uncertain fate. In June 1940 she had organised a recital by Peter Stadlen, an eminent Austrian pianist who had emigrated to Britain following the Nazi takeover of his homeland. He would shortly thereafter be interned in Britain and sent to Australia until 1942; Austrian and German members of SCM faced the same fate. 'At the end of June we had Pre-Internment Dance at which every potential internee was greeted, as he entered the room, with shouts of "still here?"' This treatment caused 'infinite distress to many of our firmest friends, whose one thought had been how they could help Britain to defeat Germany'.

Students from Abyssinia, India, France and Russia play chess at SMH.

Student Movement House produced their nativity play – an annual feature – as the year drew to a close. There was always 'a most unorthodox cast, of Christians and non-Christians, [playing] to a very large audience, the majority of whom were not Christian themselves. This year it was a particularly moving occasion and was surely one of the most remarkable presentations of the Christmas story given in this saddest Christmas since Christ was born.' The performers came from many different nations: 'All over the world, in Germany, Japan, China, Africa, India, Italy, are young men and women who have taken part in this play in former years, and some of them at least will have remembered the Watchman's cry, "God keep our land from hostile hand and fire and brand," and the message of Gabriel, "The Child that is born to set men free!"'

Mary invited a special guest this year; he was able to take the time from his work, and his fire-watching duties, to attend.

1941

I began to see him oftener. He came to the students' Nativity Play –
an adaptation of the York, Wakefield and Coventry plays – and was
so pleased with it that he came every year until I left in 1946. After
his first visit he asked if I would lunch with him one day in the New
Year and then (characteristically) disappeared for three months.
But he reappeared and the lunch took place at Viani's in Charlotte
Street. He asked me to choose a restaurant and I found myself in a
quandary, as I didn't know if he was well off or poor. It was a long
and fascinating lunch. As we walked back in the spring sunshine I
teased him a little and asked him what he was like as a little boy. He
embarked immediately on a lengthy story which started: 'Born on
the Mississippi . . .' And I was both amused and flattered at having
my hand held for an unusually long time on parting.

*Intimations of the course of their friendship appear in this passage: the
choice of a restaurant; the way she notes what she believes to be an offer
of intimacy; his characteristic disappearance following their meeting; her
teasing of him; her questioning personal rather than literary. Though she
had noted that he had been at work on 'Little Gidding', for the most part
she would not remark in detail on his writing.*

*What began to draw them together was their commitment to the
Christian faith. Peter Ackroyd has written of Eliot's 'new Christian activism' around this time; in 1936 he had been a member of the Archbishop's
committee preparing for a conference to be held at Oxford on Church,
community and service: there he read a paper on 'The Ecumenical Nature
of the Church and Its Responsibility Towards the World'. He attended
meetings at Lambeth Palace in early 1938 to consider the formation of a
British section of the World Council of Churches; later that year he took*

part in a meeting of the Council on the Christian Faith and the Common Life.

This engagement took place at a time when participation in traditional Christian life was beginning to decline. The terrible cost, both human and material, of the First World War had presented an enormous challenge to personal faith, and while the Second World War would not see a significant decline in church attendance (as far as figures are reliably available), there was certainly no increase, and church attendance would continue to fall from this time forward. Mary and Eliot were brought together by what might be seen as an embattled faith.

Mary, meanwhile, sought distraction during the Blitz by writing From the Ends of the Earth, *an account of her experiences and her travels as Warden of the Student Movement House. She submitted it to Eliot at Faber and Faber, and he was sympathetic when she expressed anxiety over its possible publication. It wasn't only his decision, he wrote to her on 23 August: 'You must just compare it to waiting in a queue for a lemon and an onion.' In a memo in the archives of Faber and Faber dated 1 August, he described Mary as 'an extremely nice woman'; he said of Student Movement House that 'it is an extremely useful benevolent institution and Miss Trevelyan runs it very well'. That said, in the memo he described the manuscript – then called* Strangers and Sojourners *– as 'rather scrappy'; while he said that her account of her students and their difficulties was 'extraordinarily interesting' he still doubted 'whether the book has enough structure to justify its publication'. He admitted he might be wrong on that front: 'It is easy reading for anybody.' His doubts were overruled: the book would be published in 1942.*

She saw his taking her hand in the spring sunshine after a pleasant lunch as a signal of possibility. She began to turn to him for counsel: in the autumn she became part of the team of a BBC radio programme called 'The Anvil', described in the Radio Times *as 'Christians meet to answer listeners' questions'. He wrote to her with his thoughts on the weekly questions; she preserved these in her manuscript. He offered*

his reflections, for instance, on 'National and International Culture'.
Prospects for culture, he opined in November, were not good. While his
dismissal of internationalism reads uncomfortably today, his analysis
shows the danger of binary systems, a danger that has not disappeared,
to say the least. Politically, he wrote, there is a tendency to sympa-
thise with either nationalism or internationalism, but both are bad
for culture. The one is too narrow; the other is not rooted in anything.
Internationalism tends to 'sterilise culture' by disconnecting it from the
local, and by its recognition as class rather than race as a marker for
division. There could be no culture, he wrote, without 'a culture'. He
questioned the pressure for writers to make their work accessible to the
maximum number of readers. His musings, however, never made it
onto the air – Mary clearly didn't think they would sound convincing
when spoken by her.

Unfortunately (or perhaps fortunately, for I could hardly get away
with these remarks on my own) although we saw the questions
beforehand we were never allowed to bring any notes to the broadcasts and even when I thought I had mastered Tom's comments, I
never managed to memorise them well enough to be of any use in
front of a microphone.

Eliot's fame continued to grow. He wrote to Martin Browne – who
had directed that first production of Murder in the Cathedral *and*
with whom he would continue to collaborate – that public activity
was a 'drug'. 'Burnt Norton', the first of Four Quartets, *had originally*
appeared in a collection of Eliot's early poems published in 1936; Faber
and Faber produced a separate edition in February 1941; a week later
'The Dry Salvages' was published in the New English Weekly. *The*
Times Literary Supplement *remarked on its quality of 'bleak resig-*
nation'. But on a lighter note – as Mary remarked – that autumn he
gave her a copy of Old Possum's Book of Practical Cats, *inscribed to*

her, and with a limerick on the title page, to boot. 'Miss Mary Trevelyan / Is like Godfrey of Bouillion. / For his name means pottage */ And her name means* cottage . . .' *(Her Cornish family name derives from 'trev', a homestead.) It was the beginning of an exchange of gifts that would go back and forth between them for the next fifteen years.*

1942

In the autumn of this year 'Little Gidding' saw the completion of some of the last – and perhaps the greatest – poetry Tom was to write (not including two plays) in the time that I knew him.

The year opened for me with a curious affair of X. Tom came to see me and asked if I would 'take on' a young gentleman for him and see what I could do with the problem. He was a wild poet from the East with a passion for T.S.E. He had married an English girl, they were very unhappy and he drank a great deal. One evening, after I had accepted the charge, he set fire to his clothes, because they had been pressed and cleaned by his wife. On another occasion, at 11 p.m., the near-by hospital telephoned that one of my flock was in Casualty, having run into a lamp-post under the impression that it was his wife. I collected the patient and took him back in a taxi to his very sordid Kensington lodging. There was a brilliant moon and a considerable possibility of air-raids. He lay back in the taxi, his feet on the opposite seat, reciting yards of 'The Waste Land'. After some weeks of struggle I telephoned Tom, to report. I could not resist telling him of a particular episode. The young poet lay back in my office chair, his eyes closed, remarking: 'I had a fantasy last night. I dreamed that you were my mother and Mr Eliot was my father.' A dry chuckle from Tom at this: 'I really think we might have done better than that!'

The whole affair was the beginning of more frequent meetings, for meals, conversations in my office, long telephone calls and Christian names. Tom would ring up and talk, sometimes for half an hour. I remember, in the course of one of these talks, he said: 'Stop me if I am becoming garrulous'. The same afternoon, at an Anvil lunch, Dr Welch (then Director of Religious Broadcasting) asked me: 'Do you know T. S. Eliot? Does he ever speak? He seems such a silent person.'

The 'curious affair of X' concerned Meary James Thurairajah Tambimuttu, a Tamil poet from Ceylon (now Sri Lanka) who had arrived in Britain at the age of twenty-two and established him-self on the literary scene as the founder of Poetry London (1939–51); Eliot admired his work. He had married an Englishwoman named Jacqueline Stanley in 1940: the marriage was difficult. Mary and Eliot together tried to persuade the young poet to return home to Ceylon, then under British control; it's hardly surprising that he did not wish to do so, as the island was on the front line of the war against the Japanese. Tambimuttu would remain in Britain – and his connection to Eliot would endure.

The episode reveals a great deal about the developing pattern of Mary's relationship with Eliot: first, that he appreciated her practicality, her ability to deal with troubled young people, or young people in troubling situations – some time in the summer of the year before he had noted that she must be a 'mainstay' for her 'waifs'. It reveals too his willingness, per-haps, to hand off problems to others, and to look away from what made him uncomfortable. But this episode also shows Mary noting – as she would continue to do – the disparity between the Tom Eliot revealed to her, and the T. S. Eliot that others saw. The former was amusing, confid-ing; the latter stiff and silent. This is the beginning of her portrait of the intimacy which would come to mean so much to her. She reproduced his notes to her 'exactly as he typed or wrote them – spelling, punctuation and all'. That too demonstrates what she saw as an intimacy: in writing to her, the great poet might let down his guard.

He often wrote to her from Shamley Green, Surrey, a village to which he retreated during the Second World War. It was the home of his friends Emily Lina Mirrlees and her daughter Hope, a writer whose long poem Paris was published by the Hogarth Press in 1920. The household was a large one, with many evacuees from all over London, mainly women and children, along with numerous cats and dogs. He would return to London a couple of nights a week for his work at Faber and Faber and his duties as an air-raid warden.

I used to hope, anxiously, that he would never be near a bomb, for he wouldn't know what to do. But he had some rough nights – and gained some of his inspiration for 'Little Gidding'.

The first complete typescript of 'Little Gidding' is dated July 1941; he revised the poem across August and September 1942. Mary includes a page of Eliot's undated notes for another 'Anvil' discussion, in which he cautions against retribution against the Germans: Britain would be at risk of 'doing ourselves a moral injury', despite a natural desire to 'see 'em suffer'. He adds a postscript, however: 'With regard to foreign nations, the maxim of Old Foxy . . . is to be adopted: ALWAYS SUSPECT EVERYBODY.' It's hard to imagine that this was Mary's attitude to 'foreign nations'; but she makes no remark. This was the first letter he wrote her that he signed off 'Tom Possum'. Possum was the nickname given to him by Ezra Pound in the early 1920s. The name – from an American animal that plays dead when threatened – originally appears in The Stories of Uncle Remus, *tales adapted from African American folklore by the American journalist and author Joel Chandler Harris. Eliot often read the Remus stories aloud to the Shamley Green crowd.*

In the spring of this year he undertook a tour of Sweden for the British Council. Mary received a 'notable' letter, all in one paragraph, dated 29 June 1942, 'SS Peter & Paul, 1942'. This is the very first of many letters dated by the calendar of saints: in acknowledging their shared faith this created another bond between them.

I ought to have explained to you long ago that I had an Irish grandmother, of a respectable family founded by a man who tried to steal the Crown Jewels. This accounts for a good deal but is far from being the whole story. In my father's family is an hereditary taint, going back for centuries, which expresses itself in an irresistible tendency to sit on committees . . . I had to dine with an old friend from Cheshire who in better days was a portrait painter of horses; and I have to do two memoranda about Sweden; I have got involved purely out of good nature with a film producer; Miss Storm Jameson wants me to write a poem for a Red Cross Book; I have had to correspond with the Master of Balliol; somebody has knitted me a pair of socks which are big enough to go over my boots . . .

He closed the letter with an invitation to have lunch or dinner and 'tell all that has happened since I have been away'. It is signed 'your faithful and humble friend'. She preserves too a couple of delightful little personal verses, written especially for her:

> To Miss Trevelyan
> Who must needs have efficient nous
> To live in a mission house
> Without cook, maid or scullion.

In scrapbook style, she pasted into the manuscript a postcard of Little Gidding church in Huntingdonshire and a copy of the poem printed in the New English Weekly. *She also preserved a review by Desmond MacCarthy in which he wrote that 'I found "Little Gidding" a singularly moving, singularly beautiful poem' on account of its 'still-deep beauty' and 'wistful, artful sincerity'.*

It is notable that in this year Mary made no mention of the publication of her own book, From the Ends of the Earth. *It is a warm-hearted account of a decade's worth of work welcoming students from all over the world to London. She saw clearly that these young people were not to be dismissed: that they were the future, and that their goodwill could foster fellowship across the globe. 'Are students so important?' she asked her readers rhetorically. 'They talk a lot of nonsense, they think they know everything. They are easily swayed, unreliable creatures, full of enthusiasm, full of contempt for the old-fashioned views of their elders . . . But it is . . . possible to sow the seeds of real friendship, tolerance and understanding and much else that is good among the products of a free and democratic country. It is possible to send back to many lands young people with happy memories of England, people who look forward to acting as interpreters between their countries and ours. These people can make a real contribution to the peace of the world.'*

The reviews – and there were quite a few – were admiring. 'The dislocating effects of war on social life are strikingly revealed by Miss

From the Ends of the Earth, front cover, published in 1942.

Trevelyan in her readable account of the activities of the London University Student Club,' remarked the Irish Independent. *According to* Tatler, 'Miss Trevelyan writes of all these young people as being so much* present *(in memory) that one can hardly realise they have gone away.' The magazine said the book was recommended 'as a help to much understanding that we shall need'. And the* Manchester Evening News *was even more enthusiastic, with hopes that a book like Mary's could have a powerful political effect. The book, wrote the critic, was 'a fascinating account of an experiment in international understanding . . . the influence of which may yet help to pull the world out of the abyss'.*

But Mary kept herself out of the frame. It's clear that her work found a wide and appreciative audience, but there could only be one writer in her relationship with T. S. Eliot.

On 15 September he wrote to tell her of all his appointments, including sharing a stage with John Gielgud at the Royal Society of Dramatic Art, and then remarked that . . .

I have an uneasy feeling that in November I have to do a talk, chat or reading, I forget which, for

Miss Trevelyan's
Tatterdemallions
And sundry rapscallions . . .

Up until this point Mary had known very little of Eliot's personal life, and nothing at all about his first wife, Vivien. Eliot and Vivien Haigh-Wood had met in Oxford in the spring of 1915; they were both twenty-six years old. She had been born in Bury, Lancashire, but grew up London. Slender and with dark hair, she was a lively woman and a fine dancer. They married at the end of June, without the knowledge of either set of parents. Many years later Eliot would write:

*I think that all I wanted of Vivien was a flirtation or mild affair: I was
too shy and unpractised to achieve either with anybody. I believe that
I came to persuade myself that I was in love with her simply because
I wanted to burn my boats and commit myself to staying in England.
And she persuaded herself . . . that she would save the poet by keeping
him in England. To her the marriage brought no happiness . . . To me it
brought the state of mind out of which came 'The Waste Land'.*

*They were badly mismatched; she was plagued by ill health. The qualities
that had attracted him – her sensitivity, her daring – came to repel him.
The struggle and tension did not only run one way: she suffered from
what she called his 'black silent moods, and [his] irritability', as she wrote
to his mother in 1917. 'Tom is IMpossible,' she wrote to a friend in 1919.
'Full of nerves, really not well, very bad cough, very morbid and grumpy.
I wish you had him!'*

*Eliot's friends were often unsympathetic to his increasingly isolated
wife. 'Was there ever such a torture since life began!' Virginia Woolf wrote
in her diary towards the end of 1930.*

*To bear her on one's shoulders, biting, wriggling, raving, scratching,
unwholesome, powdered, insane, yet sane to the point of insanity,
reading his letters, thrusting herself on us, coming in wavering,
trembling – 'Does your dog do that to frighten me?' . . . And so on, until
worn out with half an hour of it, we gladly see them go. This bag of
ferrets is what Tom wears around his neck.*

*Eliot had left her in 1933; on 10 July Virginia Woolf wrote that Eliot had
left her '"irrevocably"; and she sits meanwhile in a flat decorated with
pictures of him, and altars, and flowers'.*

*On 14 July 1938, Vivien's brother Maurice Haigh-Wood wrote to Eliot
that she was found 'wandering in the streets at 5 o'clock this morning'.
He contacted her doctor, who 'feels V. must go either to Malmaison [a
sanatorium near Paris] or to some home, and I am also inclined to think*

that, because there is no telling what will happen next'. He wrote to Eliot again on 17 August: two physicians 'felt strongly that she should be put into a home'. She was taken to Northumberland House, a private asylum, after Eliot, in concert with her brother Maurice, authorised her committal.

In 1933 Eliot had written to his friend Alida Monro that he would prefer not to see Vivien again; he wrote to another friend that he anticipated spending the rest of his life in solitude. In his Collected Poems *1909–1935 'Ash Wednesday' had originally been dedicated 'To my Wife'; he removed that dedication in 1936. Learning of this unhappy history was another opportunity for Mary to feel close to Tom.*

Early in the year I learned by chance . . . that Tom had been married, that his wife had gone out of her mind and that he had spent a terrible time with her – refusing the help of his friends – until she was finally taken to a Mental Asylum. Although it was obviously distressing for him to talk of that period of his life, he began to do so to me quite often when we were dining and he seemed to find some relief in telling me what he could about it. I have forgotten most of these talks, but I do remember one evening vividly, when he tried to tell me about 'the terrible experience of watching a mind slipping from the real world to the world of imagination'. He told me they had been married very young and they had never been happy. He thought he had never been in love with Vivien. There was some insanity in her family but he had known of this only after her breakdown. Several times, when driving about London with him, he brought out memories of that time. In Trafalgar Square, pointing to some windows: 'it was from there that Vivien threw her nightdress out of the window into the street in the middle of the night'. In Paddington, as we passed the dingy flats of Crawford Mansions: 'we lived there – I was very unhappy. There is the pub – I used to watch the people coming out at Closing Time – that's the origin of "Hurry up Ladies – its time".'

In her recollection she misremembers, or misquotes, 'HURRY UP PLEASE ITS TIME' from 'The Waste Land'.

In November of this year I heard that Maurice Reckitt was going round telling people that Tom had, during the worst period, entirely relied on him and had 'consulted him at every turn'. With some hesitation I wrote and told him this.

Reckitt was a writer and Christian sociologist who had corresponded with Eliot in the 1930s; Eliot had participated in the discussion groups he promoted. Eliot wrote to Mary on 16 November entirely refuting Reckitt's account of a close friendship between the two men; he was, Eliot told Mary, 'one of the last people I should have thought of confiding my private affairs to'. He had no recollection of sharing any of his marital distress with Reckitt. The revelation of Reckitt's claim dismayed him, he told her, but 'there is no personal friendship between us to be disturbed, and furthermore nothing of this sort could now hurt me. I sometimes have wondered, however, whether a number of untrue beliefs about this period of my life were not held by a number of people, without ever reaching my ears.' Perhaps in telling Eliot of what she had heard from Reckitt, Mary had hoped herself for more personal revelation; but none was forthcoming.

In December he wrote to thank her for a gift of eggs, and to inform her that he had bought a new overcoat, 'exactly like the old one – only fresher'. She invited him, of course, to the annual nativity play at Student Movement House, and to take a cup of tea afterwards. He wrote to her on 10 December in reply.

I find in the Book of Possum the Wise this maxim: 'The only way to get anything done is to neglect something else!' If I am silent, it only means that I have no cup of tea to propose. I should of course like a cup of tea after the Nativity, but I don't want to divert your attention due to the Nobility, Gentry and Faculty and I shall only hope for a cup of tea with the generality.

He did come to tea before Christmas.

My office was littered with properties for the Nativity Play and profusely adorned with Christmas cards. While I was answering a telephone call, I heard Tom murmur, as he prowled round inspecting all this: 'In many ways I infinitely prefer Good Friday'!

Queen Elizabeth with the Princesses Elizabeth and Margaret with Mary at Student Movement House, 1942.

1943

Tom takes his duties as Vicar's Warden of S. Stephen's Church, Gloucester Road, very seriously and when Bishops come to preach he wears his 'City' clothes and looks very uncomfortable in a stiff collar. He takes a great deal of trouble over his dress and has morning suits of varying weights, worn at different seasons of the year. He is devoted to his bowler, though I do not myself think this form of headgear suits him. Sometimes he appears in his old overcoat with mis-shapen pockets (usually stuffed with manuscripts) covering the most splendid sartorial effects and the whole topped with the *chapeau melon*. Perhaps because he tries so hard, he doesn't look quite natural when dressed up.

Eliot's murmur that he preferred the sorrow of Good Friday to the jollity of Christmas might not have been surprising to Mary. Although he would often tease her gently, or be lightly comic, for the most part his robust love of jokes, of ribald verse, was rarely on display to her throughout the years of their friendship. They found a great connection in their joint commitment to the Church of England. Theirs was a strong faith, linked too with a global vision of Christianity as a 'civilising' influence: a concept which is, of course, much more problematic today. The Student Christian Movement had evangelical origins from its founding in 1898, but as the twentieth century progressed, it became inter-denominational, and imagined a world in which British students 'who make friends . . . of people of other races and other nations are often delivered once for all from racial prejudice and all exclusive and narrow forms of racism'.

    Eliot had been raised as a Unitarian, a religious movement which had its roots in the Reformation. It advanced the idea of the unity of God, rejecting the doctrine of the Trinity; Unitarianism too rejected Puritan ideas of humanity's innate sinfulness. Eliot was brought up with a strong sense of duty; Unitarianism was not a faith of good or evil, but what was 'done' and 'not done'. Salvation came from human effort: from hard work, good cheer and benevolence. But Eliot came to dislike 'the intellectual and puritanical rationalism' of his early environment, and in his early years in England began to explore another path of faith.

He came to feel that the Reformation had brought about a kind of cultural impoverishment. He was drawn to the ritual, the structures and strictures, of an earlier time; yet he admired too the Church as it had come to exist under Elizabeth I, perceiving it to bring together faith and secular power in an ideal form. He first visited the Anglican chapel at Merton College Oxford in 1914, while on a Sheldon Travelling Fellowship; during his early years in London he was a frequent visitor to the churches in the City. In 1927 he got his British nationality – sponsored by Leonard Woolf – and was received into the Church of England. In an essay published in 1928 he praised the virtues of what he called the 'English Catholic Church': 'In its persistence in finding a mean between Papacy and Presbytery the English Church under Elizabeth became something representative of the finest spirit of England of the time.' He had lived in the clergy house of St Stephen's Church from the end of 1933 – following the final break-up of his marriage – until the outbreak of war; he was Vicar's Warden of the church for twenty-two years, beginning in 1934.

In the spring of 1943 Mary told Eliot that she would be paying a visit to Lord Lang – Cosmo Lang, who had been Archbishop of Canterbury from 1928 until just the year before. He had been succeeded by William Temple, who died in office in 1944 after only two years. Lang's Anglo-Catholic views were in sympathy with those of both Mary and Eliot; as she headed off to his home in Kew, Eliot asked Mary to 'sound him out' on the question of the discussions surrounding the formation of the Church of South India – discussions which would come to fruition in 1947 when parts of the Anglican Church of India, Burma and Ceylon were brought together with Methodist, Presbyterian, Dutch Reformed and Congregationalist groups.

The report she brought back from Kew was satisfactory in one sense: Eliot was glad to learn that Lang's views were 'sound' – however, 'It is extremely depressing to find that his impression of his successor is similar to my own,' he wrote to her on 8 March.

T. never trusted Archbishop Temple and was convinced he was 'selling the pass' in pushing the scheme for the Church of South India with complete disregard for the Catholic position . . . During this period of the war Tom was again asked by the British Council to go to various European countries to spread culture round on their behalf.

Eliot wrote to Mary of a proposed visit to Iceland with the British Council. With the war on, however, the British Council were worried about getting him back. He complained to her about lectures he had to prepare; the freedom to complain is itself a kind of intimacy. He wrote to her on 17 May wondering if she would have supper with him: 'But I am rather morose,' he said. He would contrast his own hopelessness – especially where practical matters, such as using the telephone – with her implied practicality. Eliot wrote to her on 6 August.

You know what agonies of indecision I have go to through before ringing anyone up: but this week I did make brave efforts, but unluckily Miss Swan has gone to Crowborough for her holiday, so that the first time I got your old Russell Square number (that is because you are quite rightly using up the old paper) and Miss Melton was engaged with somebody I didn't want to see, and I was told that there was no subscriber; and the second time I got the Student Movement House; and after that Dai Jones came in with a message from Bernard Wall about Ezra Pound. But it would only have been to explain that on Tuesday I have a Canadian poet to tea, and then a brisk high tea to be back at six, directly after my meeting, and for the evening. So will you dine on the evening of September 29? Meanwhile I hope that you will be enjoying a carefree holiday among the haunts of

1943

The boast of heraldry, the pomp of power
And all that beauty, all that wealth 'er gave,
Forget awhile the somber street of Gower . . .

A letter like this might indicate that she was enmeshed in every aspect of his life, but that was not so, as she admitted. Miss Swan, the receptionist at Faber and Faber; Miss Melton, his secretary at the firm; Dai – Eliot's diminutive for David – Jones, a poet and painter; Wall, a Catholic intellectual who had reviewed Eliot's Essays Ancient and Modern *. . . the names scrolled by her.*

Many people referred to in these letters meant nothing to me. It was a particular delight to Tom to write about people and things with no explanation. He would write on any notepaper that came to hand; often the CRITERION paper – of which he must have had quantities to spare when the Criterion closed down – or the VIRGIL Society – or the Alliance Française – or the notepaper of St Stephen's Church, Gloucester Road.

Her claim to be ignorant of the people he mentioned to her is startling: yet it almost seems like a subliminal indication that she had her own life to attend to, though she keeps it out of the text.

Mary paid close attention to his health; at the end of a busy year, he came down with influenza. She had, she said, 'put in an enquiry as to his whereabouts' in December; he wrote back to her on 14 December from Shamley Green – having just spent a week in a nursing home, recovering. He had found the experience pleasant, he said, despite fearing the ministrations of a visiting vicar: 'I was afraid he would want to give me ghostly comfort and perhaps suggest my occupying myself by writing something for his parish magazine.' He remained, however, unmolested, as he said. He expressed keenness to take Mary's advice on 'public affairs'. Throughout their friendship, his frailty would be a running theme.

Nothing, however, would stop him smoking – these were the days, of course, when advertising promoted the health benefits of cigarettes. She sent him some cigarettes for Christmas, and he replied most appreciatively, his answer urging greater familiarity between them. The letter is dated 28 December, 'Holy Innocents'.

My dear Mary,
(And don't you address me as Poet: I am not a Poet, Ma'am, but a Poor Gentleman who occasionally scribbles to divert himself. Give you an inch and you'll take an ell: it will be Bard next. In Swedish: angelsk-americansk skald – next.) . . .

Meanwhile this is just to thank you for your extreme generosity in sending me what is not to be bought and which you could have done with quite as well as I: except that these savoury tubes come very conveniently to eke out my dwindling supply of inferior weeds in the country. Cut off as I have been . . . I feared that I might be reduced to smoking dried bracken, which is plentiful in this neighbourhood. I appreciate your kindness of heart and your generous gift.

He signed off 'yours gratefully', with the initials, 'T. P.' – 'Tom Possum', in Mary's careful annotation.

1944

Between the end of the Blitz in the summer of 1941 and the first months of 1944 there were many fewer raids over London. This changed when, in retaliation for raids on German cities by Allied air forces, the Luftwaffe returned in force to attack British cities. Around 1,500 Londoners were killed, and twice as many injured. After the D-Day landings in June, the attacks by Hitler's 'vengeance weapons', the V-1 flying bombs and V-2 rockets, began. These attacks would only end when the weapons' launch sites were destroyed by the Allied armies; more than 1.5 million homes were damaged or destroyed. The V-1, often referred to in Britain as a 'doodlebug', was a winged bomb powered by a jet engine, its roar heralding the approach of the deadly device; silence meant the engine had cut out, and the bomb was about to fall.

In June the flying bombs became very active, both in London and in Surrey. I stayed at Shere twice and thought, on the whole, that the nights there were more terrifying than in London – the quiet of the country made the throb of the approaching bombs very clear from very far away.

Eliot wrote to her on 19 June that things in Surrey are 'very rough' because of the bombing at night; he declined an invitation to dine with her before he gave a reading as the prospect of performing made him unsociable, he told her. He said he would ring to fix to meet her: 'but you are always out'.

The doodle bombs became so bad that I wrote to Tom to say I really could not let him fulfil his promise to do a Poetry Reading for the students, since the only big room we had was covered with a glass roof.

On 24 June he wrote her what she called 'a long and intimate letter', agreeing with her judgement about any event conducted under a glass roof. A doodlebug had dropped early Friday morning on Russell Square, destroying the pavilion in the square and blasting the Faber and Faber offices. Windows were blown out, the ceiling had fallen, doors were blown off – though no one was hurt. 'The business can carry on,' he wrote, 'extricating itself gradually from lath and plaster, but the flat will be out of use for some time to come, and I can't say I am altogether sorry, as it has not struck me as an ideal spot for sleeping.' He told her that he would come to 'camp' for fire-watching, but otherwise he would only come up for the day.

In a diary entry, the company chairman Geoffrey Faber kept an account of the night's dramatic events – he had been safely away in the country, but had heard the news over the phone:

The thing fell bang in the exact middle of the square, about 3 a.m. The square covered with green leaves, the trees stripped and no doubt killed. All the houses stripped of doors and windows, but no really serious damage at 23 & 24. Ceilings down in many rooms and a bad mess. If I had stayed up and been asleep I should have been more or less badly hurt. Since the ceiling came down on my bed. Flat uninhabitable, at least for some weeks. No one hurt; but Mrs Lister [the caretaker] unable to stand any more.

She did not preserve copies of her own letters, but must have asked him about Vivien's safety at Northumberland House. 'I actually wrote yesterday to my solicitors to ask them to find out whether she had not better be moved,' he continued on 24 June. But he had no 'official status' in the matter; her brother did, but he was 'engulfed in AMGOT somewhere' (the Allied Military Government for Occupied Territories). 'I am considerably worried by all this.'

She suggested visiting him in Shamley, but he was not encouraging; there would be several buses involved, or a walk of five miles; bombs remained a danger. None had fallen close to the house, he told her, but they *heard 'cracks' two or three times a day, and the house was shaken at night. He confessed his anxieties to her:*

I suppose I'm as frightened as most people. So far as it comes from a lively imagination – as I can make myself feel rather faint by shutting my eyes and imagining myself on the edge of a precipice – I think one must just put up with it, and try to think of the advantages one has over unimaginative people at times when there is nothing to fear. If one is of a worrying disposition, as I am, one worries about all the possible consequences short of death, even the more trivial ones like how one is to get any clothes, or carry out an important engagement with nothing but a shirt and trousers. But there is something else which I can't get to the bottom of, disgust, horror, physical nausea, the <u>nightmare</u> of evil.

But one of the dangers of fearfulness is that it can, at moments, make you reckless. The imperturbable person who can calculate that there are 999 chances to one that nothing will happen to him, and sleep like a top, will also see when the chances are the other way, and avoid the risk: whereas the person who is frightened all the time, and ashamed of it (one always is) may try to overcome it by doing something too bold – just to reassure himself, or others, about his own courage. The moral is, I think, to try to keep up to just the extreme of what one can do, and not be ashamed of not being able to do more. And this is difficult.

I don't think people ordinarily see through one's attempts to appear calm as easily as you seem to imagine.

On 24 July he wrote her the kind of letter which, the reader can see, gave her perhaps reason to believe that there might be something more to their relationship than a simple friendship. She had clearly invited him on a visit which would have been important to her. 'Well, about Oxford: it is very sweet of you,' he wrote, 'and I should much like to meet your mother; but I do feel too tired for any expeditions at present.' And they had, it seems, exchanged timepieces: 'Of course take my watch; and so long as I have yours (which is much more useful to me than mine would be), my watch is your watch. And the poems will be ready (though one can never be sure nowadays) in their binding on September 1st, and you shall have a copy at once.' The first British edition of the Four Quartets *was published by Faber and Faber that autumn.*

She went up to Edinburgh for a brief visit; while there she bought him some excellent – very rare, she wrote – wine. In a letter of 15 August he pronounces himself 'ébahi' – delightedly shocked – by her gift.

In the autumn of 1944 I obtained special leave from Student Movement House and went out with the Y.M.C.A. to France and Belgium, in the wake of our troops, to act as Programme Director in an enormous Hostel for Front Line men.

I wrote as often as possible to Tom, giving him my impressions of events in Belgium as they occurred – letters which he seemed to appreciate and which, so he said, he read aloud to the ladies (and dogs and cats) of Shamley.

We met often before I left England and had a farewell dinner on my last night in London. I went off with several carefully thought-out presents from Tom and had some difficulty in finding a place in my luggage for a very large prayer-book, which looked more suitable for use in a church than for the bed-side table. On my rare leaves in London he was always at hand and I used his office as a store for the German literature I picked up. He also housed a huge crucifix which I rescued from a devastated town in Germany. His letters to me in Belgium were an invaluable distraction.

The work she would do on the Continent was remarkable. She was running a hostel, as she wrote, for Allied soldiers on leave, co-operating with fellow relief workers who came from backgrounds very different from hers – Catholics, Socialists, Communists. She would write that this collaboration was 'one of the few good results' of Nazi domination.

Perhaps it seems peculiar to speak of any good result coming from such oppression: but the notion is revealing of Mary's optimistic personality, especially when it came to interactions between people of different cultures and classes.

It seemed to her that – even as she considered travelling to Europe – she thought that the experience would make an interesting book; she had wanted to write another book for some time. She asked Eliot's advice, though she revealed nothing about the notional book to Eliot other than its proposed form. He replied quickly on 12 February 1944 – he was rushing, he told her, because he had to be present as churchwarden when the Bishop of London would be preaching in Kensington the next day:

Well of course I haven't the faintest notion from your letter what your book will be about, BUT with authors who have anything serious to say, we always use our best endeavours to dissuade them from using the epistolary form. That gives the PERSONALITY TOUCH and is therefore suitable for authors of an exaggeratedly egocentric type: a good way to talk about yourself, but unsuitable for the development of any serious or continuous argument . . . So please don't.

Perhaps unsurprisingly – after this firm, not to say dryly withering, dismissal from the greatest literary man of the age – she took his words to heart . . . at first.

This letter effectively stopped me at the time, but the following year Longman's published my letters from Belgium (to T.S.E., though this was not stated), which were very successful.

They were published as I'll Walk Beside You: Letters from Belgium, September 1944–May 1945. *The book took its title from 'a little song', she wrote, 'a great favourite of the soldiers'; with music by Alan Murray and words by Edward Lockton, the sentimental tune originally appeared* in 1936, and would be covered by many artists including Vera Lynn. 'I'll walk beside you through the world today / While dreams and songs and flowers bless your way / I'll look into your eyes and hold your hand / I'll walk beside you through the golden land,' the lyrics run. 'I have often wondered, as I have watched groups of men singing this song, of whom they were thinking,' Mary wrote in the introduction to her little book, which comprises seventeen letters 'to a friend in England'.

It is a slim volume, but one that reveals Mary's fortitude, empathy and boundless curiosity even in the face of danger and suffering. The YMCA had become involved in relief work almost as soon as the war broke out, developing mobile canteens to bring refreshments to troops, rescue workers and victims of air raids. As the conflict went on the second-hand vans of the YMCA headed to Europe, trailing advancing and withdrawing troops: the first YMCA van arrived on the Normandy beaches less than eight weeks after D-Day. This work was part of an international alliance of YMCA organisations that would go on to expand its work into prisoner-of-war camps, and help deal with the refugee crisis that followed the Second World War.

It was a highly organised relief programme that appealed powerfully to Mary, and her sense of excitement is palpable as she wrote to Eliot of setting off from the YMCA headquarters on Great Russell Street on 29 September 1944 – in that long convoy of vehicles, driving the single high-powered car. They would arrive on 1 October on the Normandy beaches, where the Allied forces had made their D-Day landings. In the first days of October the convoy arrived at a 'huge deserted-looking château', about four miles from Bayeux; Mary was cagey with place names, for the most part, so that her letters were acceptable to the wartime censor. There was no heating, hot water or sanitation, but Mary didn't seem to mind; what she did note were the bullet holes everywhere, and the graffiti on the walls in both German and English. She thought of the soldiers on both sides: 'they were all so young, and they were trying to kill each other.'

It was a brief stop before they carried on to Brussels, which had been liberated from German occupation on 3 September. It took three days *of driving to travel from Normandy, she wrote to Eliot on 6 October. 'Every village approaching Caen was in ruins,' she told him; she noted the 'horrible' devastation of the city of Rouen – devastation largely caused by Allied bombers in their attempt to disrupt German lines of transportation. Yet despite the devastation, she had a 'delightful adventure' in Rouen, encountering in its battered streets a small boy, René, who offered lodging with his family; in exchange she brought them tea, soap, cigarettes and chocolate, none of which they had seen for years. M. Bonnet was 'not more than thirty but looks far older'; he expressed his bitterness against the French government which had capitulated to the Nazi regime. 'I wondered how long it would take for France to begin again,' she wrote.*

On 20 October she sent a letter from Brussels, liberated from the Germans six weeks before. She had gone searching for a house they might use for the troops on leave – and found one which had been used as the German Ministry of Propaganda for Youth. There were portraits of Hitler everywhere: 'It seemed as though the occupants had just gone out for a cup of tea and would be back any minute.' She collected up papers left by the Germans, including a child's game of bombing England. 'Almost every family seems to have lost a father or son in action or by imprisonment.' She heard flying bombs whizzing overhead: 'The war is certainly not over, even for Belgium.'

Eliot's letters to Mary almost seem to make light of her situation; perhaps he didn't like to consider the real danger she could have been in. Or perhaps there was some shame in his own relatively privileged position. He noted that she had told him that she was on active service: he would be 'interested to know what you do besides distributing tea to Princesses', he wrote. 'Do be careful about stray bullets and mines.' He promised to send her Four Quartets *since it seemed 'safe' to do so. By November he acknowledged the hardships she was seeing: 'I fear that your account of your local civilians will be grimmer and grimmer as the winter wears on.' He offered the diversion, a few days later, of a couplet on the subject of his indigestion: 'In the year that King Uzziah died, / Rumpuscat felt bad inside.'*

But her work was to provide respite for Allied troops: she threw herself into it wholeheartedly and she was clearly proud of what she was able to achieve. Eventually the YMCA took over a hotel, the Albert 1er, which the soldiers simply called the Albert. Exhausted men found themselves 'living like civilians, in a luxury hotel, requisitioned with all its luxuries intact. They come down to tea a little dazed, saying "Where's the catch?" – and by supper-time are perfectly happy.' And no wonder: there was dancing, a variety show, a library, gramophone records. There was a barber's shop, a bootblack, a photographer. From 10 p.m. to midnight a buffet of tea, coffee and biscuits was laid out for the time when the men would come in from 'decent places of entertainment'. 'It is much our best opportunity for personal contact, these two hours at night, for the men begin to feel at home and relaxed and they like to be able to come and talk about their adventures,' she wrote. 'In the last month I must have inspected hundreds of photographs, produced like lightning the moment one displays any interest, of parents, wives, children, and an immense succession of best girls.'

The men, by her account, couldn't have been more content. 'I asked one man the other day if he'd been happy, and his reply was "Oh, miss, it's been like 'eaven with the gate shut!"' She paid close attention to them, describing the different perspective she got on each man as she bent over a tea urn to serve them: 'Hands are as interesting as faces. Each seemed to have their own character, each can tell something about their owner.'

But, as she wrote to Eliot, the world outside the walls of the Albert could be very grim. In mid-November she described a visit to an air evacuation centre at an airport four miles outside the city. At first she went to observe, but thereafter went once a week to give a regular worker a day off, 'for the work is a considerable strain, especially on the sensitive', she told him. 'I have never seen such a mass of human suffering.' Two hundred and fifty stretchers at a time could be laid out awaiting evacuation: there were men with bad head wounds and amputated limbs. It was her job, as she saw it, to bring them treats and buck them up. 'I ask every man where he comes from at home and generally have the luck

Troops relax at the 'hostel' for Allied troops, set up by the YMCA
in Belgium, where Mary volunteered in 1944. These photos
appeared in *I'll Walk Beside You* (1946).

of knowing something about their part of the world.' She was humbled
by their good humour and bravery despite what they had suffered. 'This
really is the Light shining in darkness – the darkness which is Germany,
which cannot understand what it has done to mankind . . . Surely in
some ways these men are all helping in the redemption of the world –
perhaps it is only because of them and many others like them that we can

be saved.' But some of what she saw and felt she kept from the published edition of her letters. 'I think quite differently about euthanasia now,' she wrote privately to Eliot. 'A man came into that hospital with no arms, no legs, no eyes – I hardly think the doctor did his job. Do you think that quite wrong?'

She did not think well of everyone she met, it must be said. She kept her opinion of one segment of the Allied forces out of her finished text: 'The only trouble we have is with the Americans,' she wrote to Eliot on green German notepaper, 'who drink a great deal, not only at night, but all day, mostly bad cognac which they smuggle into their bedrooms.' He could only concur. 'I share your opinion of the Americans: they are only nice as individuals,' he pronounced. That he was American by origin himself didn't seem to occur to her – or indeed to him.

On 28 November he wrote to her half-jokingly, half-fretfully. 'Be careful to keep out of harm's way and remember to DUCK when there are missiles flying about: you are giving your family something to worry about, being where you are.' By then she had visited Paris, thanks to the arrival in Brussels of an old friend of hers, André de Blonay, then General Secretary of the International Student Service; after the war he would be head of external relations at the UN educational and cultural agency UNESCO.

He drove her there: 240 miles on a sunny day. They arrived on Armistice Day, 11 November – the same day that Winston Churchill had come to make a speech, commemorating the end of the First World War while the Second ground on. The weather was cold and the atmosphere festive – despite the fact that there was no heating or hot water anywhere, and only spasmodic supplies of electricity. She walked through Paris, which was pockmarked with shellfire – but Notre Dame and Sainte Chapelle were mostly untouched, to her eyes. The Hôtel de Ville had been badly hit. She stepped into a little bookshop; there was nothing on the shelves published later than the summer of 1939. 'I bought a Guide Bleu of Brussels, for the sake of talking. The elderly assistant seemed surprised that someone actually wanted to buy something. He took a very long time making out the bill and I found myself wondering how long it was since he had performed that ceremony.' She called the place 'haunted'. The bookseller told her that the Germans destroyed anything English and the booksellers destroyed a good deal themselves.

On 8 December she had enclosed her Christmas gifts to him; she kept this intimate exchange out of I'll Walk Beside You. *One was a diary ('it is more interesting to have an engagement book in French'); the second would form an enduring bond. It was a novel by the Belgian crime writer Georges Simenon. Simenon, creator of Inspector Maigret, was extraordinarily prolific: he published three novels in 1944 alone. 'I don't know if you are familiar with the works of this gentleman, but I think he is an excellent writer of detective fiction and this is a particularly good example of his work.' Eliot would become quite addicted to Simenon's works: in years to come the pair would often exchange his books. In the '50th Anniversary Report' of the Harvard class of 1910 Eliot reported some notable developments over the years: 'I now prefer Burgundy to Claret and Inspector Maigret to Arsène Lupin.' (Lupin was a fictional creation of the French author Maurice Leblanc.) Simenon became part of Eliot's personal pantheon; in 1954 he would come to think that he might have introduced Mary to the works – though he wondered whether she might, in fact, have done the introducing. 'Did I first introduce you to Simenon, or you to me?' he would ask her. He had, in fact, been reading Simenon for many years before he met Mary; it seems a little gift to her, this potential misremembering.*

He read her letters aloud to the company at Shamley Green ('the Shambley family'): everyone, he told her, was 'consumed with admiration for you both as a letter writer and as a Man of Action': the last, perhaps, a telling remark regarding his perception of her. She told him in confidence that her letters to him were a kind of 'safety valve' – yet certainly there can be no doubting her strength and resilience. She wrote to him too that she had become wary of seeming too sympathetic to the men: they had but brief respite in Brussels, and then would need to go back to soldiering. 'I am beginning to find that a small remark as to their toughness, a hint of admiration, not given seriously enough to embarrass them, will make a whole group stiffen up again.'

Christmas was in the offing. She was aware of how fortunate she was, surrounded by plenty when the Belgians had so little. Privately she had written to him: 'Yesterday I had a friend to tea, a German Jew, and his wife and tiny baby. I gave them as good a tea as possible, but they ate it with the greatest caution because they thought it might make them ill as they were not used to so much food.' And the war was not over yet: just before the holiday, news reached the Albert that the Germans had broken through US lines and were advancing on Brussels; the fighting in the Ardennes would be Hitler's last major offensive against the Western Front. Men had their leave cancelled and had to return to their units. But the preparations for Christmas went on: Mary was arranging a 'Christmas Tableau', done by local children. 'The Angel Gabriel had been a prominent member of the Maquis, though still a schoolboy, and had done some excellent sabotage work. His brother, one of the Kings, had acted as interpreter to the British troops when they entered Brussels in September last.'

She continued to exhibit her characteristic phlegm – 'At 6 a.m. on Christmas morning I was woken by two enormous flying bombs coming over us, very noisily, at a tremendous pace. But at least they woke me in time to get to church,' she wrote briskly. But she also noted that for the first time she felt personally the terror of knowing the Germans might come at any moment. It made her revise her opinion that the Belgians had become complacent, had forgotten war too easily. 'What I have seen lately makes me feel that, though they have recovered some kind of stability on the surface, they are in no state to face a strain which would, this time, be beyond human bearing.'

1945

Have you ever read *The Old Curiosity Shop*? A character who is only mentioned in the book, the father of Sampson and Sally Brass, was known affectionately as Old Foxy; and he maintained a prosperous legal business on the motto: 'Always suspect everybody'. When I was a very small boy, I was given a tricycle or velocipede: a beautiful shiny japanned and nickelplated affair, with brake, bell etc., and was riding it proudly up and down the pavement, under the eye of my nursemaid, when an odious small boy who lived a few doors away, who wore a kind of frilly blouse, sidled up and said ingratiatingly: 'Mother says I may ride your velocipede if I let you blow my whistle.' That aroused my first disgust with human nature.

A tale like this from Eliot offered respite, perhaps, to Mary, who was still witnessing the effects of front-line fighting. On New Year's Day she heard German planes overhead, and she was powerfully struck by the conversations she had with boys of eighteen and nineteen who told of the terror of digging trenches in ground too hard to dig – the Germans were able to shoot them before they could take cover. 'A huge Scot could talk of nothing but the atrocities he had seen,' she wrote. Over and over again she would stress how important she felt it was for people to understand what soldiers were going through, and how it might continue to affect them.

Eliot wrote to her on 2 January from Shamley Green, where he had been 'watching a godson trying to skate'. He told Mary he had written to her mother, mentioning that he'd got a 'reassuring note' from her – but he had revealed nothing of a longer letter. 'I have no doubt she has been very perturbed.' His personal concern and pride is clear. 'What you say of the troops, and the behaviour of the Belgians themselves, particularly the children and your gallant Resistance girls, is very moving. You are doing a wonderful job . . . It's like private benevolence: the more you do to help a person the more claim it gives that person upon you: so the better you do the job the stronger its claim upon you.' He would continue to haver about how much information to pass on to Mary's mother; a letter of 10 January is very interesting, he says, 'but the letter closes with a reference to a German raid with bullets flying about, so I shan't send it unless you direct me explicitly to do so'.

This letter of 21 January, like so many others, is dated by the church calendar, but Eliot is muddled at first, giving the dateline: 'S. Simeon: no, I keep getting confused in this Diary. It is S. AGNES.' The feast of St Simeon Stylites, or Simeon the Elder, is on 5 January; St Agnes's feast day is indeed 21 January. He was perfectly aware of his relative comfort and safety: he questions it and accepts it, all at once. He is buried, he told her, in 'one-hoss', small-town Shamley affairs: the trouble with grocery and coal deliveries, the lack of clean laundry. 'Somebody gave me a few grapes the other day which a soldier had brought back from Belgium,' he told her. 'They were the best I had eaten for a very long time, but I didn't like eating produce of Belgium when I couldn't send the Belgians anything in return.' Undercutting himself again, he promises to send her his lecture 'What is a Classic?', delivered at the Virgil Society in October of the year before – noting its price: '3s 6d, a swindling price for 32 pages.'

As spring came, Mary was able to witness the destruction wrought by Operation Veritable, the pincer movement planned by Field Marshal Montgomery as part of the Rhineland Offensive. The main aim of the offensive, which took place between February and March 1945, was to clear the area between the Meuse and the Lower Rhine of German forces. In a letter dated 5 March she wrote of travelling out north-east from Brussels, watching anti-aircraft guns 'chasing' a flying bomb. 'I went because I know that the more one can share people's experiences, the more one can help them,' she wrote.

Crossing over the Dutch frontier to the town of Nijmegen, where the YMCA maintained a base, she could hear shelling. 'The town gave me the impression of a town continually in the front line, indeed it is still in *range of shelling.' Hardly a house in the town was undamaged. All night* *the guns pounded away, and a bomb dropped not far from where she was* *sleeping, shaking her bed.*

They drove out in a jeep towards the German border: Mary noted *a sign as they entered: THIS IS GERMANY. YOU HAVE BEEN* *WARNED. Her description of what she saw, the extent of the destruction, remains powerful to this day:*

At first it seemed as though we were in a dead country. Every tree along each side of the road had been blasted, every farm or cottage by the roadside had been razed to the ground . . . There was no sign of a human being, no birds to be seen or heard – it was just a wilderness, a land over which the hand of death had passed, and we seemed to be the only living creatures.

In the pouring rain they drove through Kleve, formerly a health resort: *she noted the shell of a church, a blasted fish shop, crosses by the side of the* *road: the graves of the men who had died to take that place. 'I felt that all* *the world was wrecked and this could not be real. You know how a child* *builds great castles of bricks on the drawing-room floor and then, when* *he gets tired, kicks them all down again. That is what Germany looks like.* *It is a terrible retribution.'*

Eliot wrote back to her a week later – 13 March, 'Ste Euphrasie' *– calling her letter sent from liberated Germany 'thrilling and important'. He despaired at her descriptions of the Netherlands pummelled, as* *he saw it, to near-oblivion: 'What a field-day for thugs and hooligans* *the rest of our lifetime (mine at least) is going to be.' He signed himself* *off to her as grateful and appreciative – and opined that she deserved* *both the rank and pay of a brigadier. However busy she must have been,* *she still found time to send Eliot a bottle of cognac, for he wrote to thank* *her: 'Unless you pinched it out of the ruins it must have cost you a pretty* *penny, and so all the more shameful that I did not write at once,' he said.*

Kleve, a town just inside Germany, destroyed by Allied
bombing. The photo appeared in *I'll Walk Beside You*.

*Back in Brussels in April – the war in Europe nearly over – there
was an air of excitement, she wrote. She was tasked with constructing a
huge YMCA canteen and recreation room for released prisoners of war:
'the most tragic and pitiable body of men', she called them. 'Many of the
men are skeletons, all are hollow-cheeked and sunken-eyed . . . for the
most part they have had no change of clothing for months and some still
have lice . . . Many are dazed and still cowed.' They longed to get home,
she observed, but knew that 'home' wouldn't solve their problems. 'Their
cure is likely to be a long and costly process.' Her understanding of the true
cost of war on the men who fought it was another way in which Mary
was ahead of her time. Arriving back in Britain, she wrote, 'The fighting
man, a stranger to his own people, who has had little chance to read a book
or hear a political speech, will be bewildered and dazed.' Her job, as she
saw it, was to make them feel at home and wanted for the few hours they
spent at the YMCA before crossing the Channel. She could at least provide comfy chairs and games of ping-pong, magazines and newspapers,*

a piano, and a bar selling very mild beer. Fifteen hundred men arrived every day. A couple of weeks later, in early May, men arrived in Brussels who had been at the liberation of Bergen-Belsen; as they told their stories, she wrote, 'their eyes were full of horror at the things they have seen'.

Her last letter is dated 10 May – two days after Germany surrendered unconditionally to the Allied forces. The war in Europe was over. She observed a 'sober mood' in Brussels, but also great joy and relief. On 4 May, Eliot had written to Mary to tell her he would be in Paris: he would be delivering a lecture on 'The Social Function of Poetry', as well as bringing gifts of small luxuries to old friends such as Sylvia Beach, the bookseller who had first published James Joyce's Ulysses in 1922.

We met successfully in Paris. I flew there from Brussels and I remember arriving early in the morning, travelling by Metro (only a very few stations open) in a great crowd. Standing in a swaying mass of people I read over my neighbour's shoulder a heading in his newspaper: 'M. Eliot est actuellement à Paris'. We spent the afternoon and evening together and had an extremely nasty dinner at my Officers' Mess Hotel in the Rue des Arcades – the only time I have ever entertained Tom to dinner in a restaurant and probably the only time he has ever had a meal for 1/10 – but there was nowhere else to feed except some quite exorbitant black-market places. We talked until the last minute before my train left.

She returned to England in June. There were few letters between her and Eliot for the rest of the year because they met most weeks, 'for tea in Tom's office, or in mine, or for dinner', an easy, relaxed informality that contrasted with increasing tension, for Mary, at work. She told a younger friend, Ann Stokes, that the Student Christian Movement apparently found her way of running the Student Movement House too informal, too lacking in seriousness. Eliot, sure enough, was on her side: 'They won't get anybody else who could do the job,' he told her. But whatever else was going on in her life, she could count on Tom Eliot to provide some

*amusing distraction. He did write to her in the early autumn of that year
to inform her that out at Shamley,*

The elderly dachshund (15 yrs. some months) has passed on . . .
assisted by Mrs Danby's chloroform, last night: and the funeral is
about to take place in a grave 5 in. by 25 in. under the oak tree. Cooky
believes we shall meet our pets in the next world, but keeps forgetting to ask Fr. Mangan about it. Life is very rum.

1946

This was a year of change for both Eliot and Mary. Early this year Eliot began sharing a flat with John Hayward at 19 Carlyle Mansions, in Chelsea. Eliot and Hayward had met in the spring of 1926, when Hayward was still studying at King's College, Cambridge; he had gone up to King's in 1923. Eliot had come to the university to give the Clark Lectures on 'The Varieties of Metaphysical Poetry': six undergraduates were chosen to have breakfast with the visiting lecturer, and Hayward was among them. The breakfast began awkwardly; after Eliot appeared there was a long silence, finally broken by Hayward. 'Mr Eliot, have you read the last volume of Proust?' 'No, I'm afraid I have not,' Eliot replied, after which silence resumed. An unpromising beginning to what would be a long and intimate friendship, or as intimate as Eliot would ever allow.

Hayward, seventeen years Eliot's junior, was the son of a Wimbledon surgeon. As a schoolboy he was friends with John Gielgud, who also attended Hillside School near Godalming. While still at school he was diagnosed with muscular dystrophy because of a weakness in his knees, and because his father observed that he slept with his eyes wide open – one of the symptoms of the condition is that it can weaken the muscles around the eyes. He won an Exhibition to Cambridge; by the time of his arrival he was already afflicted by the disease which would eventually cause him to use a wheelchair. His brilliance as a man of letters was apparent almost immediately: while still an undergraduate he edited an edition of the work of John Wilmot, the 2nd Earl of Rochester, then a largely neglected figure in seventeenth-century studies. It was published by the Nonesuch Press in 1926, the year of his first encounter with Eliot; the critic Edmund Gosse called Hayward 'the best, and in fact, the only competent editor of Rochester'. He would go on to produce editions of Donne and Swift, and write a brief life of Charles II. His disability did not hamper his engagement with the London literary scene. He was relentlessly social, setting off in taxis to book collectors' dinners, his wheelchair carried up and down stairs like a throne.

He was one of a tight coterie of men who formed 'a court circle' around Eliot in the 1930s: Hayward, Geoffrey Faber and Frank Morley, an American publisher who was an early director of Faber and Faber (Geoffrey Faber had offered to name the company 'Faber and Morley' in 1929). In schoolboy fashion, each had an animal nickname: Faber was 'the Coot' (because of his baldness), Morley 'the Whale' (he had published a book on whaling in the 1920s), Eliot 'the Elephant' (an elephant appears on the Eliot family crest), Hayward 'the Tarantula' at the centre of the web. Their Sunday evening gatherings were a boys' club, 'a world of men without women'.

Yet his wider sociability was often remarked upon and fondly recalled. One friend of Hayward's remembered: 'One's easy and dominant memory is of his purposeful gaiety, of his delight in exactitude (and in the exposure of sloppiness), of the impressive head and bright eyes, of the comic imitations of people and puffing trains.' 'Everyone wanted to know John Hayward,' remarked Lady Violet Bonham Carter; 'I know of no one more vitalising to talk to, whether seriously or in fun,' Edith Sitwell said.

Hayward became a regular reviewer for The Criterion, and he and Eliot would meet often. Hayward, an English literary insider, was useful to Eliot as a careful reader of his work. As Hayward's biographer John Smart wrote: 'To Eliot Hayward was the arbiter of English correctness: as an American by birth, Eliot relied on his friend's scholarship and knowledge of grammar. Part of Hayward's role was to act as a representative British reader and filter out any Americanisms that might be unclear or confusing.'

Eliot and Hayward would share the flat right up until the time of his marriage to Valerie Fletcher. Eliot had two small dark rooms at the back of the flat, which was directly beneath a flat once owned by Henry James. Hayward's rooms were much more open and airy, but the arrangement

*gave Eliot the privacy he needed. Eliot would visit Hayward once a day
in his rooms, and take him for a walk at the weekend. In the mornings
after mass Eliot wrote, standing up, before heading for the Faber offices
in Russell Square.*

*It was in this year too that Mary left Student Movement House,
after beginning an appeal to fund a new building. She would continue
to dream of 'the great International House which we would set up in
London', modelled after the International Houses she had seen in the
United States. Such a place would offer greater opportunity for students
of different backgrounds to 'get to know each other better': the ideal of
cross-cultural fellowship which had always driven her. Her dream would
become reality in May 1965 when International Students House was
opened in Park Crescent, near Regent's Park, where it remains to this
day. But her personal life was bound up with Eliot; although he was now
living with John Hayward, she did not feel displaced. As she noted, there
are few letters in this period because they met so often.*

After my return to London, there were few weeks when we didn't
meet. We had a period of experimenting with restaurants – the
Moulin d'Or, Antoine's, the Three Vikings, the Étoile. Hoellering
was busy on the film of *Murder in the Cathedral* and gave Tom com-
plimentary tickets for the Academy Cinema, which we utilised from
time to time. Longman's published the book of my letters to Tom
from Belgium.

*Hoellering was George Hoellering, the film-maker whose acclaimed pro-
duction of* Murder in the Cathedral *would appear in 1951. Born in
Vienna a year before Eliot himself, he had come to Britain in 1936 and
was interned on the Isle of Man during the war, where he first encountered Eliot's play. Hoellering was also a director of the Academy Cinema
on Oxford Street, one of the premier art-house venues of its day. Mary
also remarks plainly on the fact that* I'll Walk Beside You *was not published by Faber and Faber but by Longman's – as of course Eliot himself*

had tried to dissuade her, in 1944, from publishing a book of that sort at all. Once again, however, a book of Mary's was well received: I'll Walk Beside You *was 'confidently recommended', as one reviewer wrote: 'To those of us whose sons were engaged in the fighting from Normandy to Germany, the narrative makes a particular appeal because the author has so much to tell us that the fighting men are too modest to reveal.'*

Mary of course sent Eliot a copy, despite his lack of encouragement. He wrote to thank her in a letter dated 28 March. He apologised to her for the delay in opening her parcel, which also contained gin 'though during Lent I never drink gin deliberately except on Wednesdays'; she had sent him some eggs, as well. His thanks for the book are polite; he calls it 'nicely-produced' and assures he will read it again. 'But', he wrote, 'it is very odd to read in a book what had been letters to oneself, and I murmur proudly

> *e cio lui fece*
> *Romeo, persona umile e pergrina*

Or something like that, for my Italian is very weak, and *I never quote correctly even in English . . .'*

He quotes from Canto VI of Dante's Paradiso; *the correct Italian is* e ciò li fece / Romeo, persona umìle e peregrina. *Romeo, a man of little standing and a stranger, made that happen. Here is Eliot's traditional self-deprecation in corresponding with Mary; it is interesting too, however, that the lines, which she reproduces, refer to himself as a 'stranger', perhaps hinting that the closeness she believed existed between them was not as mutual as she would have liked to believe.*

But the letter is chatty and amusing too, recounting an 'odd party' at the Royal Court Hotel 'which included an Elizabethan specialist named Percy Allen, who has been getting messages from Wm. Archer and Marie Lloyd through a medium (but some of the messages from Marie were intended for Sybil Thorndike: it appears that Marie and Sybil had bathed together on the beach at Brighton and struck up quite a friendship, which impressed Mr Allen very much.)' William Archer, a Scottish theatre critic,

*had died in 1924; Marie Lloyd, the music hall artist, had passed away
two years before that. Whether the actress Sybil Thorndike, who lived into
the 1970s, was receptive to these messages from beyond the grave, Eliot
does not recount.*

Tom was now installed in a flat in Carlyle Mansions with John
Hayward, his close friend, constant literary adviser and Literary
Executor. John was paralysed from the waist down. 'Taking John
for a walk' meant pushing him in his chair. For years Tom took him
out on Saturday afternoons often to the Royal Hospital gardens to
watch football.

*On 5 May Eliot wrote that he didn't ring her because 'I quail before a
telephone if it is more than to say yes or no to something or to fix an
appointment.' (Anne Ridler wrote that when he spoke on the telephone,
'his voice had a curiously strangled sound'.) He thanked her for gifts of
eggs and rhubarb.*

But your eggs do worry me, I think you ought to be eating them
yourself at odd moments; if you could procure some Worcester
Sauce (or even the Worcestershire Sauce, which is inferior: the
Reading Sauce, which I have not seen since the war, is unobtainable,
it came in a flat bottle with a thick neck) it goes very well with raw
egg (a thin not a thick neck). So please lay off eggs.

*He suggested dinner rather than a visit to the cinema, concerned that the
cartoons often shown before the main feature 'fill my mind with junk
that I never altogether get rid of'. He was still troubled – though he
didn't say why – by a film they he saw the Christmas before, René Clair's
adaptation of Agatha Christie's* And Then There Were None, *though
he referred to it by the book's original title, now no longer used.*

*In the summer Eliot travelled to the United States. The year before, his
friend and supporter Ezra Pound had been arrested in Italy by American*

forces. In broadcasts made over Italian radio between 1941 and 1943 Pound expressed his support for Mussolini's fascist regime and his disdain for the Allied cause; he spoke in virulently anti-Semitic terms. Addressing the British in March 1942 he spat: 'You let in the Jew and the Jew rotted your empire, and you yourselves out-Jewed the Jew.' Pound was taken to a detention centre in Pisa before being extradited to the United States to stand trial for treason.

Eliot was unstinting in support of his friend; upon hearing of his arrest, he had cabled Archibald MacLeish, poet and Assistant Secretary of State for Public Affairs, offering his help. Before travelling to the United States in 1946 Eliot sought the support of other poets, soliciting public and private support: it was certainly possible that Pound would face execution for his crime. He would eventually be declared unfit for trial by reason of insanity, and confined until 1958 in Saint Elizabeth's Hospital for the criminally insane in Washington, DC, which is where Eliot visited him on this summer trip, and would continue to visit him in subsequent years.

Mary says nothing of this in her account of their interactions and correspondence. It is as if there is a mutual concealment at work, with Eliot referring only vaguely to what occupied him on his travels, and Mary seeming to admit of no curiosity. There is no record of what she might have said to him of her life when they spoke privately, yet it seems unlikely that she would have revealed her feelings or activities to any great extent. Her gaze, her interest, was fixed on him.

Eliot wrote to her on his return in late July of seeing friends and relatives – those friends included Emily Hale, of whom Mary makes no mention. She noted only that he had returned from the United States, bearing nylon stockings (he was afraid he would only be able to get rayon) and a silk scarf designed by Marion Dorn, a Californian-born textile designer famous for her organic, geometric patterns for the London Underground.

Mary ends 1946 by reproducing two poems, sent to her as Christmas presents. The first was 'Billy M'Caw: The Remarkable Parrot' – which had in fact appeared some years before in The Queen's Book of the Red

Cross, *a volume produced in 1939 as a fundraising effort; fifty British authors and artists had made contributions, including not only Eliot but also A. A. Milne, Daphne du Maurier, Eric Ambler, Ivor Novello and Cecil Beaton. The second is Eliot's jovial hymn to a pig, a 'Worcestershire heavyweight' called Mr Pugstyles. Pugstyles is the denizen of a village which disdains any foreign-bred pigs; the verses begin by dismissing such animals in no uncertain terms: 'Other counties have schemers, contrivers and plotters; / Their underbred swine only merit our smiles.' At the end of six rollicking verses, Mr Pugstyles exceeds even the feats of winning blue ribbons at local fairs: he is elected to Parliament.*

> *So now we live quiet, and leave well alone*
> *And ignore all those Parliament folk and their wiles.*
> *Let 'em mind their own business, we'll manage our own,*
> *While we're represented by Mr Pugstyles.*
> *Mr Pugstyles, Mr Pugstyles,*
> *Our Worcestershire heavyweight, Mr Pugstyles.*

Perhaps it is interesting to consider this as comment on British parliamentary democracy, a consideration especially striking in the twenty-first century. Eliot's irony – if we perceive it as irony, and that is up to the reader, of course – is powerful. Mary makes no comment on his work; she was his friend, never his critic.

1947

Early in January Tom went into hospital for an operation, but he developed bronchitis, so the operation was postponed. I took him jam, eggs and soap! A young doctor took his blood pressure, glanced at his card and asked: 'Any relation of <u>the</u> Eliot?' 'Yes,' said Tom, meekly. Lying flat on his back one day, he announced in sepulchral tones that he was about to disown *Murder in the Cathedral*, as it had recently been made 'Prescribed Reading for Higher Certificate'.

On 22 January Tom's wife died suddenly. I was in Scotland at the time and saw the news in the press.

Eliot wrote to Mary on 30 January; she had written to him, having seen the notice of Vivien's death in the papers. 'Her death was quite sudden and unexpected,' he told Mary.

She was supposed to be in quite good physical health, but her heart was weak. It was therefore a particular shock, and has left me more disintegrated than I could have anticipated. Curiously enough, I believe it is much more unsettling to me now, after all these years, than it would have been fifteen years ago. It is partly because of the diminution of resilience that occurs in that length of time.

Fifteen years previously, 1932–3, was when he had resolved to leave her. Eliot had learned of her death in a phone call from her brother on the morning of 23 January; John Hayward took the call and broke the news. '"O God! O God!" Eliot said, and buried his face in his hands.' On her death certificate, the cause of death was listed as 'syncope' and 'cardiovascular degeneration'. Peter Ackroyd writes: 'She had worn herself to death.' She is buried in the cemetery in Pinner, North London; Eliot and her brother Maurice were in attendance at the burial. Just over a dozen years later he would write that while his first wife was 'nearly the death of me', she kept him alive as a poet. He called their seventeen years together 'a nightmare agony' but said that agony protected him from what would otherwise have been a 'mediocre' life.

Mary saw Eliot most weeks between January and Easter.

He talked much of his wife and did, indeed, seem to be very much upset at her death.

She gave no more detail than that. She was protective of him; it seems clear that she saw his feelings as private – rightly so – yet wished to demonstrate their closeness by revealing his confidence: the fact of it, not the substance. If she speculated that he would now be free to marry she gives no indication of that here. He wrote to her on 17 February that he was still ill with bronchitis, in bed with it when his electricity was cut off; he felt he would not get better until the weather improved. 'I go on coughing and spitting. The alternatives are a cold flat or a cold office.' He can't work; he's 'stupefied'. Before that, however, he had managed to go to a performance of Murder in the Cathedral *in aid of the Friends of Canterbury Cathedral; he wrote to Mary of having to go a tea party afterwards and being placed next to the Dean of Canterbury – Hewlett Johnson, known as 'the Red Dean' thanks to his support of the Soviet Union. Johnson 'irritates me exceedingly,' Eliot wrote to Mary. '(He never asks an intelligent question, he just tells you.)'*

She wrote that in Holy Week Tom's church was one of the few places that held the service of Tenebrae, performed during the last days before Easter, a darkness before the light. It is a beautiful service; candles are gradually extinguished, and at its end there is a 'strepitus', or loud noise, bursting from the darkness. 'For the last few years we had been to this service together.'

Soon after Easter I went off to UNESCO headquarters in Paris (on the avenue Kléber), from where I travelled around northern France and then to Greece, making my first surveys of priority needs in education in war-devastated countries. T. sent me many C.A.R.E. parcels – the food in Paris was still scarce, expensive and sometimes bad. Often the parcels contained groceries which I was able to give away to my French friends, for I was not doing my own cooking.

Her title was Head of the Field Survey Bureau in the UNESCO Department of Reconstruction in Paris; as she wrote, 'This new work promised opportunities of helping towards the rebuilding of education in many of the war-devasted countries.'

In April Eliot flew to America; his older brother, Henry Ware Eliot, was dying, and passed away twelve days after Eliot arrived. Mary wrote that he was 'very fond' of his brother: 'Later he told me how he had paid his last tribute by kneeling by his brother's body, saying some prayers and then kissing him good-bye.' He stayed in the States for two months, lecturing to keep an income: an address on Milton at the Frick Collection in New York, a poetry reading at the National Gallery in Washington, DC. He received an honorary degree from Harvard – the ceremony also conferred a Doctor of Science degree on J. Robert Oppenheimer, director of the Los Alamos Laboratory and widely known as the father of the atomic bomb.

He did not speak to Mary about his meetings with Emily Hale on this trip, or at least there is no evidence for this. The two women existed in different spheres, for him. While in America he went, at Hale's instigation, to Concord Academy in Massachusetts to give the Commencement address on 3 June. If Hale had imagined that Eliot might have felt able to marry her after the death of his wife, she discovered her error when they met. A few months later she wrote to a friend:

I am going to tell you, dear friend, that what I confided to you long ago of a mutual affection he and I have had for each other has come to a strange impasse whether permanent or not, I do not know. Tom's wife died last winter very suddenly. I supposed he would then feel free to marry me as I believed he always intended to do. But such proves not to be the case . . . He loves me – I believed that wholly – but apparently not in the way usual to men less gifted i.e. with complete love thro' a married relationship.

It is clear from Eliot's letters to Hale that their relationship was one of great intensity. To Hale, with whom he also shared drafts of his work – as he never did with Mary – he would write of his powerful feelings. 'You have made me perfectly happy,' he told her; 'that is, happier than I have ever been in my life; the only kind of happiness now possible for the rest of my life is now with me; and though it is the kind of happiness which is identical with my deepest loss and sorrow, it is a kind of supernatural ecstasy.'

His letters to Mary never expressed such emotion. On this trip he wrote of the 'pomp and ceremonies' of Harvard, Yale and Princeton – he had met Secretary of State George C. Marshall and Veterans Affairs Administrator Omar N. Bradley, who had been Army Chief of Staff and Twelfth Army Commanding General, respectively, during the war and who were also given degrees at Harvard, as well as the Governor General of Canada; he had heard President Truman speak. Yet it had been 'a sad and distressing visit indeed'. On top of it all, he had not enjoyed the trip by air: in those days the journey took nearly 14 hours, with stops to refuel in Ireland and Newfoundland.

When he returned, he underwent an operation for a hernia; they had dinner before he went into hospital. After the operation he was 'emaciated and tottering', he wrote to her on 14 August. He told her that he found the freedom from responsibility in hospital 'rather debilitating morally'. 'I feel very weak and stupid: it is surprisingly easy and pleasant to pass one's time in utter idleness, reading nothing but theology. Innumerable unanswered personal letters.'

It took Tom a long time to recuperate from his operation – he was very nervous about himself – 'apprehensive' he would say and he was not to be laughed at – only consoled.

He wrote on 29 August and told her that he had received 'a juvenile composition by Stephen Spender'. Eliot and Spender had first met when the latter was just twenty; Spender's description of that encounter is memorable. 'His appearance was grave, slightly bowed, aquiline, ceremonious, and there was something withdrawn and yet benevolent about his glance,' the younger poet wrote.

His voice alone, grave, suggesting a bowed gesture, almost trembling at moments, and yet strangely strong and sustained – his voice alone is Eliot . . . At our first luncheon he asked me what I wanted to do. I said: 'Be a poet.' 'I can understand your wanting to write poems, but I don't quite know what you mean by "being a poet",' he objected.

Eliot told Mary that he wanted to see her 'before you go to China' – another Far Eastern trip was in the offing. 'Keep out of the Balkans', he writes, and signs off with deep respect to her mother.
She was still working in Paris.

In September I came home briefly on business. My aeroplane was very late and I remember the sight of Tom standing patiently on the steps of Faber's doing the crossword puzzle while waiting for me. I was going to the Far East for six months and we dined the night before I set off. T. was much troubled by his new false teeth.

Indeed he was. 'I have always wondered how people who have a complete false upper set manage to keep it in and now I wonder more than ever,' he would write to Mary. 'I am afraid to look out of the window, lean over a bridge, spit into a lavatory basin: and if you give me a piece of bread I take it away to a corner to eat, like a suspicious dog.'

On 30 September he wrote that 'I discovered by accident to-day, picking up a copy of Burke's Landed Gentry, my family listed as Landed Gentry Settled in America. I am not landed, except with all these foreign men of letters invited over by the British Council, and how can anyone feel settled under Sir S. Cripps?' Stafford Cripps was Chancellor of the Exchequer in the post-war Labour government, one whose priorities were 'exports first, capital investment second, and the needs, comforts, and amenities of ordinary consumers last'; Eliot was never happy with the attention paid to his earnings by the Inland Revenue. 'Well,' Eliot continued, 'I suppose you will be in Burmah trying to be pleasant to little brown men named Baw and Saw, when I come to France if I come in November . . .'

That reference to those 'little brown men' is uncomfortable; it is a glimpse of the prejudice which still taints his reputation. It was not one shared by Mary: her open-mindedness in this regard was in notable contrast to Eliot's attitudes. 'After the Holocaust, after the exposures of the Nuremberg Trials, Eliot still kept the "jew" he had aligned with rats and the "jew" who was "spawned" in Antwerp in the lower case until 1963,' as Lyndall Gordon wrote. 'Eliot's greatness, I believe, shows itself not in glib jibes but in a struggle with certain flaws in his nature, a long struggle that gave birth to the spiritual journeys of his maturity.' Those glib jibes, however, still have the power to shock.

On 22 October he wrote to Mary that he had a cold and couldn't leave his flat: it is often hard to refrain from contrasting Eliot's apparent vulnerability to any ailment with Mary's hardiness. He told her that he had written to Jacquetta Hawkes, who was just leaving for Mexico with a UNESCO junket, 'to explain why it is most undesirable to translate all the "classics" etc. Unesco is very weak at definition: but a classic is any book printed before 1900, which any official committee of any government wants to put across to other peoples.' (Hawkes was a remarkable woman, an archaeologist and a writer: she and Eliot had had some correspondence about her poetry at this time. Today she is best known for her book A Land, published in 1951. Her second husband was the author

J. B. Priestley; it was on this trip to Mexico that the pair met and fell in love.)

On *1* Advent, in the weeks leading up to Christmas, Eliot wrote to Mary that he was preparing to go away to France; in fact that trip would be cancelled, though he would head to Amsterdam and Rome under the auspices of the British Council. As for Mary's travels, he hoped they were going well, and that she would be 'sailing into a milder climate'. 'I hope that the worries of the Burmese will distract your mind from the worries of Europe, without being too serious in themselves.' He promised that he would try to write to her over Christmas, and report on his adventures.

Mary arrived in Burma three days before Christmas, and would be travelling until February of the following year. Once again, she displayed indefatigable curiosity and energy on another remarkable journey.

1948

Mary's trip to Burma was part of her work with UNESCO, her task to investigate how the education systems of war-devastated countries could be rebuilt. She arrived in the country at a time of drama and radical political change. Burma had been made a province of India by the British in 1886; resistance against British rule had been building since the 1920s. By the mid-1930s the arguments for autonomy were led by a young law student, Aung San. Following the Japanese invasion of Burma during the Second World War, Aung San co-operated with the British to drive out this second group of invaders; after the war's end, Aung San negotiated Burma's independence from Britain, which was declared in January 1948; Aung San, however, was assassinated in July 1947. Mary was arriving in a brand new country; she spent 'two months in the almost exclusive company of the Burmese as their guest, coming to the country a fortnight before Independence broke out', as she wrote in her report on her journey.

Her fearlessness, as ever, was on display. 'A week before Independence, Mrs Lingeman (wife of the General Manager of the B.O.C. [Burma Oil Company]) was shot and killed in her garden at Greenbank, at midnight. It was eventually established, and possibly truly, that she was the victim of a nervous sentry across the lake, who thought he saw something moving in the bushes. But the tragedy created panic among the English who were to remain in Burma and some did not go out of their houses for the whole of Independence week. As an International representative, I thought the only possible line of action was to procure a new Burmese flag to put on my station wagon and go about as usual. Although once caught in an excited Burmese crowd for more than an hour, I had no trouble whatsoever – fortunately it is often possible to make the Burmese laugh,' she wrote with equanimity.

She moved in high circles, spending much time with U Tin Tut, Burma's first foreign minister and the man who had been Aung San's principal deputy; he had been a key figure at negotiations for independence. According to Mary, he remained warm towards the British: she reported him as saying, 'We need our British friends in the new Burma.' She spent time too with Sao Shwe Thaik, Burma's first president, and travelled to the Shan States, as she called them, in northern Burma, encountering Karen nationalists: both the Shan and the Karen sought autonomy. For all Mary's open-mindedness, however, she did bring with her the legacy of a British imperial upbringing. 'Nationalisation of everything is the motto of the Government,' she wrote, 'but they are like children and have no idea how to manage the big concerns they are taking over.'

She was taken with the place – so much so that her report for UNESCO, 'New Moon on Burma', reads like a history-cum-travelogue. It is beautifully written, if perhaps a little flowery. But her affection for the country rings true: 'And at nightfall the deep yellow moon shines undisturbed by cloud or storm, save in the monsoon period. The radiance of the moon throws a new light on Burma, a softer light which gives relief after the brilliant, unrelenting sun of the day. The curious, musty smell of the East mingles with the strong perfume of the temple-flower and a little breeze moves the pagoda bells to soft music.'

In the Birthday Honours this year Tom received the ORDER OF MERIT – to him the greatest of all honours. In September he took the precaution of spending his 60th birthday at sea – and a Symposium to celebrate the occasion was edited by Tambimuttu. In November his painfully written 'Notes Towards the Definition of Culture' was published after five years' hard work and had a mixed reception; there were complaints of its obscurity. My copy was inscribed 'in all simplicity'. In December came the NOBEL PRIZE. The letters which followed me faithfully to Burma, Malaya, North Borneo and Thailand made little mention of these notable events.

Mary's pride in her friend's achievements is evident, not least in her CAPITAL LETTERS. The Order of Merit was founded by Edward VII in 1902 and is awarded to those who have especially distinguished themselves either in the armed forces or in science, art, literature or the promotion of culture. It is limited to twenty-four living members at one time. The symposium to which Mary refers was edited by Richard March and Meary James Tambimuttu, the Tamil poet assisted by Mary and Eliot six years before. The celebratory publication included contributions from Conrad Aiken, Lawrence Durrell, Edith Sitwell, Stephen Spender and many others. It's worth noting that an essay by Desmond Hawkins – an author and critic who would go on to be one of the founders of the BBC's Natural History Unit – in this collection is entitled 'The Pope of Russell Square'. Evidence, at least, that the moniker was in circulation at the time.

The Nobel Prize in Literature would indeed come in December, though Eliot had been informed of the Swedish Academy's decision the month before. In the manuscript of The Pope of Russell Square *which is kept in the Bodleian Library, there are clipped and saved newspaper articles marking all these feats carefully pasted in. She preserved George Orwell's review of* Notes Towards the Definition of Culture *which was published in the* Observer: *'Is it too much to hope that the classless society will secrete a culture of its own? And before writing off our own age as irrevocably damned, is it not worth remembering that Matthew Arnold and Swift and Shakespeare – to carry the story back on three centuries – were all equally certain that they lived in a period of decline?' And she also saved the critic Raymond Mortimer's remarks on Eliot's OM. 'The Order conferred on Mr Eliot honours two men, the dramatist who has moved a large public in churches as well as theatres, and a recondite poet who has further widened the gulf between literature and the general reader.' Mortimer's description of Eliot as 'two men' resonates with his and Mary's friendship – though she was, as yet, unaware that she did not see the whole man.*

Eliot wrote to her on 5 January, dating his letter 'St Gerlac. Vigil of the Epiphany' – his choice of Gerlac (or Gerlach), a twelfth-century saint with origins in the Netherlands, perhaps unsurprising given his travels to Amsterdam. He had, he said, got two letters from her which he read 'with (as Edward Lear would say) the utmost apathy and delight', and joked with her about her writing a History of the Rise and Fall of the Burmese Republic: '(pp. 32, price 3/6) with a prefatory note by Brass Tak, First Prime Minister and Second Education Officer of the Burmese Republic'. Given the turmoil in Burma, his continued mockery of Burmese names rings ever more hollow; but Mary passed no judgement.

He told her of his adventures – his travels to Rome, via Amsterdam, where he ate oysters, steak, 'with considerable Hollands gin and beer, at the expense of the British Council'. He 'looked in on the Pope' and was made a member of the Italian intellectual academy, the Accademia dei Lincei,

to whom I delivered a short, modest and refreshing address in the most excellent French, and then listened to a discourse on the Russian reply to the Italian invitation to the Russian scientists to come to the celebration of the anniversary of Marconi's discovery of wireless telegraphy. The Russian Academy expressed gratification, but pointed out at some length that wireless telegraphy had been discovered some years earlier by a Russian and therefore they could not come.

He met, he told her, many Italian poets 'whose works I shall never read'. In veritably the same breath he advised her not to travel by BEA – British European Airways, as was – because you have to pay extra for food. He looked forward to hearing of her adventures 'among the wilder tribes', and mentioned his cousin Martha, 'the boss of children's health in America'. While it is true that Martha May Eliot's focus was on paediatrics, it's worth noting that in 1948 she was president of the American Public Health Association, the first woman to hold the post; she was also the only woman to sign the founding document of the World Health Organization.

'I wish you good food and few cockroaches,' Eliot concluded in his letter, 'and trust this will reach you before Easter to convey my New Year's Greetings.'

The letters that followed in the coming weeks were long and cheerfully chatty. The Pope, he assured her, made a good impression on him, and seemed less like a headmaster than the Archbishop of Canterbury. Geoffrey Fisher had been installed in that post in January 1945. Eliot didn't know, however, how he would compare if put up against Fisher and his wife. Does she want a rosary blessed by the Pope? he asked. His hot water bottle had leaked, he informed her; he had to change mattress and blankets both. 'Please DON'T give any letters of introduction to me to Burmese poets, I am very busy. I do hope you will not catch leprosy or spiders or anything or eat too many mangoes.'

He depended, he told her in a letter dated 26 January, 'Septuagesima', or the ninth Sunday before Easter, on her Burmese gossip. '(Does U mean Mister? If so, what is Miss and Mrs? Are you known as U Nesco?)' He was, he said – apparently never one to let go of a joke – 'eager for further news about Buz Saw and Go Bang, and all these touching little Burmen and Burwomen. Oh dear, how pathetic their Independence Day Clelebrations (my machine is beginning to talk in Burmese) and how sordid the sequel to all these jubilations and firecrackers will be!' This, of course, was an echo of the same sentiment Mary had expressed in doubting whether an independent Burma would be able to manage the 'big concerns' faced by a new nation. Burma's fight for independence, he told Mary, recalled for him his ancestor, the Rev. Andrew Eliot, who had preached a sermon on Easter Day 1765 in Boston addressing his audience as 'a generation of vipers', the text taken from the Gospel of St Matthew. 'He was much wiser about the American Revolution than the Burmese seem to be; but then, after all, he was an Eliot, and Eliots are wiser than Burmese.'

Her letters, he told her in February, depressed him. Everything she told him about Burma made him feel dismayed for the future of the East; but *then, he noted, he was dismayed about the future as a whole. He had met King George VI – to receive his Order of Merit – and thought he compared favourably to the Archbishop of Canterbury, but gave equal weight to noting that the front door of Buckingham Palace had neither doorbell nor door-knocker: the first such he had ever encountered. He listed his obligations: talks at Jesus College, Cambridge, presenting 'magic lantern slides' at the Royal Horticultural Society, giving a lecture on Apollinaire at the Institut Français. If the lantern slides seem surprising, that talk came about as a result of his relationship with John and Edith Carroll Perkins, Emily Hale's aunt and uncle; Edith Carroll Perkins was a keen gardener, and spent many summers in England, admiring and photographing English gardens. It was her collection of lantern slides Eliot was presenting to the RHS, but he did not tell Mary that. He closed his accounting gloomily: 'so life on the Thames is almost as unpleasant as life on the Irrawaddy.'*

Early in May, after a terrible series of delays owing to aeroplane breakdowns, I returned to civilisation and five days in England. I had tea with Tom on the day after my return and a long evening and dinner the night before leaving for Paris again. He gave me a detailed story of his visit to the King (to get his O.M.) which both seemed to have enjoyed very much. Two months later I returned again for three nights and we dined in Soho. These meetings I recall as being 'talking matches' followed by taking taxis late at night, which went so fast I could have murdered them. I gather, from the following letter, that I had failed to get any reply to requests as to when we were to meet on this second visit.

'I gather from the following letter' is interesting: it suggests a lapse of recollection, that she wished to put to one side any anxiety she may have felt regarding the nature of their friendship, or what his silences might have meant. For on 2 July he wrote to say that he was 'distressed' by the letter he had just received from her; the fact of his not writing 'does not,

my dear Mary, bear any of the usual interpretations'. He was in arrears
of correspondence, is all. 'I will only ask you to believe that I value your
friendship; and that if at any time I am invisible or inaudible, that is no
indication of disloyalty.'

On August 22nd, with bag and baggage, I finally left Paris and
UNESCO. We dined on the night of my return. Then I went to
Switzerland to recuperate after the long series of farewell parties etc.
I had had before leaving France.

In June of that year Martin Browne noted that he and Eliot discussed the
first draft of a play, then called One-Eyed Riley; *it would later be called*
The Cocktail Party, *and mark a significant inflection point in Eliot's*
relationship with Mary. In August he mentioned his new work to her for
the first time. 'I am to be taken to a cocktail party at the Perths',' he wrote.
'I hope it will be less depressing than the cocktail party in my play.'

In the first week in October Tom left for the United States and spent
three months at the Institute of Advanced Studies in Princeton.

He had originally been invited by the Institute's director Frank Aydelotte,
but had been unable to take up the offer until 1948; by that time, J. Robert
Oppenheimer had taken over the directorship. He had no duties except
to get on with his work: when Aydelotte had extended the invitation,
he had written that he might 'come to the Institute for Advanced Study
for a period of two or three months with no duties except to go on quietly
with your own work and to engage in such discussion with Members of
our group here as may seem interesting and profitable to you'. He was, in
effect, an artist-in-residence.

He sailed at the end of September and wrote to Mary from the
SS America *on his way, as he called it, to 'Gomorrah'. The ship pulled*
into Cobh, in Ireland, before crossing the Atlantic. He wrote to her on 28
September – the letter is dated 'St Wenceslas' – that a group of priests came

aboard, 'and aren't they the jolly boys with the colleens, except when they are in the bar playing cards, drinking brandy and soda and smoking big cigars', rather scandalising, Eliot surmised, some other clergy making the crossing. He noted too among the passengers 'the usual representation of Central European ghettoes, and the lower middle class of everywhere', as ever, keeping people in their proper places – as he saw it, at least.

He settled into a house on Alexander Street in Princeton, not far from the university. Everything was taken care of for him, he told Mary on 15 October: there were plenty of secretaries and administrators to look after him; he was even provided with a servant, Blanche, to look after him at home. On 15 October he wrote happily from the Institute, where 'they seem to be able to do almost everything for one', that there were a great many secretaries and administrators to help.

I have not seen any of the atom bombers or Einstein or Dirac, but the place is swarming with mathematicians and with physicists, but some of the latter are working on a Thinking Machine under separate cover: somebody has promised to take me over and introduce me to it, but I feel rather diffident because I know it already thinks so much better than I do.

The 'Humanists' huddled together at lunch, he said, being in a minority – though it was at Princeton that he met the American poet Robert Lowell; Faber and Faber would publish Lowell's Poems, 1938–1949 *two years later.*

It was while at Princeton that he learned he had been awarded the Nobel Prize. The Times *noted in a leader that while once Eliot was the object of criticism for his obscurity, he was now 'widely considered the chief formative influence in the language at present'. He would cut short his stay in New Jersey to travel to Stockholm. Eileen Simpson, then the wife of the poet John Berryman, noted his reaction to the award in her memoir: 'When John congratulated him on the prize, and added, "High time!" Eliot said, "Rather too soon. The Nobel is a ticket to one's own funeral. No one has ever done anything after he got it.'" Simpson found him reserved, in his formal banker's dress. 'Shyness had been disciplined into courtesy. On being introduced he made an effort not to avert his eyes, as one felt he would have done as a young man.'*

He returned briefly to England before heading off to Sweden. He and Mary dined together upon his return.

On December 10th Tom returned from America and, almost at once, left for Sweden to receive his Nobel Prize. After several short meetings we dined on the Sunday before Christmas – I called for him at Carlyle Mansions where I found him desperately typing letters of thanks etc. to people in the U.S.A. It was very cold and T. wrapped himself in a huge fur coat (his deceased brother's and too large for him) and, after drinks, had dinner at the Russell Hotel. He talked a great deal about his adventures in America, too detailed to remember and confusing because of his habit of referring to everyone by their first names.

In Sweden he attended a performance of 'Family Reunion' [*sic*] in Swedish and his description was very comic. 'The drawing room looked very like a waiting room in St Pancras Station. The Library was like a Public Library, but the bookcases parted obligingly to admit the Eumenides – and they appeared to be a sort of Rugby team, of 15 huge, leprous giraffes.' On December 13th, the day started surprisingly. At 6.30 a.m. the Nobel Prizeman got out of bed and went to his private bathroom to make his toilet. Attired in vest and pants, he was shaving when the door into the vestibule of his suite opened and a procession of six young ladies dressed (so it seemed to him) in nightdresses and carrying crowns of lighted candles on their heads, marched into his bedroom – singing. Poor Tom – but by stretching an arm round the bathroom door he reached his overcoat, into which he rapidly inserted himself and appeared before them thus clad and half shaved. They sang solemnly, while he stood in front of them feeling very foolish. Then the leading lady gravely presented him with a cup of coffee and a sweet biscuit which he, with equal gravity consumed. After which, to his great relief, the procession departed – still singing. Nobody had thought to warn him of Saint Lucy's Day and the customary Swedish celebrations.

He had written to her earlier in the year to enquire whether she would help him with writing out the score for 'One-Eyed Riley' – a bawdy Irish folksong which he wanted to use in his play; at this point she knew little about it, but was of course happy to help. He would sing it to her, and she would transcribe.

After his return we managed, with some difficulty, to transcribe 'One-Eyed Riley' – a song he had heard in his youth – for use in 'The Cocktail Party'. Tom's singing was rather like an out-of-tune bassoon. However, I got it down on the back of an envelope and then played it to him on the piano.

Two days before Christmas Tom came in for a drink and brought me, as well as many books, a beautiful old crucifix which had hung in his own room for twenty years and of which he could not remember the origin. He discussed confession: 'The awful thing about it is that one keeps confessing the same sins every time. And when one has led a comparatively good life for some months and can't think of anything to confess, one always feels that more advanced Christians would discover many more subtle sins.'

1949

After 1948 the character of Mary's account of her friendship with Eliot changes; it becomes clear too that she hoped the relationship itself would change.

From the beginning of this year we met – or telephoned – so often that I am only including such extracts from my diary as indicate some particular points of interest in the make-up of this very intricate character. I hoped, now that I was returning to London, that we should be able to come to some clear 'working relationship' with regard to our relationship. I really didn't know where I was at all. Tom gave me many indications that he reciprocated my feelings for him – not only in a continuous stream of presents, but in such ways as holding my hand for an almost embarrassingly long time on saying good-bye, even though we were to meet again very shortly.

There is a poignancy in the way that Mary notes his attention to her: a wish to see someone better than he saw himself, and in the account that follows, an unwillingness to perceive the authenticity of his reticence. She believed she saw the whole of Eliot, assuming that his practical reliance on her was an emotional reliance as well. But there was so much she did not or could not see, given the way he kept such a strict separation between the spheres of his life. That she barely knew Emily Hale's name, for instance, is evidence of this; nor did she have any awareness of the way in which Eliot's connection to Hale had marked him.

The year of 'The Cocktail Party' – the only play in which I can claim to have had a small share myself. In my copy there is a characteristically formal inscription: 'To Miss Mary Trevelyan, with the author's compliments' and, in addition, 'See Appendix and with thanks for her contribution to the character of Julia. E.g. p. 151.' The Appendix consists of 'The Tune of One-Eyed Riley, as scored from the author's dictation by Miss Mary Trevelyan'. Page 151 includes:

Julia: My dear Henry, you are interrupting me . . .
Riley: Who is interrupting now?
Julia: Well, you shouldn't interrupt my interruptions.

Tom used to derive great amusement from interrupting some of my longer and more fascinating stories, in spite of my protests, so that I lost the thread entirely.

Did Eliot find those long stories 'fascinating'? There is a possibility – the reader can't help but feel – that he might not have done. And Mary's involvement in this new play – helping him with a tune, a little inspiration for a character – cannot be compared with the way in which he had corresponded with Emily Hale about The Family Reunion, *sending two drafts of the play to her for comment. The American poet Marianne Moore wrote to Hale to tell her that Eliot often spoke of her; Moore says she almost thought of Hale 'as a collaborator in some of [his] plays'. And Hale had found, reading* The Cocktail Party, *'many a passage which could have hidden meaning for me and for him'. Mary was not a woman, in any case, to look for hidden meanings: she was forthright and matter-of-fact, and it seems clear that this was what Eliot found refreshing about her company. He relied upon her for practical advice. She noted a letter received from him on 13 March: he could not see her, he told her, in part because he was 'hermetically sealed up with my seven imaginary characters who I am already heartily sick of'. What he wanted from her was information: one of his seven imaginary characters was Celia Coplestone, who meets an appalling end – offstage – as a result of her missionary work. 'Perhaps you can give me some tips about my East Indian Island: are there monkeys, and do people tie their victims up in the jungle and smear them with sticky stuff to attract insects. There is no information on these points in any of your Reports.' But Mary now hoped for something more. She had taken a flat in Brunswick Square, close to the offices of Faber and Faber in Russell Square.*

Tom's experiment of sharing a flat in Chelsea with John Hayward was being very successful. Besides a strong personal affection, he depended greatly on John as his literary critic and seldom felt quite easy in his mind about anything he had written unless John approved.

Tom had no telephone; John took messages.

Only very occasionally did I visit Tom at the flat – in the evening after dinner, or when he was recovering from something or other, for tea in his room . . . It was not DONE to visit both of them at the same time and they had few friends in common.

On 3 January, I drove back from Oxford, after a Christmas holiday, in bitter cold. Tom turned up at 6.30, bringing his Nobel Prize medal to show me – also a little book containing his 'Poe to Valéry' lecture to the Library of Congress (printed in U.S.A.) as an extra Christmas present.

In this lecture, delivered in November, Eliot had spoken of Poe's 'negligible' influence in Britain and how much impact he had had on the French poets, especially Baudelaire, Mallarmé and Valéry. They ate dinner in a restaurant, and then returned to Mary's flat, where they talked, she played the piano and they listened to a BBC lecture on Eliot given by the scholar Jacob Isaacs, a longstanding friend of the poet: part of a series of talks later published as An Assessment of Twentieth-Century Literature.

Very odd it was, listening to a broadcast with the Subject of the Talk sitting beside me. Much of it was about his early life. Tom got very restive and kept muttering 'Nonsense', or 'that was the wrong year'. He said it made him feel quite dead already. He seems oppressed at having obtained the O.M. (which he prizes above everything) and the Nobel Prize – 'there is nothing left – like a schoolboy who has won ALL the prizes worth having.'

They did not see each other again for three weeks. She called this 'an unusual gap', beginning to draw attention to the times in which they would be apart, noting his mysterious abruptness. She began to ratio-nalise these absences, linking them to a feeling of closeness; at least, that is how she perceived them.

T. suddenly telephoned that he couldn't see me again until 27 January – with no reason stated. I was to become used to this. He tended to 'disappear' after a particularly good time together; he seemed to take fright and going away was his instinctive defence. But during such intervals letters and books used to arrive – 'to keep in touch'.

Mary turned fifty-two on 22 January. On 27 January there was a birth-day tea-party in her flat: she invited the actress Athene Seyler – one of the finest comic performers of her generation – to meet Eliot. He had long admired her – having written an enthusiastic notice of a 1924 per-formance in Wycherley's Restoration comedy, The Country Wife. *'She played the part of Lady Fidget with a kind of cold ferocity,' he had writ-ten, 'a pure and undefiled detachment which makes her worthy to rank in that supreme class which includes Marie Lloyd and Nellie Wallace.'*

She was all of a twitter at meeting the Great Man. He came in with a large attaché case, dumped it on the floor and unpacked his Nobel Prize Book (which he gave me) and many tins of food. Athene looked rather astonished. They got on excellently together and were very comic.

He wrote to her on 14 February – which he did not note as Valentine's Day, but rather 'Ste. Georgette', though most sources mark the following day in that saint's memory. He reflected on a reception he had to attend: 'Einstein said that there were three periods in the life of a scientist: one where he does his work, second when he gets his laboratory, third when he entertains distinguished visitors. I appreciate that.' It is a light-hearted remark which, however, hints again at the divisions in the poet's life. They had lunch together around this time.

I thought T. looked very white and tired. He brought to me to vet with him an orchestral score by a Dutchman of 'The Hollow Men'. He was pleased that we had the new record player and threatened to give me a disc of his Old School as a Valentine. In the afternoon he sent a lovely book on Van Gogh round to my office. At dinner later in the month [23] we discussed the recording he had made of the 'Four Quartets', which he had sent to me. I teased him about his pronunciation of 'worried' as WERRIED and 'poetry' as POITRY.

The 'Dutchman' was Kees van Baaren, who set Eliot's poem as a cantata. Eliot's reading of Four Quartets *is available online; readers may verify for themselves Mary's opinion of his pronunciation. He was, Mary said, 'vexed' by his writing: 'the seven characters are a nuisance,' he told her, adding that he was very depressed about them – but he had promised Martin Browne that he would complete* The Cocktail Party *by the summer. He was very busy, he told her, and indeed he was, speaking at the Alliance Française, attending a lunch at the Anglo-Swedish society, giving a speech in Oxford. He dated his letter on 11 March 'les 40 Martyrs (count them)'; on 23 March they went to the Academy Cinema to see Luigi Zampa's film* Angelina *with Anna Magnani – Magnani and Zampa were in London for the premiere. 'I thought Zampa was the name of an obscure opera,' he told Mary.*

I thought the film only moderate and I think Tom went to sleep. Afterwards Tom was mobbed by distinguished ladies. One of them told him coyly that she had a bone to pick with him. 'But you so often have bones to pick with me,' says he, 'very soon we shall have a whole chicken!' – which was almost rude and considerably disconcerted the lady. I was told, as we drove home, that she deserved it.

Two days later T. brought the records of the 'Poe to Valéry' lecture, which had just come from the U.S.A. A good deal of talk about his 'seven imaginary characters' who seem to be causing him some trouble. The play will be called 'The Cocktail Party' – partly because it has already been so announced in the press. The first act is a cocktail party which has been cancelled, but to which some guests come nevertheless. He seems attached to a lady called Julia. I guess it is going to be an unusual play.

The Cocktail Party *has been described as a morality play disguised as drawing room comedy. In it a separated couple, Edward and Lavinia Chamberlayne, reunite at a cocktail party held to preserve social appearances; Lavinia is brought to the party by an uninvited guest who is later revealed to be the analyst treating both husband and wife. Celia Coplestone is Edward Chamberlayne's lover. The 'lady called Julia' hovers at the edges of the couple's social circle, talkative and never quite welcome. Although the play has been revived in the years since its first production, its allegorical quality made it hard to take even for some contemporary audiences. 'Mr Eliot as a dramatist has a lot of fun in him, but the fun is kept in strict subservience to a moral judgment which applies itself with high, even bleak seriousness to the vagaries of human character,' wrote a critic in* Tatler.

Again: Mary was not a critic, she was not of his literary circle and it is clear that this is precisely what Eliot found refreshing and relaxing about her company. The intersection of their relationship was in their desire to do good (as they perceived it), their religious faith, their interest in music. It seems as if it was, to Eliot, an uncomplicated, straightforward relationship. But he did not perceive – or chose not to perceive – that this might not have been the case for Mary.

On 29 March he told Mary that John Hayward had discovered that there was an HMV recording of 'One-Eyed Riley', perhaps a version recorded by the Irish tenor Robert Irwin. Eliot instructed his secretary, then Mary Bland, the wife of Faber and Faber's production director, to get it. But she noted that she and Eliot listened to something else when they next met.

31 March: Under the influence of gin we played a splendid record of the 'Poe to Valéry' lecture to the Library of Congress, when the Chairman invites T. to sit down and there follows a groan from the Great Poet and a most resounding thump. It's really very funny – especially when played out of its context . . .

13 April: (Holy Week). (Drinks) During Holy Week we attended Tenebrae, then had dinner very late at a little restaurant by S. Kensington Station. The service is very long, but interesting and dramatic – many psalms and the candles put out one by one until the church is in complete darkness – then there is a loud bang (which made me jump) and silence . . . We were both so exhausted by this experience that dinner was somewhat silent and gloomy.

Tenebrae – which Mary had also mentioned two years before, in 1947 – seemed to have appealed not only to their shared faith but also to their sense of the dramatic. They met again on Easter Monday, 18 April, together in her flat. There is a tone of quiet intimacy to what she records.

A contrast to our last meeting. Bank Holiday and a Heat Wave. We pulled the blinds down, Tom sat in shirt sleeves and we drank long, cold drinks. T. brought a quantity of 'Picture books' as he calls Faber's Art Productions and we had a little music – it being no occasion for anything that demanded the slightest effort. T. looks less tired and I think that 'the seven imaginary characters' are falling into line.

In the typescript copy of the manuscript of The Pope of Russell Square, *what follows is entirely crossed out in pencil. It is impossible to know whether it was crossed out by Mary, or by a later reader. The parentheses are her careful punctuation, a kind of typographic shelter: a half-concealment. It is almost as if her pain – agony is the word she uses – could be contained. And in a sense, it was, for she did not reveal it to Eliot. It seems as if Eliot destroyed her letter to him; but the contents and intention are clear.*

(On 18 April I went to Paris and Switzerland for a short holiday. Before leaving I wrote to Tom, having come to the conclusion that I could no longer go on with our increasing intimacy without the assurance that he knew my feelings. It was characteristic of Tom that he sent NO reply to Paris, in spite of my urgent request that he should do – one glance at my letter and he had put it on one side until 'the burden of the unwritten letter became greater than the pain of writing'. And he will never know the agony he caused me. His letter was waiting for me on my return to London.)

He finally replied on 27 April 1949, giving the day as 'S. Frederick', though this St Frederick's day appears to be in July. The catastrophe to which he refers may well be his break with Emily Hale two years earlier.

Oh dear, oh dear. I haven't been so distressed since a catastrophe which I can't tell anyone about because it involves another person. It was thoughtful of you to write before going to Paris – and I did not really take in on what day you were returning – because I simply could not have collected myself to write before now: only when it's got to the time at which the burden of the unwritten letter is greater than the pain of writing.

Well, one so easily falls into assuming that another person under-stands what one feels, without facing the fact that they can't do that in ignorance of things one has not told them, and which reticence makes impossible to tell. Which, even when it comes to a show down, one can only hint at.

As for yourself and me, I honestly didn't know that it was any-thing like that. Not that it had not crossed my mind, some time ago, that something might have developed if other things that had happened to me in the past had not made it impossible for me – but that's all, and I did think we had arrived at a stable friendship. I should hate to lose that, because you have become an important part of my life, though I have to parcel my time out in such ways that I cannot ever see a great deal of any one person. It is always a long time before I can convince myself that anyone (of either sex) really likes me very much and wants my friendship, and I am always surprised and grateful when someone does. But even in the curious life I lead, it would mean a great gap if you were not there at all.

As for myself, I realised – with a shock – several years ago and in quite another context, that I was burnt out, and that I could no longer feel towards anyone as I once had, and up to that moment I believed I still did. This was a tragedy of which I cannot say more, but which has made me feel, ever since, a haunted man. I realised too, that I had become fixed in one mode of life although for years I had rebelled in spirit against it; and that the thought of trying to share my life with anyone had become a nightmare. I went through a kind of psychological change of life; and now I feel that I am merely living against time with my eye on the clock, to accomplish the best I can in creative work – or if not that, in some usefulness – and in making some progress on the Way before the gong is struck and the last round is over (mixed metaphor). It may be just a some-what premature ageing; it may be partly that what I went through in a good many years of agony had exhausted and crippled me more than during the five or six years before the war, I had recognised.

I should like to dissipate from your mind, if they are there, all of the painful or embarrassing things which you may think I think or felt, and don't think or feel. But at present I must just want to find out what you find out is best for you. I don't know whether you will wish to dine with me at the Garrick on Sunday, so I shall just wait for a message from you (or none) about that. I should be very sorry for any long interval, but it would be worse to have you force yourself to see me. In waiting, I shall be always your affectionate and appreciative friend.

There is, after his signature, an addendum:

And now I suppose I ought to destroy your letter. And I enclose a diversion – a copy of the best Indian letter I recall receiving.

The letter to which he refers is from one Sarwan Singh, who writes from Patiala in the Punjab; it refers to Eliot's 'sweet and thrilling' poetry, and requests money, 'as I have a very limited source of the financial aspect'; Singh said he wished study in England and the United States. And so Eliot offers what he perceives to be an amusing foreigner (!) to distract her from her suffering – and from her humiliation, which he begins to imagine. His letter is remarkable for what it withholds and conceals, while revealing what he paints as his own inescapable suffering. Phrases jump out at the reader: reticence makes impossible – other things that had happened to me in the past – parcel my time out – curious life – burnt out – cannot say more – a haunted man – a nightmare. And towards the end, the convoluted, not to say confused, expression of tangled emotion in the painful or embarrassing things which 'you may think I think or felt, and don't think or feel'. Expressed this way, painful sentiment bounces back and forth between them with nowhere to land, no way to be resolved.

'I said to my soul, be still, and wait without hope / For hope would be hope for the wrong thing; wait without love, / For love would be love of

the wrong thing,' Eliot wrote in 'East Coker'. It was impossible for her to see the full picture of Eliot's life, what he desired or did not desire, for he worked hard to keep it invisible. None of us, of course, is ever wholly visible to others, and not even to ourselves, but Eliot worked harder than most to show only certain aspects of himself to certain people. Peter Ackroyd has written of the nine years Eliot spent working at Lloyd's Bank as 'arguably the most important years of his creative life'; but during this time he was also 'a bank official indistinguishable from other such officials except perhaps for the absolute decorum of his dress . . . a little cog in the machine of Britain's commercial empire. Here are the makings of a truly remarkable double life.' 'Prufrock' was published just a few months after he began working at the bank.

Mary records her response to Eliot on 1 May.

After reading this letter (which I was not to understand fully until a year later) I sent Tom a note to say I would like to see him and had a telegram to say he'd call for me at 6.30 p.m. – which he did, and we both burst into talk on the doorstep – about anything, simultaneously. I mixed some strong drinks – conversation helped by Tom's vivid account of The Bump Supper (i.e. Academy Dinner – Munnings, not too sober, speaking his mind). Dinner at the Russell Hotel – SO slow and SO bad – coffee in the lounge and both miserable at the thought of our prospective talk. But it wasn't too difficult. I just amplified my letter a little, very gently, and T., who had put on his 'distraught refugee' face, relaxed. I said as much as I could and I guess it's all right. We drove to Chelsea rather silently but quite peacefully, about 11 p.m.

She would learn, as she hints here with the timing of a dramatist, more of his personal life the following year. Her technique allows the reader to be present in the emotional moment she conjures, which acknowledges her shock, her pain, but moves swiftly and briskly to what had been the status quo between them: amused, practical, relaxed. He felt safe within the bounds of their friendship as he conceived of it; for the moment, she seemed willing to accept what was on offer. The supper to which Eliot referred was a notorious one at the Royal Academy at which its president, the painter Sir Alfred Munnings, attacked 'highbrows' and 'experts' who 'think they know more about Art than the men who paint the pictures'. She was game for distraction, determined as she was to put on a brave face. Five days later she received a letter from him.

To-day a letter came from Tom, mostly concerning various dates for meeting and adding, 'at the same time I am worried about you and all this. Perhaps I have not been very lucid yet'. I replied cheerfully and firmly and asked for (and got) a frivolous reply (which seems to have been lost).

This is where the crossing-out in the manuscript ends.

They met again on 15 May. He turned up early at her flat and 'with greatly increased confidence'. They had supper, listened to the Mozart clarinet quintet '(which he had given me)', as she noted, still annotating, as it were, his special attention to her.

Nothing later than Brahms (whom he doesn't really care for much) is of any use to him. We talked of his programme for the visit of his sister Marian and niece Theodora, who arrive soon from the U.S.A. and, of course, 'The Cocktail Party'. The rehearsals (to which I am asked to go) take place in London for the first three weeks of August, and then Edinburgh. John Masefield seems to be dying – and we discussed the probability of T. becoming Poet Laureate – a prospect he dreads, but seems to think inevitable. 'I am putting wheels in motion in the direction of Edith Sitwell. There is a precedent for this; in Wordsworth's Life there's a mention of the fact that Elizabeth Barrett Browning was the favourite – though Tennyson got it. It means app. £300 a year – the price of a butt of Malmsey Wine – becoming a member of the Royal Household, hard work at official occasions, and the wearing of Court Dress!' I asked what he would do if he had to write a poem on the birth of a Royal Child – 'I should take refuge in obscurity'. The King, when he gave Tom his O.M., said: 'Poets, when they become Laureates, never write again.'

His older sister Marian and his niece Theodora were to arrive in July; as for her reference to Edinburgh, The Cocktail Party *would have its first outing at the festival in August, produced under the aegis of the theatrical impresario Henry Sherek. It is fine to think of Eliot in favour of a female Laureate; sixty years would pass, however, before Carol Ann Duffy took up the mantle in 2009.*

By the following month, she wrote on 12 June, 'we were almost back to "normalcy" as the Yanks would say'.

I was commanded to dine at the Garrick Club, to which Tom has lately been elected a member. I was acting as a guinea pig, since he had not yet been brave enough to take advantage of Ladies' Night in these august premises. On arrival I was met by an elderly waiter who led me to an immense smoking room on the first floor, with nobody in it but Tom. Many portraits (Holbeins and Zoffanys) of famous actors in famous parts, the CHAIR David Garrick had used and a glass case full of relics . . . After several attempts on an ancient bell we secured drinks and sat down and gossiped mildly . . . After a good dinner we returned to the flat for some music – a new record of the Coriolan Overture and a Mozart Oboe Quartet – T. brought a lot of food (from U.S.A.) and some books.

On 12 July she wrote of Eliot's involvement in the forthcoming produc-tion of his play.

We talked much of the play – he is going to record the whole thing himself and he urges me to come and hear it, and see if he can bring out the different characters. The casting is being very difficult. He requires very sudden changes from comedy to gravity and, rather than risk sentimentality, would prefer it all in the comic vein.

Irene Worth and Alec Guinness were among the original cast. At the first rehearsal Eliot announced to the assembled company, 'I will now read the play to you to show how I want my lines spoken' – he did not want the 'voice' of his poetry to be subsumed by acting and direction.

Marian and Theodora arrived from Boston – and the quartet made a companionable group, she wrote on 13 July.

Soon after their arrival, I spent an agreeable evening at the Ladies' Athenaeum with Tom's sister Marian, 71, straight-backed, bright-eyed, charming 'Bostonian', just a little alarming and the niece, Theodora, quiet and nice-looking. T., very amiable, introduced me as 'the Vicar's daughter'. Such a bad dinner, but easy conversation, only occasionally needing prodding.

It is notable that Eliot in describing her this way casts Mary in a junior relation to someone else, not as the independent woman she was. Mary was in her fifties, usually a time when women are no longer catego-rised as daughters. The vicar's daughter: unlikely too to be the object of romance. Mary records the description, as much comment as she is will-ing to pass. Another description of her in a letter of Eliot's has Mary as 'industrious, honest, and moderately temperate': a worthy, if not enticing, portrait.

On 16 July she suggested an outing to Windsor, to visit the Morsheads: Sir Owen Morshead was the King's Librarian at the time. His wife, Francisca de la Escosura Hagemeyer – known as Paquita – had been born in Florence to American parents. Eliot checked on her origins with Mary before the trip, asking whether Mary had indeed told him she was 'a foreigner'. They went with Marian and Theodora to Windsor in early August, and Mary recorded the visit on 7 August.

We took the family to tea with the Morsheads. We arrived at the TRADE DOOR in the Castle, where we were met by Owen and spent a fascinating hour with him in the Library, seeing miniatures, medals, letters and pictures of great interest. A friendly tea with Paquita, evensong at St George's followed by a short tour conducted by me in the Little Cloisters. After depositing the ladies at their hotel on our return, I drove T. to Chelsea and we discussed play revisions.

8 August: The next day Tom and I spent a very peaceful two hours drinking gin and discussing, of all improbable subjects, euthanasia – 'which must never be legalised, but should sometimes be practised'. On death: 'Christians are braver than others because they face another life. I am afraid of death, but I believe that in the last moments most of us are calm.' On *The Cocktail Party*: 'Julia, Reilly and Alex are immortals who do not progress – the other four are human and develop.' He fears that the public are expecting too much of the Nobel Prizeman.

On 18 August they had a 'most exciting' time, at a London dress rehearsal for the Edinburgh production of The Cocktail Party.

Tom very sociable and being photographed. It was fascinating, after attending so many rehearsals, to see the shape of the whole. Later Tom rang up from the office, as excited as a schoolboy. I fetched him at 5.30 and we had a post-mortem before depositing him at the Ritz to dine with some Americans. I think it is going to be all right – the play I mean. Alec Guinness sings 'Old Man Riley' quite creditably. Julia (so much of her is me!) is excellently played by Constance Cummings – indeed, she, Guinness and Irene Worth are first rate.

The Times *praised the play when it opened later that month in Edinburgh: 'In this brilliantly entertaining analysis of problems long since staled by conventional treatment Mr Eliot achieves a remarkable*

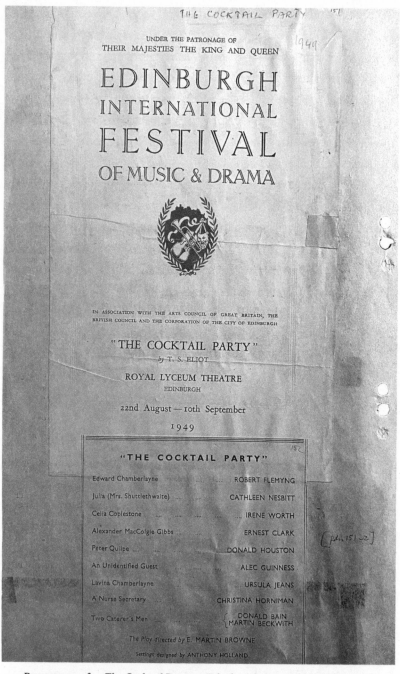

Programme for *The Cocktail Party* at Edinburgh International Festival of Music and Drama, 22 August–10 September 1949.

refinement of his dramatic style.' Though there were admissions that the poet's work could be an acquired taste: 'The Eliotians were saying it was just too marvellous, and the Oppositions were observing that it was all pretentious mystification and a blether of words,' wrote Ivor Brown in the Observer.

Right around this time the offices of Faber and Faber received an enquiry regarding employment. 'I understand indirectly that Fabers require a personal secretary. Perhaps you will consider my application,' wrote Miss Valerie Fletcher. Fletcher had been a Leeds schoolgirl when she heard a recording of John Gielgud reading Eliot's 'Journey of the Magi' and her life shifted on its axis; later in her life she would call the experience 'a revelation'. She took a secretarial course; she worked at the Brotherton Library at the University of Leeds; she worked for the novelist Charles Morgan before she heard that a post was opening up at the publishing house where Eliot worked. She was called for an interview. 'I was terrified,' she recalled long after Eliot's death. 'In my excitement I'd cut my hand the night before and had a light bandage on it. There were people on the stairs waiting to be interviewed. Tom chatted with me about [George] Herbert and the 17th century. At the end he held the door open for me – I can still picture him with his chin against it – and said: "I'm not allowed to say anything, but I hope that hand has healed enough for you to type in 10 days' time." I thought: "Well, I'm in the lead at the moment."' So she was; she was offered the post of 'Secretary to Mr T. S. Eliot' on the last day of August, at a salary of six pounds, ten shillings a week.

Eliot was full of stories for Mary in September when he returned from the north 'full of his Edinburgh adventures', she wrote. There were suppers at the Garrick and an evening listening to Beethoven's Coriolan Overture.

T. told me of a white-Russian ex-army man whom he knew at the end of the 1st war. This man described to him how he had, after a battle, watched a huge army horse dying by the road-side – a splendid creature – and his last moments brought vividly to the officer's mind the last bars of Coriolan.

On 17 September she wrote that they discussed lepers and midgets – no more information is provided – and on 22 September that he came to tea to meet her mother. 'They had already met several times and like each other very much.' There is a yearning for intimacy in this detail; she noted too that his next letter contained the first mention of his future wife – Valerie – regarding some small secretarial confusion. Her tone, as Eliot prepared for a lecture tour of Germany is concerned and almost motherly. He had told her that what he needed was a month without speaking to anyone, hoping simply to 'keep alive' before his next bout of travelling. As the autumn drew in she reflected that he must be a very poor Churchwarden: 'but it's stabilising for him – something he has to do every week, so removed from his usual ploys – when he is first Churchwarden and then Poet'. On Sunday 16 October she recorded another relaxed evening.

Before he left for Europe, we had Dinner at the Garrick (where I am fast becoming a habitué and get quite a greeting, especially from Barker, the wine waiter). On the way back to the flat we burgled Faber's and T. extracted from his offices a wonderful book of Degas Dancers, two volumes of records of American Poets (including himself) reading their poetry to the Library of Congress. Then we played the whole of the Beethoven Quartet Op. 132 – and a ceremonial exchange of Daily Service Books, which we have given each other, took place. Helen Gardner's book on *The Art of T. S. Eliot* has just come and is to be loaned to me. 'It is good – though such books ought not to be written about people's work during their lifetime.'

The Beethoven had inspired Four Quartets, *as Eliot had written to Stephen Spender many years before. They discussed the poet and novelist*

Charles Williams that night too, and she recorded more of Eliot's remarks on the Sitwells: 'Edith and Osbert are 70% humbug – but kind – and cruel.' With the preparations he was making for his trip to Europe, he would not, he told her, have time to go with her to see The Third Man, *which came out that year. She paints a portrait of Eliot's slightly bumbling helplessness, as she perceives it.*

The dedication Festival of St Stephen's 22 October, with the Bishop of London pontificating – and Tom in tails – and galoshes – a peculiar ensemble. He was to lunch with the Vicar and the Bishop, and I left him plunging about in his pew trying to retrieve a large galosh which had fallen off. They belonged to his deceased brother and are too large for him.

24 October: An hour and a half for a farewell gin before T. leaves for an exhausting three weeks tour in Germany, lecturing and poetry-reading. His last instructions were to get two English Missals, keep copies of the *Listener* and, if he is not in church on 20th to telephone the following day.

He returned in late November.

Sometimes we seemed to be living in *The Cocktail Party*. One morning in a chemist shop in Southampton Row, a voice behind me said, 'Oh, it's YOU again, Julia!' That evening, a detailed description of his three weeks in Germany over supper.

There is a public/private aspect to Mary's record of their friendship. On the one hand her account is a demonstration of their closeness; on the other hand she guards their intimacy, holding back that 'detailed description'.

On Advent Sunday, 27 November, they took their new missals to church for the first time – 'very appropriate, at the beginning of the church's year', she wrote. Later they dined at the Garrick again.

He had been to the Natural History Museum yesterday with John and observed a buffalo head 'the dead spit of Lord Athlone'. (Lord Athlone was then the Chancellor of the University of London.) At dinner some mention was made of Enid (Mrs) Faber. 'She went to visit Vivien in the mental asylum right through the war. I didn't know until afterwards.' He talked much to-night of his youth and of his mother. Being much the youngest of his family he only knew his parents as 'ancestors', having a closer relationship with his sisters. His mother came to England once and met Vivien, whom he never took to America. In discussing genealogical trees he said he had worked out the pedigree of the Monchenseys (*Family Reunion*) very carefully – only two generations of title! And their names he took from Browning's play *A Blot in the 'Scutcheon*. On the way home T. insisted on singing, in a loud and tuneless voice, songs about Robinson Crusoe – memories of his youth.

On 29 November she recorded a Hampstead dinner with the Huxleys – Julian Huxley and his wife Juliette. The Hungarian violinist Jelly D'Arányi was a guest, as were the Henry Moores. Huxley, zoologist and popular scientist, was the older brother of Aldous Huxley, author of Brave New World.

Jelly was very friendly to me and we discussed old friends at Oxford. Henry Moore (the greatest British sculptor, says Tom) is a delightful little Yorkshireman with a charming, half-Russian wife.

There is something brisk and no-nonsense about Mary's description of Moore, who had won the international prize for sculpture at the XXIV Venice Biennale the year before; she was happily outside his cultural circle. They dined at the Garrick in mid-December with the literary scholar Leslie Hotson – still noted for his discovery of the identity of the murderer of Christopher Marlowe – whom she called 'nice and friendly'. She was less kind about his wife, 'a terrifyingly plain "natural". Neither had any

*inhibitions. After a lively dinner, the exhausting Mrs H. shrieking away,
we sat upstairs until 10.30 p.m., Tom looking more and more frantic. But
he unwound on the journey home.'*

23 December, Sunday: I had been rather worried about T. a few days
ago. He seemed full of tension, but this evening he was all right
again. He busied himself in the flat pulling corks, with telling stories
of *The Cocktail Party* in Brighton last week. [George] Hoellering is
going to film *Murder* in a bombed church and John Groser will play
Becket. Then to Beethoven: 'Don't forget to tell Cheetham that I
want the Allegretto from the 7th Symphony for my funeral march.
If the organist can't play it, you can provide the records. But NOT
Coriolan – that would be too pretentious of me.'
    On his grandfather, whom he had never really known: 'Better so,
perhaps, because I have always admired him and I might not have
done so if I had known him!'

*Hoellering's film of Eliot's play used non-professional as well as profes-
sional actors. Groser was an Anglican priest based in London's East End,
serving at Christ Church in Stepney and at St George-in-the-East,
in Wapping; he was very much involved in movements for social justice in his day, fighting on behalf of the poor in his district and against
fascism. He was later Warden, and subsequently Master, of the Royal
Foundation of St Katharine, a Christian community of medieval origin,
in Limehouse. The Rev. Eric Cheetham was vicar at Eliot and Mary's
church, St Stephen's in Gloucester Road.*
    *Mary includes in her manuscript a letter Eliot wrote to her before
leaving for six weeks in South Africa, a trip with the Fabers to find
warmth away from a London winter; it is dated 'St Rigobert 1950' – St
Rigobert's feast day is 4 January, though 1950 is crossed out and 1949
written in.*
    *He was, he told her, 'embarking into the unknown', and so wished to
be 'shriven, houselled, and relieved of my debts' – he therefore returned*

to her three shillings he apparently owed her: 'You can show this letter to my executors (Bird & Bird, of Burley House, 5/11 Theobalds Road) if I am shipwrecked and lost at Tenerife or Adamastor, and recover what I owe.' He asked her to keep note of any interesting conversations; 'It is pleasant to think that for six weeks you will go on being useful, and I shall persistently be useless. CONFIDENTIAL: I have just written to Butler ('Rab') to decline nomination to the Presidency of the Royal India and Pakistan Society.

'I shall nourish myself on Simenon and S. Francis de Sales.'

Mary was useful to him. He made that very clear.

1950

1st January, Sunday: A very trying evening, unexpectedly so, for there were no signs of 'bad weather' after church. But Tom leaves to-morrow on a visit to South Africa with the Fabers and will be away for six weeks. This might have been a prospect that would send his spirits up, but he hates the thought of going <u>anywhere</u> more and more and becomes almost suicidal with depression as the hour of departure draws near. He worries himself to fits as to whether he has the right tickets and takes days packing. Added to all this, he had to look in on Martin Browne's party later in the evening to which I drove him, wrapped in his brother's fur coat, gloomy and sleepy. What jolly company he'll be at a party!

Meanwhile in New York, on 21 January The Cocktail Party *opened at the Henry Miller theatre on Broadway; the Duke and Duchess of Windsor were in the audience on opening night. In the* New York Times *Brooks Atkinson wrote: 'Whatever its merits may eventually turn out to be,* The Cocktail Party *is a remarkably provocative play – a fascinating experiment in the suitability of poetic drama to modern themes and in the religious interpretation of modern life. But to me, it is insufficiently poetic. It needs more eloquence, passion and imaginative courage.' Martin Browne wrote to Eliot that the play 'is a very big success'; the text was published by Faber and Faber in March of that year.*

19 February, Sunday: Ah – quite a new man – very brown. I sat behind him in church, being late, and much enjoyed his writhings during a characteristic sermon from Clarence May. The preacher, in his peroration, referred to 'one of our great poets', at which Tom

nearly fell under the pew, but it turned out to be Ella Wheeler Wilcox who was thus quoted!!

Wilcox (1850–1919) was a rather different sort of artist than Eliot, hence those two exclamation marks. She was a Wisconsin-born poet whose work, written in plain, rhyming verse, was very popular. 'Friendship after Love' mourns the transition from the latter to the former, ending: 'Why are we haunted with a sense of loss? / We do not wish the pain back, or the heat; / And yet, and yet, these days are incomplete.'

22 February, Ash Wednesday. A lovely sunny morning. We attended Matins and Ante-Communion and the Imposition of the Ashes at 11 a.m. and then drove through St James's Park towards our respective offices. The almond blossom and crocuses were gay – the Household Cavalry rode past, in their plumed helmets and red cloaks and T. was in high spirits at being home again. But he takes Lent <u>very</u> seriously and has many rules and regulations, one of the oddest being that he doesn't play patience <u>before</u> breakfast!

The following day was the general election in which Clement Attlee's Labour party saw their landslide post-war majority reduced to just five seats. Mary, however, keeps her personal account free of national politics.

23 February: After a very exciting and exhausting day with the General Election I slipped into the small studio at Broadcasting House where 'Family Reunion' was being televised. Tom and John, with whom I had some talk in the interval, were sitting in front. There was an amusing moment when a lady sitting in the second row hit Tom in the back and told him not to talk! The play was awful and I slipped out before the end.

The televised production of The Family Reunion *was part of the BBC's long-running series* Sunday Night Theatre; *most of the productions, which ran between 1950 and 1959, are now lost, the tapes they were recorded on were wiped, like so many from this time.*

The following entry in Mary's diary is striking. It reveals their comfortable intimacy – the door key, her ability to be honest in her opinions of his work – but also the way in which, perhaps, she is expressing her feelings through this discussion of 'the people in his plays'. 'Perhaps he doesn't love them,' she says. She calls him 'blind', carefully records that he cannot defend himself, and, in essence, turns away from her line of enquiry.

26 February, Lent 1: T. now takes my front door key when we are dining together so as to come up to my flat without my having to go down many stairs to let him in. The Garrick was very empty and at dinner we had every detail of his holiday. Characteristically, he enjoyed the voyage home best. After dinner and back at the flat, we talked of the people in his plays. I suggested that his people are mere puppets, speaking what he wants them to speak – that they don't really come alive at all – and what often puzzles me is that although, in some ways, he seems to know so much about people, in other ways he seems quite blind – perhaps because he doesn't love them. And I added that, although he <u>says</u> he is frightened of people, it seems to me that this is just a protection because he is afraid of being disturbed by them. Tom was interested . . . and put up no defence except to say 'you mustn't want to know too much about people'.

She noted too Eliot's apparent anxiety regarding a reception to welcome Vincent Auriol, President of France, who had come to London. 'I am really frightened at going to this Reception alone – I shall be so lonely,' she reported him telling her. And the reception would also mean missing out on a shared pleasure: a Marx Brothers film. A decade later Eliot would develop a kind of friendship with Groucho Marx, though the two were a peculiar match; Groucho's biographer Lee Siegel wrote of the 'strenuous bonhomie' expressed by Eliot in his correspondence with the comedian. Mary also recorded that 'he is pleased that I am pleased at my Hon. Mention in the preface to The Cocktail Party *which has just been published.' There is a pragmatic thanks to Mary for the transcription of 'One-Eyed Riley' in the text published by Faber and Faber.*

5 March, Sunday: A lovely sunny morning. T. was lunching at the Spanish Embassy so we drove to St James's Park, where my companion observed the decorations for President Auriol's visit with a very jaundiced eye. The weather was so pleasant that I actually persuaded T. to get out of the car and we walked among the crowds to the bridge. He was, of course, very gloomy – his Luncheon Party hanging, so to speak, over his head. And I must say he looked very odd – bowler hat (too small) blue overcoat (too large), stiff collar, striped trousers and all. He felt very unhappy and he declared he never did <u>anything</u> except from a sense of duty. What a jolly life! And yet, though he often makes that kind of remark, he never really loses his sense of humour – or, at least, his sense of the ridiculous.

They eventually saw A Night at the Opera *at the Academy Cinema on 7 March.*

17 March: I had an odd little note saying he couldn't see anyone more than once a fortnight – so comic, seeing that we meet, these days, at least once, often twice a week – really, POETS! Anyway, I shall be away next Sunday so he came round this evening, cheerful and chatty. We talked of the hydrogen bomb – 'I find myself planning another play for 1951 and hope I can arrange to get a copy to America to be preserved. But expected catastrophes often take unexpected forms.' I made no direct reference to his note, except to tease him about rationing friends. I think it's a game of pretence, when it suits his convenience.

On 26 March she recorded a letter from his sister Marian – asking Mary to call her by her first name, another gesture of intimacy inscribed in her book. On 3 April, there was another

... odd visit, much gin and a great deal of talk about Tom's habits. 'I never see ANYONE for pleasure etc . . .' which is just plain nonsense. I remarked that he was an unusual friend; 'and, in the end, unsatisfactory' was the complacent rejoinder.

Church on 7 April, Good Friday, and of course on Easter Day.

People nudge each other as Tom collects from them. It is said that some of the receipts he signs as Churchwarden are sold by the recipients at a handsome profit!

They dined the evening of Easter Sunday at the Oxford and Cambridge Club.

We talked of the Easter Liturgy, our Missals, Hymns, Tom's rosary (blessed and given to him by the Pope) which has a bead missing and puts him off his stride! . . . After dinner we sank into large armchairs in a corner of the drawing room and Tom talked of his childhood: 'I loved my brother – 8 years older than me – but I think he was a bad influence on me. I was never whacked – I was spoiled, but never made to feel important. I grew up a mournful young man!' I asked how he came to the Church from Unitarianism. 'Not through the influence of any one person, but on the rebound from my past.' And then, how did he come to marry as he did? 'I can't tell you. Not because I don't want to, but because I cannot find ways to express it.' Then he suddenly looked tired, like a child, and I ordered him to bed.

She quizzed him; he evaded her. It hardly seems as if she was aware of his evasions, although she was aware of his sudden exhaustion at her questioning, and reverted to taking command, a dynamic in which they both felt comfortable.

In early May came the opening night of Martin Browne's production of The Cocktail Party *with Rex Harrison as Sir Henry Harcourt-Reilly – 'an absolutely crowded theatre', she wrote on 3 May, and the performance was 'good and well-received, Tom made a modest little speech of several words!' She noted that 'John (in flowered waistcoat) said to me: "I look on you as part of the family".' The play would run until February 1951; on 2 August there was a celebration of the hundredth British performance. The play had over 200 performances in New York.*

They dined together at the Connaught Hotel on 28 May; he was, she wrote, 'very white and strained . . . saying pathetically, "What can I do if I get ill?"' It had been just over a year since Mary had tried to clarify their relationship – or rather adjust it, to cause Eliot to acknowledge that surely his reliance on her meant that they must be more than simply friends. She felt that he was sending her signals which he himself was

Invitation card from T. S. Eliot to Mary Trevelyan, 3 May 1950.

not willing to recognise; she would press the point. In the typescript, all of what follows is crossed out.

29 May, Whit Monday: However – the worm turned – and this morning I came to the conclusion that I couldn't stand any more of this 'I feel so lonely going to Receptions alone', and 'What shall I do if I get ill?', and 'I can't plan a holiday – how can I find a retreat where I can be protected from molestation?'. So I wrote again saying, in effect, why should we both be lonely?

4 June, Trinity Sunday: I opened Tom's reply this morning – couldn't face it yesterday. Here was the truth at last and I began to understand. I had thought last year that his explanation of his being unable to marry again 'because of what has happened to me in the past', referred simply to his wife and her mental collapse. And I hoped that, having got over telling me about it, he might get over his nightmares about that period of his life. I couldn't have guessed the truth.

Eliot's letter follows in full, dated 2 June 1950.

It is perhaps a good thing that you wrote your letter of Whit Monday, though it was distressing to receive and distressing to answer. For I had been conscious for some time that our relations were not as settled and explicit as one likes all relationships to be, and I had been feeling embarrassment and unease.

This is not the first time, in the most general way, that I have thought I have said enough to someone to clarify a position once for all; and then found I had left a misunderstanding. It is partly from reticence in talking about oneself and one's past experiences; in some cases the desire not to inflict pain (but the desire not to inflict pain can often approach very near to cowardice); and also the inadequacy of language to express feelings and to explain how those feelings came about – so that at times one seems faced merely with the alternative between conveying two or more different misunderstandings. I am afraid I must try to expose (as I have done to no one so far) the most agonising experience of my life.

For a great many years I was very much in love with some one, and would willingly have sacrificed everything for the possibility of marrying her. Then, when finally I was free, I realised quite suddenly that I was deluding myself with emotions I had felt in the past, that I had changed more, and in ways unsuspected, than I had thought. I found that I actually could not bear the thought of it. You will of course at once infer that this was merely a particular relationship which, when it reached the possibility of completion, was found no longer to exist. But it is much more than that, and that is what cannot be expressed in any words that I can find. I take it to mean that I am still in love with her, in a way, even though I prefer not to see her, feel embarrassed and unhappy when I do, seem to have very little in common now. There is also of course the feeling, which only a man can understand, that a man, in all these situations, is somehow in the wrong. Anyway, I do care enough about her to be unable to contemplate except with horror the thought of marrying anyone else, or of any relationship except that of friendship. And I have never wanted to marry anyone except this one person.

No doubt I ought to have explained all this before, instead of wrapping it up in phrases which might be taken to apply to my married life. But it is something which gnaws at my liver, and the liver is an organ which one does not willingly expose. I shall never be relieved of this pain, except, I hope, at the moment of death. And that seems all I can say at present.

He closed the letter 'Affectionately'.

He does not appear to name Emily Hale. Mary will come to know the identity of 'this one person', and at some point – the details are unrecorded in this text – he will reveal a little more of what passed between them, as her later entries will show. But whatever he told her, or would tell her, did not alter what was between Mary and Eliot. She is brutally forth-right with herself in the aftermath of the receipt of this letter.

Tom joined me as usual after church and I simply thanked him for his letter without further comment. We arranged to meet to-morrow for a talk. I spent a bad afternoon and evening, but came through it and was able, by the time I saw him again, to look at the picture from a new angle. And indeed, such an experience was surely enough to frighten any sensitive man for life.

5 June: Tom arrived very early, with new records. I was playing the piano and he was quite silent until I had finished whatever it was that I was playing. It was very hot again, he took off his coat, was very chatty in shirtsleeves, poured out drinks and put some records of 'East Coker' in German on the gramophone. Then we had to get down to business. I first, of course, thanked him for telling me straight and explained that I couldn't have understood a year ago. T. said: 'I am so thankful I have told you. I have never told anyone else and I am very grateful to you for forcing the truth from me.' We both agreed that we felt a new freedom. Then I heard him murmur, with a little chuckle – 'I don't suppose the lady will ever understand what it was all about. She, and others no doubt, would say I ought to have seen a psychologist.' (See Celia and Edward in *The Cocktail Party*!) I said that I was glad to know that he really could understand what I felt about him! to which he promptly replied: 'Yes indeed, and I know that I must leave the decision to you – you must do now what you feel is best.' I told him that what I now knew could make NO difference to my feelings for him – that I knew there was something between us which just couldn't be killed – and I hoped that my letter which, though written without full knowledge and absolutely sincere, would cause no embarrassment between us. Indeed, I hoped that in the future he would enjoy, without embarrassment or unease, the knowledge that there is one person who loves him, and him only, and that from now on he had better adopt me as one of the family.

Tom, with a beaming smile, said, 'Yes, indeed – and I'll give you a toast – TO THE GUARDIANS' – so we drank to our guardians of our future. Speaking of my letter he said: 'I read it through three times, then tore it into strips, then burned it – for ashes endure, you know!' On our way home he said: 'I am sorry you had to force this out of me' – but I said I realised that he couldn't tell me before and that even now it must have been very difficult. 'That is kind – and very understanding.'

I wonder – he is a man in prison, a prison largely of his own making I suspect. Maybe all this had to happen – I had to spend all these years loving him and being hurt often – and now, perhaps, the prison door has opened just a chink.

The pair of them echo Celia and Edward's toast to the guardians in The Cocktail Party – *Celia and Edward, lovers who must be parted, who note that Julia might herself be a guardian, a watchful force. Mary also requests 'adoption'; a few years later Eliot, in writing to Mary, will refer to himself as an adoptive nephew. However one looks at this turn and turn about of generational games, it remains distinctly unsexual. And at this point too it is worth remarking on Mary's apparently happy identification with Julia, the play's annoying busybody. In the play's first twenty pages Julia is variously described (by herself and by others) as a 'gluttonous old woman', a 'silly old woman', a 'maiden aunt', a 'dreadful old woman'. She is someone who turns up 'when she's least wanted'. This casts perhaps a painful light on Mary's remark that she had to spend so many years loving him – and being hurt often: hurt which could be seen to include very public humiliation in the form of this play.*

Over the course of the next few days he alternated between being 'beaming and cheerful' on 8 June and 'all buttoned up again' on 11 June. But they were back to their usual routine; she noted, amused, on 5 July that

The great success of *The Cocktail Party* means other problems – including employing an accountant to find out what his new income is! He is inundated with begging letters daily, but says he wants to help the Chinese. Before leaving T. remarked: 'I am inclined to think I must have had too much gin' – quite right, he drinks more gin at a sitting than anyone I have ever known, but it does not seem to affect him except when he is very tired.

But she also remarked to herself that it is 'exactly a month since our conversation'. She wrote no more; and this is where the deletions in the typescript – whoever made them – end.

7 July: Dinner at the Connaught to meet (and help with) Miss Abigail Eliot (Queen Bee of Rachel Macmillan Training Colleges in U.S.A.) and her friend Miss Holman. I was rather over-dressed – both ladies being in 'costumes' and looking very Bostonian. Cousin Abigail was rather nice, with Tom's nose (and nostrils!) and the other lady a pale shadow. I chose a lamb chop, forgetting it was Friday. 'Well, I AM surprised,' said Tom.

Abigail Adams Eliot was a pioneer in nursery school education in the United States. Rachel and Margaret Macmillan had campaigned in England, in the early years of the twentieth century, for better health and education for underprivileged children; Abigail Eliot brought their mission to the United States. Anna Holman was her companion and partner.

19 July: The Huxleys asked us all to dinner to meet Aldous, over here for a few days from California. T. came round about 6 p.m. and stoked up with gin. A nice dinner. Only John and I didn't 'belong' to a group which, as young men, saw so much of each other in the Ottoline Morrell circle. Conversation very general and easy. After dinner we sat out in the garden until 11.15. I reflected, driving home, how curious it was that so distinguished a party of celebrities should have produced no notable conversation – but nobody held the floor and the talk was not only general but quite unimportant. Tom took

his share amiably enough and perhaps regretted having only fifteen minutes to talk alone with Aldous. I tried to imagine them all as young men at Garsington.

Morrell was one of the great salonnières of the early twentieth century; her home, Garsington Manor near Oxford, had been a gathering place for Eliot and Aldous Huxley and a great many others – Lytton Strachey, Virginia Woolf, Dora Carrington, Clive and Vanessa Bell, D. H. Lawrence and Siegfried Sassoon. 'Sometimes I felt as if Garsington was a theatre, where week after week a travelling company would arrive and play their parts,' Morrell would recall, though at first Eliot did not seem a promising member of the troupe.

They discussed this dinner on 30 July, when Mary recorded Eliot as remarking: 'No, Aldous is not a great man – his characters are not real, not alive. Sometimes characters are created by an author, though they may come basically from someone known to him – e.g. Mrs Gamp – a real person, but never alive. A second-rate author's characters are usually smaller than himself – a great writer sometimes creates characters who become greater than himself. Aldous is not interested in people or characters except in so far as they can be used by him.' On Garsington days: 'Ottoline Morrell wanted and expected more affection than she got.'

23 July, Sunday: Sheeting rain. Tom gloomy, because he had to give lunch to an American lady friend (THE lady, I suspect!) Miss Emily Hale. Theodora, Tom's niece, is here for her annual visit – I entertain her more than Tom does – but he is a punctilious man about his family.

Hale remained a distant presence for Mary, though here she reveals at least an awareness – 'THE lady' – of her significance to Eliot. She did press him, at least a little, towards more personal discussion. On 20 August, in the Russell Hotel ('that oddly anonymous place'), he began to speak of his marriage to Vivien. 'I didn't realise for a long time what was

*happening and I thought it was my fault for a period,' she reported him
as telling her. 'I got away by going to America and not coming back. The
difficulty is that you either suffer too much or too little with the sufferer.'*

Tom is already reaching the stage of dreading his visit to America
– except for seeing sister Marian. His nervous fear of anything that
lies ahead seems to be growing on him and he works himself into
such a state of nervous apprehension that he almost makes his fears
come true.

*He would be making a trip in the autumn to see his family and to give a
series of lectures – in part to finance the trip – in New York, at Harvard,
where he would deliver the first Theodore Spencer Memorial Lecture, and
at the University of Chicago. Mary, perhaps, recorded Eliot's dread to
reveal how she was, at least in part, able to soothe him; therefore, he had
need of her. But she relied on him too, for her own mother was unwell.*

27 August, Sunday: After a particularly troubled visit to my mother
it was good to be back at St Stephen's, with Tom so comfortingly at
hand. A nice, frivolous dinner – on which I commented, the frivolity
I mean. 'Yes, but one has to talk seriously with people one doesn't
like – with people with whom one has serious things in common
one can talk frivolously.' We talked of acceptance of the fact that
some problems seem insoluble – 'one should start from that premise
and then see what can be done to solve them. But usually there is
no ready solution, because new factors develop continually. Most
problems are the result of sin. We accept responsibility for sin by
doing something.'

*On 5 September they went to a dinner party at the Étoile on Charlotte
Street given by Eliot in honour of Sarah Gertrude Millin, 'the South
African authoress' and her husband, Judge Millin. Millin was one of the
most popular South African novelists of the day; she also wrote biographies*

of Cecil Rhodes and Jan Smuts. Mary took the trouble to record that Eliot came to her flat first, then went on to the restaurant, 'giving me orders to arrive ten minutes later', as if they must not be seen arriving together – but she knew, and wished to state, that they had been together in her flat.

The filming of *Murder in the Cathedral* is well under way and Tom had spent the morning in the bombed church. He doesn't seem to be happy about Father Groser as Becket and is quite sure he is going to detest the processes of filming.

Sometimes, but not often, she gave inklings of the shape of her own life.

7 September: Tom came to say good-bye to Maung Ohn, the young Burmese Ambassador who had been at the First Night Party of *The Cocktail Party* and who is now bound for another Ambassadorship in Moscow. It was terribly hard work as Maung Ohn, a gentle dreamy Burmese, with a great awe of T., was almost speechless with fright at first. However, he sipped orangeade and Tom gin and the party warmed up a trifle. Tom put in what hints he could about Russia: 'Russians are afraid – and I am afraid of people who fear, because they become what they fear...' Maung Ohn said he was taking with him Plato and books on National Income, no servants and a staff of three only – and is delaying his departure as long as possible.

On 11 September she reported that 'he wrote down the outline of his movements for this next trip to America. "I am uneasy about this trip. I hate going."'

In September she herself went away – on holiday to the isle of Sark, where she broke her arm immediately after her arrival. Eliot wrote to her from Chicago on 16 October:

What were you doing? Running away from a Guernsey Bull or merely gesticulating violently? I don't condole so much for the immediate pain and the complications of getting home again, but how on earth you are managing your affairs all by yourself I can't think. I hope that somebody has taken you in and that you are being looked after.

On 28 October he wrote from Chicago again, from the Hotel Windermere, saying jokingly that 'it seems extraordinary that you are still alive, and your letter fails to explain why you are'.

Upon his return from the United States Eliot was badly affected by the weather, suffering attacks of bronchitis. Mary noted the change in his appearance, as her entry for 17 December, a Sunday, shows; yet it also shows her own ability to revive him, and the way in which she continued to treasure what she regarded as their intimacy.

In church to-day he looked very old – but this evening, laden with nylon stockings, French books, candies and cigarettes he was most cheerful. He insisted on getting out his engagement book and describing each day in detail. It took so long that he cancelled our table at the Garrick and we cooked eggs and bacon etc., instead. He interrupted perpetually, while I was trying to get some food together – and didn't leave until very late – insisting on some music before moving. On the way home he said: 'This continual meeting of people who only want to see you because you are famous is the most desperately lonely business. You begin to wonder if the real YOU exists.' He was looking forward to returning to St Stephen's, collecting on Sunday morning etc., which made him feel himself again, with a real private life.

What was the nature of that 'real private life'? In considering Eliot's divided nature, Lyndall Gordon quotes 'Little Gidding': 'So I assumed a double part, and cried / And heard another's voice cry: 'What! are you here?' / Although we were not. I was still the same, / Knowing myself yet being someone other—' Mary believed she was connected to Eliot's 'real YOU'; it was a belief that continued to sustain her.

1951

14 January, Sunday: Tom out for the first time two days ago, after a fortnight in bed. I sometimes think he prolongs his indispositions as long as possible – it's such a delightful excuse for not seeing ANYBODY. We drove round London for an hour after church and this evening he reappeared about 7 p.m. When I went to prepare the dish he always demands for supper – eggs and bacon – (perhaps because he thinks that is all I can cook!) I left him doing the *Times* crossword. On my return I found him sitting on the floor, using a chair as a writing table, jotting down a name that had struck him for the new play – Mrs Gozzard – he'd found it in the *Sunday Times*. Some of the others are to be: Sir Claud Mulhammer (Bradford Millionaire), B. Kragston (the stranger), Lucasta Windybank (lady of doubtful virtue), Simpkins – and Eggerson (a Lloyd's clerk – 'perhaps he lives at Gidea Park – he calls his wife "Mrs E." and has an allotment').

After supper T. told me that he had 'broken' with Sarah Gertrude Millin. She had written him a letter saying that, after reading his early poems, it was clear to her that he is an anti-Semite – which made him very angry. The letter reached him just before he left for the U.S.A.

The question both of anti-Semitism in Eliot's work, and whether or not he himself was anti-Semitic, is a complex and challenging one. There are lines in Eliot's work which are difficult to read. 'Burbank with a Baedeker: Bleistein with a Cigar' is a relatively early work, yet it remains in the Collected Poems. *'The rats are underneath the piles. / The Jew is underneath the lot.' Anthony Julius, in his important book* T. S. Eliot, Anti-Semitism, and Literary Form *discusses the 'radical . . . challenge to the Jewish reader' in encountering poems such as 'Burbank': 'There is a difference between reading a text that challenges the worth of one's ideas, and one that challenges the worth of one's person.' Julius writes of these specific anti-Semitic poems as being 'charged with malevolent meaning'. He calls these instances 'hurts of intimacy', violations of the bonds that tie us to certain texts.*

Millin was herself Jewish; her biographer, Martin Rubin, notes that 'her sensitivity on the subject of anti-Semitism was legendary'. Eliot wrote to Millin that he was 'horrified, shocked, and hurt' by her critique.

A week later Mary and Eliot dined at the Garrick.

21 January, Sunday: Dinner at the Garrick. When our drinks came and we settled down by the fire Tom said, with a sigh: 'how nice this room is when we have it to ourselves!' at which point I observed Robert Speaight coming up behind Tom's chair. His lady friend turned up soon after and we carried on a desultory conversation, until Tom whispered to me: 'Let's go down now – I think we could' and we escaped. An addition was reported to the names in the play – Slingsby Simpkins – and if I think of any others I'm to keep them in the same rhythm.

Speaight was the actor who had created the role of Thomas Becket in Murder in the Cathedral; *he was acclaimed for his restrained eloquence and became a leading actor in London's West End.*

At the end of the month Mary and Eliot went to Cambridge, and took tea in the Trinity Master's Lodge 'as he had dined two nights ago next to G.M.T. at the Pembroke Feast and they'd actually made friends. He stayed a long time and there was some good talk,' she wrote. G. M. Trevelyan would retire as Master of Trinity later that year.

28 January, Sunday: A very icy day and we drove to Ely in the after-noon – explored the Cathedral thoroughly and had an excellent tea in a small hotel in front of a roaring fire. T. was staying with the Willinks and we arranged to drive back to London together.

Sir Henry Willink had been a Conservative MP; in 1948 he had taken up the post of Master of Magdalene College, Cambridge, which he held until 1966. Once again, Mary paints a cosy portrait.

11 February, Sunday, Lent: Last Thursday T. was wheezing like an accordion, but better this morning. Supper at the flat – what he likes best – soup, eggs and bacon, an excellent Brie, Cox's apples and coffee.

They discussed the play he was at work on: The Confidential Clerk *would eventually open in Edinburgh in August 1953, produced once again by E. Martin Browne.*

The Lady Elizabeth Mulhammer (wife of Sir Claud) married beneath her, for money, and he for her connections. She goes to Séances and Dress Shows. This time the last Act is already plotted – 'so that people shan't say it's an Epilogue, like they did of The Cocktail Party'. But 'I can't get anything else done (such as the Johnson Essays) until I've got over being a playwright. Lent? I have given up smoking before breakfast and patience after lunch.' (In the course of the evening T.'s braces broke, so he took them off for me to mend – his trousers securely tied with string!)

19 February: We dined with Margaret Rhondda and Theodora Bosanquet in their new, grand flat in Arlington House. The evening was a great success, easy and gave great pleasure to our hostesses. Nobody else there. Driving home we had more of the play: 'So far it's a roaring farce, I'm afraid. I am becoming very fond of Eggerson, B. Kagan (ex-Kragston) and Lucasta Angel (ex-Windybank) – they are the only ones who have come alive yet. Mrs E. calls her husband "Eggerson" – and his name may be Harold.' A new doctor has taken on the great man – the other died, no, went away. The new one says that Tom will die of pneumonia, but may live for 25 years.

1951

Margaret Haig Thomas, Viscountess Rhondda, was a businesswoman, editor and suffragist; she had founded the feminist weekly journal Time & Tide *in 1920. She lived with Bosanquet, the secretary of the International Federation of University Women, from 1933 until her death in 1958. Eliot was a frequent contributor to Rhondda's influential journal; he also enjoyed its puzzles, revealed here as spring wore on.*

On 25 February Mary recorded 'a splendid, long evening', making sure to note how he drew attention to their closeness, as she did in recounting her visit to him in hospital, where he was being treated for piles.

T. arrived early at the flat with 'only two packets of cigarettes, but I now have a special corner in the office where I put aside books for you.'

4 March, Sunday: T. in the London Clinic 'for a little operation on my posterior'. I visited him and found him very spry, sitting up in bed in pink pyjamas, his room full of flowers. After five minutes, some people called Simmons came in – also invited. I was a little cross about it, for it would have been better to let them have their innings alone. However, I soon left them to it.

He was back in the office, she said, by the end of the month, and at church on 25 March, Easter Day. On 1 April ('Low Sunday') she wrote that she had been 'showered with Faber Gallery books and silly notes' all through-out the week. N. M. Iovetz-Tereshchenko, mentioned below, was a White Russian émigré scholar, a writer and psychologist whom Eliot had come to know.

The play is making no progress, no time or opportunity. But he'd gone by bus to see Tereshchenko this afternoon – 'it's so easy to slip into being a rich man – and must be so difficult to get used to not being one'. A propos the operation on his posterior: 'It's odd to think that people all over the world know exactly what has been the matter with me' – and I was then treated to an account of his health in general and his inside in particular. The programme for his holiday in Spain with the Fabers sounds very restless. He doesn't think he'll bathe, because he can only get gent's bathing drawers, which didn't seem indecent in S. Africa, but you never know in Spain – 'they make me feel I'd be more decent naked.'

On 14 May, on his return, he would tell her about 'Bull Fighting and bathing': 'I borrowed a bathing dress from Geoffrey Faber, but my drawers would have been all right.' She opined that she doesn't think he enjoyed the holiday much.

2 April: After telephoning, T. turned up at 6 p.m., very pleased at having his name in print for a correct solution of the *Time & Tide* crossword puzzle. But he stated that he must be back in good time to do his exercises before dinner. However, he settled down to tell me stories of London in 1911, which he then visited as a student at the Sorbonne. With an American friend who had been at school with him, he stayed at Bon's Surrey Hotel, in Duke Street, with a coffee room, a butler and maids in starched aprons bringing hot water in great brass cans. They bought lovely ties in the Burlington Arcade for 9½ d. and suit the most expensive they could buy, for £7.7.0. They visited Salisbury and Winchester, thought England fine, but Paris less lonely than London, and he didn't return until 1914. Then he had a great friend Janes, an ex-police detective, who became his handyman at his house in Chester Terrace. Janes used to tell him stories of Disraeli. When he fell ill, Tom visited him in hospital and took him champagne, which Janes hid and then shared with other patients in the middle of the night. 'I buried him – and his sister. If I ever write my reminiscences, which I shan't, Janes would have a great part in them.' We talked of Merton College, Oxford. He greatly resents them not making him a Fellow until he had become respectable, with his O.M. and Nobel Prize . . .

On the way home: 'Shaw did great harm – he hadn't a great brain. He was a mischievous child and a nasty old man.' We talked of snobs: 'I know there are Eliots, non-Eliots and foreigners.' And of memory: 'I have no control over my memory – but I always remember when people hurt my feelings – even people I am still very fond of. I can say this to you, because you've never hurt my feelings. I am ashamed, but I can't forget.'

George Bernard Shaw had died the year before: a socialist, a freethinker, a man who moved in his life from atheism to mysticism, he was in many ways the antithesis of Eliot, who saw him as a manipulative writer: 'No one can grasp more firmly an idea which he does not maintain, or expound it with more cogency, than Mr Shaw,' Eliot had written of Shaw's play Saint Joan *in* The Criterion.

In the late spring he travelled to Granada with the Fabers, returning in May.

10 June, Sunday: T. had been at Brighton for the Alliance Française, so an unusually long interval. At 2.30 p.m. we set off in the car for Windsor – T. slept all the way to Datchet – a tribute to my driving. Owen Morshead took us [on] a fascinating tour . . . In one of the State Drawing Rooms T. insisted on lying on the floor to admire the painted ceiling. 'Splendid – this is the first opportunity I have ever had of observing a ceiling from the proper angle.' As we were examining the miniatures in the King's private study, Owen suddenly turned pale and gasped: 'Don't MOVE – please stay exactly where you are, both of you – I shall be back in a moment'. We remained rooted to the spot, wondering what we had done. Owen returned in a few minutes and explained that he had forgotten to have the burglar alarm disconnected – and had we crossed a certain line in the carpet of the study we would have set in motion, in Scotland Yard and the Police Stations of Windsor and Reading, a gramophone record which would have repeated: THE KING'S PRIVATE

APARTMENTS ARE BEING BURGLED – THE KING'S PRIVATE APARTMENTS ARE BEING BURGLED. I was quite disappointed that he had remembered and got it turned off in time.

After an agreeable tea with Owen and Paquita we drove back to London, in time for Tom to entertain an American Professor and his wife to dinner at the Garrick. En route we talked of the *Murder* film: 'I don't think the cinema is my medium at all – indeed most of the play seems to me to be second-rate now and I am bored to death with it.'

17 June, Sunday: T. had been to Chichester, for a 'Friends of the Cathedral' do and stayed with Dean Duncan Jones. 'The bathroom was a long way away, down a corridor and through a baize door and the bath looked as though it ought to have had a celluloid duck and a broken boat in it. Luckily it was fine, so the Friends' Tea-Party was in the garden.' We made arrangements for next Wednesday's jolly evening in Hampstead.

His talk to the Friends of Chichester Cathedral was on 'The Value and Use of Cathedrals in England Today'. The dinner mentioned was evidently at the Huxleys'; they arranged to be driven there and back in a 'Godfrey Davis limousine': the name of a car hire firm of the time.

20 June: At the H's, supper in a tiny basement – then we sat round the fire in the small sitting room, close and cosy. The guitar was brought out and we had song after song. Tom turned very white and gripped the arms of his chair. Suddenly he burst out: 'Do you know the Song of the Reconstructed Rebel?', which he proceeded to sing, very loudly and raucously, with extreme violence. It was embarrassing and alarming. He said afterwards that he had completely lost his temper. To make matters worse, the car returned at 10 p.m., but Mrs H. told it to wait and didn't tell us it had come. At last I made a move, and all was revealed. On the way home T. said he had been

frightened and felt we were in a cage with two wild animals. He'd sung his song because otherwise he would have exploded and the whole evening was 'quite creepy'.

Mary's willingness to record what is embarrassing and alarming in Eliot seems a way of indicating how closely she was able to observe him, how apparently unguarded he was in her company. Her unliterary qualities – the way in which she was, in many ways, completely unconnected to his cultural milieu – makes her a reliable witness in her recording of Eliot's scathing remarks regarding his contemporaries.

30 July: T. brought books and records and described Ashley Dukes' party for the 21st birthday of the Ballet Rambert. 'Madame Rambert is common AND vulgar – a more rare combination than people suppose' . . . I was off to Switzerland: 'I want to give you my addresses – write to me and I'll write to you.' On getting out of the car: 'By the way, Lucasta is becoming a person!'

Lucasta Angel is a character in The Confidential Clerk; *the party was for the twenty-fifth anniversary of the Ballet Rambert, which had given its first performance – Frederick Ashton's* A Tragedy of Fashion – *in 1926. Dukes was Marie Rambert's husband.*

15 August, The Assumption: We met at church and I didn't expect to see Tom later. I was ironing when he turned up. I had booked a room for him at the Chardonne, my 'second home' in Switzerland. He had given me the Ezra Pound letters, which I had been reading. 'I never knew Amy Lowell nor Harriet Monroe personally – and the £500 that was to be raised for me never materialised! I didn't leave the Bank until later, when I had an offer from Faber & Gwyn.'

Two days, later, 17 August, Eliot said of Pound: 'He was never normal – he is an egocentric with no ability to laugh at himself' – and at dinner with Margaret Rhondda on 22 August (when he 'drank gin for nearly an hour' before dinner; there would be 'more gin, champagne and liqueurs and whiskey' to follow) he said that Pound was 'always eccentric, generally very irritating, and mad long before the war'.

Clearly Mary and Eliot were discussing the early years of Eliot's career, when his work was first finding attention and he was struggling to make ends meet. Ezra Pound had attempted to raise funds for Eliot in order that he might devote himself to writing and avoid alternative employment; that had proved impossible, and Eliot continued working for Lloyd's Bank, a job he took in 1917 – though it appears that here he misremembers slightly, for he did receive some funds which Pound had managed to collect. Yet his recollection here fits the picture of suffering and struggle which he liked to paint for Mary, and which Mary liked to hear. Both Lowell and Monroe – poet and editor respectively – were instrumental in bringing modern twentieth-century poetry to American audiences. Lowell (sister of the American astronomer Percival Lowell) championed the work of both Ezra Pound and H. D. (Hilda Doolittle); Monroe was the founding editor of the influential magazine Poetry *(originally* Poetry: A Magazine of Verse*); 'The Love Song of J. Alfred Prufrock', Eliot's first publication, appeared in its June 1915 issue.*

2 September, Sunday: After church I was introduced to a little man, a don at Magdalene – as we drove away, after some chat, T. said: 'He is such a nice little man I had to introduce him to you' – and it occurred to me how very seldom he says he likes anyone.

The following day, before he travelled to Switzerland, he brought her a proof of the poems of Marianne Moore; her Collected Poems *were published by Faber and Faber that year. 'The greatest living woman poet – far better than Edith Sitwell, but for goodness sake don't quote me.'*

He was back in London by 26 September, his sixty-third birthday; she gave him a glass goblet commemorating Gibraltar which she had found in an antique shop in Edinburgh. 'He really was delighted.' They visited the Festival of Britain: 'On the whole he survived it well.' He began to leave notes on her car window: 27 September: 'The goblet is MUCH admired – so sorry to miss you'; 2 October: 'Another note on the car window saying, in red letters, GOOD MORNING.'

On 14 October she recorded how he was nearly always in good spirits in the morning, 'and very often becomes tired and gloomy by the evening'. 'At the Garrick the "barometer" was lower than I'd seen it for a long time.' He was struggling with The Confidential Clerk, he told her: 'Dreadful – just drudgery, but I'm keeping myself at it daily. The first part is so exciting – then I have to go through this.' By 21 November he said he was still making no progress: 'Everyone tells me I MUST get down to writing, but everyone says they'd like me to do one thing for them first!' He had told her on 12 November that his niece planned to visit in the summer; Mary had replied that she might not be around. 'Oh, you MUST be. You are her only friend!'

Mary again draws attention to just how necessary she is to him, and her closeness to his family members. As for that 'barometer': it was around this time that Donald Hall, the American poet, met Eliot before going up to Oxford as a graduate student: 'Eliot was only sixty-three, in the autumn of 1951, but he looked at least seventy-five . . . His face was pale as baker's bread. He stooped as he sat at his desk . . . He smoked, and between inhalations he hacked a dry, deathly, smoker's hack. His speech – while precise, exact, perfect – was slow to move, as if he stood behind the boulder of each word, pushing it into view. Eliot was cadaverous, in 1951.'

At the end of November they discussed Eliot's forthcoming trip to Paris to collect an honorary degree from the Sorbonne; Mary gave him a map of Paris. 'He pushed it over to me and said: "you might inscribe my name in it please" and gave me his fountain pen.'

She went on:

I demonstrated the recovery of my broken wrist by playing the overture to 'The Queen of Sheba' and remarked what fun it must have been for Mr Handel to have written that. 'But what fun to be able to play like that – you sound like a spirit released!'

A very strange conversation on confession: 'I only go three times a year. Sometimes my Confessor has no idea what I am talking about – and I can hardly tell him when he has missed the point! Sometimes I make up sins that I think he'll understand, to help to cover up what is too subtle and complicated for me to explain . . .'

A most agreeable and 'ordinary' evening really yet, as he got out of the car, after I had driven him home, I said mildly that I hoped he would enjoy himself. At which he suddenly shouted 'DON'T say that! It's what people always say when you've got to do something you don't want to do. It's as bad as saying "you'll enjoy it when you get there".' He retrieved his case and umbrella and repeated, furiously, 'DON'T say things like that!' – banged the door of the car and shot into the flats at a run. Well, well!

On 29 November she got a note from him, 'perhaps by way of apology', wondering if she'd only intended to lend the map of Paris – lend was underlined – saying he would return it to her if so, along with a copy of the Swedish or Finnish edition of The Cocktail Party, *inscribed by him. She called him, told him he was 'an idiot', and that of course the map was a gift. 'But you see, you didn't inscribe it until I asked you to do it,' he told her.*

She wrote:

I retorted that I wouldn't dream of inscribing a map unless asked to do so – and that I still hoped he would enjoy Paris a little. I begged him not to be so sudden, but if he must, to run up a red flag of warning – to save my nerves.

He made two visits to Paris that autumn: in November to open an exhibition and give a speech at the Bibliothèque Nationale; then to receive his honorary degree. But it wasn't a city he enjoyed any more; places he had known in his youth now held little attraction for him. She saw him upon his return. The appeal that raised his ire was printed in The Times *in late November, raising funds for an 'international tribute' to the memory of George Bernard Shaw.*

9 December: A very shrivelled poet – he'd been in bed for some days, thinking he'd got influenza. I think he really hated Paris, especially all the publicity. He worked himself into a great state of fury over the Appeal for £250,000 for a Bernard Shaw Memorial. 'He has successfully hoodwinked the public for 50 years – a monstrous sham, which ought to be exposed – but perhaps people will think I am jealous.' I said I thought that unlikely. 'Well, I am being treated very rough at the moment. I have just got a book, which I haven't yet read, called "The Myth of T. S. Eliot", which will probably be good reading.'

The book was The T. S. Eliot Myth, *by Rossell Hope Robbins, published by Henry Schuman in 1951; it was described by the critic Irving Howe as 'a bitter and insensitive polemic against T. S. Eliot's social opinions'. Howe wrote: 'This book is an extension of an article which appeared in* Science and Society, *the last "respectable" journal of intellectual Stalinism in America. If to most of us Eliot matters primarily as poet and critic, to Mr Robbins he is significant mainly as a spokesman for "clerico-fascism".' While Howe admits that some may be repelled by Eliot's views on certain political matters, 'Is it really necessary to accept Eliot's political views or religious commitment in order to be moved by* Murder in the Cathedral *and excited by the* Four Quartets? *I think not.'*

On 12 December Mary noted the arrival of her Christmas present from Eliot, two volumes of a French–English dictionary: 'The postman wilted.' There was a quiet end to the year.

23 December. Sunday: Supper at the flat – another long talk on confession and on the Midnight Mass and prayer, topped up with Beethoven Op. 59, No. 1.

30 December. Sunday: A very peaceful evening, mostly in front of the roaring fire in the smoking room at the Garrick. Vernon Bartlett and a few others there. We exchanged Simenons, apples and olives.

1952

Following a bout of gastric flu in which Eliot wrote to Mary that his insides felt 'like a session of the Colonial Legislative assembly', he recovered and she recounted a dinner at her flat. He arrived 'in his "millionaire coat" – a curious tweed with a large brown fur collar'. She wrote on 20 January:

He turned up about 7. p.m. and stayed until 11 p.m. We had a roaring fire – he brought chocolates and cigarettes. He is annoyed with George Thompson in the *Evening Standard* saying that his father wanted to be a clergyman and had an impediment in his speech – neither of which statements are true. On dentists: 'When I was ten I had to go to the dentist twice a week for two years. He had the collected works of Poe in his waiting room and I read them right through. I wish I'd thought of putting that into my Address on Poe to the Library of Congress.' And on G.B.S. again: 'He ought to have died thirty years before he did, after he had finished *St Joan*. I only saw him once. He flirted with Hitler and Mussolini, but they call me a Fascist and a Hyena.' T. is becoming an expert washer-up.

In 1949, of course, he had given her that 'little book containing his "Poe to Valéry" lecture to the Library of Congress'; he had delivered it in November of that year. Before he left, on this January evening in 1952, they listened to Beethoven's Coriolan Overture again, and the whole of the Mozart clarinet quintet – he had brought her the Beethoven in 1949, too.

27 January: T. failed to materialise on my birthday – perhaps he forgot – perhaps he didn't want to, as it is the anniversary of his wife's

T. S. ELIOT'S

MURDER [U]
IN THE
CATHEDRAL

Press flyer for the film of *Murder in the Cathedral*.

death in 1947. This morning he was in his enormous coat again. 'If you want a cigarette, say so now, as I'll have an awful job to get inside my coat once I've done it up.'

1952 was a year of momentous change: on the morning of 6 February, King George VI was found dead in his bed – after a shooting outing the day before – by his valet. 'A deep sorrow has fallen on all the peoples of the Commonwealth and Empire,' opined The Times. *'Until yesterday they were united in allegiance to a SOVEREIGN to whom they were proud to yield it. Now they deplore his grievous and untimely loss.'*

6 February: We had arranged last Sunday to go to a concert at the Festival Hall tonight – but the concert was cancelled because the King died early this morning – and all London stopped. T. turned up about 6 p.m., with six books and a black tie. We had a remarkable evening – 'After all,' says Tom thoughtfully, 'we've buried four sovereigns.' While I cooked supper he read all the evening papers I had collected, then, because the wireless programme had stopped, Tom kept dialling TIM [the speaking clock], so that we shouldn't miss the 9 p.m. news – when it came it was very impressive and moving. THIS IS LONDON – and a round-the-country description of how the news had been received – the Lutine Bell tolling in the City, Great Tom of Liverpool, the Oban fishing fleet coming in at sunset with their sails dipped . . . It was strange, listening with thousands of other people, yet oddly isolated in a Bloomsbury room in a stately house which had 'seen better days'. Later we discussed the possibility of the *Murder* film being postponed yet again – and Eggerson in the new play: 'No, he is quite stationary – I hope he won't suffer from it. I've grown very fond of him.' We drove back to Chelsea through a curious, silent, dark London – no theatres, cinemas, dance halls open, few people on the streets.

The loyal, decent Eggerson is integral to The Confidential Clerk. *Eliot's work on the play was going well. On 10 February, after church on Sunday, Mary recorded how she wanted to buy flowers for a friend; he offered to buy them instead. 'Why shouldn't I get them for you? I buy your newspapers sometimes.' She declined, and bought inexpensive flowers because tulips – which she had wanted – were too costly. 'Oh dear, I ought to have got them and disguised the expense,' she noted him saying to her. There is, in this, once more a kind of intimacy, as when she waited for him at the Garrick.*

My neighbour in the smoking room said to his lady friend: 'Tom Eliot is below. He comes every Sunday and always comes alone.' At that moment Tom came up, sat beside me and said: 'Same as usual?' He talked again of the voices he hears when going to sleep – 'quite indeterminate voices, neither male nor female – I hear what they say – but it's never anything notable, nor anything connected with anyone I know. I'll try and snatch a phrase one night and note it down, to give you an example.'

The smoking room neighbour claimed that no one was close to him, but Mary showed that she was. Not only was she with him at the Garrick, but he also went on to tell her of the voices he heard as he drifted off to sleep. On 17 February she noted that he was ill all over the time of the funeral processions of the King; and once more there was the push-pull of their friendship: his resistance, her insistence.

This morning I asked if we were dining to-night or if he was supping with me. 'No, Mary, you know I can't see anyone more than once a fortnight – they would get on my nerves!' I preserved a stunned silence so that Tom, rather anxious, began to engage me in conversation. I observed mildly that we did seem to be meeting rather oftener than once a fortnight, to which Tom said: 'Well, that must have been for a special occasion' – what nonsense – but I understand that we dine next Sunday.

Indeed they did on 24 February, at which point he told her that he had finished a draft of The Confidential Clerk: *'Now the hard work starts,' he said.*

On 28 February, they had agreed to go and see the film of Murder in the Cathedral, *but he was not feeling well. Furthermore, he told her that he was*

. . . very depressed with the Press reviews of *Murder* and he's been to the first showing and it went on so long that he didn't get any lunch and the critics made such silly remarks and so on. 'I shall invite you later. I want you to come with me, though I never want to see the film again, but I want to see the audience.' . . . Then on he went to other matters and I reminded him of the concert he had arranged for next week. 'Oh yes, if I'd remembered the concert I should not have had supper with you last Sunday' – at which I burst out laughing and said he made such complicated rules that he couldn't remember them himself. This doesn't really describe our extraordinary conversation – perhaps this is all caused by the bad reviews of *Murder*.

Eliot had been very enthusiastic about the film, writing to Hoellering that he had become convinced that the play could make a fine and unusual film, having set aside his earlier doubts, but the reviews did not necessarily echo Eliot's hopes. 'Whatever literary merits T. S. Eliot's "Murder in the Cathedral" may have and whatever strange dramatic virtues it may possess in performance on a stage,' wrote the New York Times's *film critic,*

> *it is obvious that this stylized verse drama is not felicitous material for the screen . . . In spite of an excellent production and bold direction by George Hoellering and in spite of an eloquent recital by a virtually organ-voiced cast, Mr Eliot's long poetic discourse on the preparation of Thomas a Becket for martyrdom completely eludes projection in cohesive and exciting visual terms.*

On 5 March Mary wrote that Eliot was very disappointed by the final result; Groser is 'an amateur, he can't act and he is a stupid man. Besides, he is not in sympathy with what I am trying to say.'

They went to see the film together at last on 17 March, though he remained reluctant.

He was distinctly peevish. 'I lost all interest in *Murder in the Cathedral* when it became prescribed reading for Higher Certificate.' I had not looked forward to this party – the film really hadn't had a chance, three times postponed and then no First Night because of Court Mourning – and it has not started well, tepid press and small audiences. 'Well, this is a gloomy expedition!' said Tom as we arrived. A fat little Manager met us in the almost empty foyer, bowed like corn in the wind and ordered a minion to conduct us to our seats in the Dress Circle. A good deal of fuss was made that we had exactly the numbered seats on our tickets, in the front row, which was comic, because there was only ONE OTHER PERSON in the Dress Circle – an elderly lady in Row F! We looked over the Dress Circle into the stalls with interest – a very sparse audience, mostly 6th formers with their teachers I think. Throughout the 2 hours and 20 minutes of the film Tom kept up a running commentary – so perhaps it was as well that we were practically alone. 'Too much of this sky . . . I mistrust it . . . all these carvings were photographed all over Europe and copied – there is no complete set of 12th-century chessmen – a few were discovered and the rest made up – Groser makes one false move with his castle, the fault of the producer.' We returned to the flat for gin. 'There! now (privately to you) I hope NEVER to have to go to see that film again. It seemed longer than ever this afternoon. It all goes to show that the film is not, I think, a good medium for poetry. I always thought that, but I didn't want to hurt Hoellering's feelings. But it did get some really good notices at Venice!'

He left for Nice on a short holiday; while he was gone Mary saw John Hayward – apparently Tom had been 'snapping his head off', and so they consoled each other for his temper. Eliot's holiday didn't do him much good: on 7 April, Palm Sunday, he told her the weather was bad and he saw 'far too many people'.

13 April, EASTER DAY: Lovely sunny morning – we took a long drive through the parks and the milling crowds – 'how vacant their faces are!' – and splendid daffodils. He arrived rather late for supper after a long tea with a family of small children. 'I need gin, sympathy and symphonies' said my guest. A very mixed bag of talk after supper – on Confession: 'when they are too lenient one doesn't feel one has a clean bill'. 'I begin to dread old age – the difficulties, the impossibility of saving money, the complications ahead . . .' 'Everybody is pathetic – you and I too – but we can't see it ourselves. On Bertie Russell: 'We knew each other too well to tell on each other.' Another nightmare: 'I dreamed that I was being abducted by the Dean of Canterbury; he took me off in a lorry, and I couldn't make people understand. There he was, smiling away . . .'

Eliot travelled again to the United States in the spring. He would see Emily Hale in Andover, Massachusetts, where she was teaching at Abbot Academy; as her 'special friend' he gave a talk to the girls, but Mary's record gives no indication that he informed her of this.

2 June, Whit Monday: A great agitation about T.'s return – owing to an oil strike and cancellations of planes. This morning he telephoned having succeeded in getting here last night, to know if he could come and 'crack an egg' with me. In excellent form, with nylons and sugar and the records of *The Cocktail Party*. After supper we had his usual day-to-day recital of his adventures . . . 'I am so glad to be home, I've been homesick all the time – I longed for a rainy, grubby Fulham Road.'

11 June: Oh dear, right down again, after a visit to Edinburgh for the Alliance Française. Now that he is President of the Alliance he has to take the chair and speak often himself. He obviously finds great difficulty in keeping speakers to time and even left one out by mistake. (I expect he did it badly – NOT his line) and the many official dinners, receptions and expeditions and two 8-hour journeys 'shouting to frogs over the noise of the train' almost finished him. Desmond MacCarthy had died suddenly – 'It's strange to hear of the sudden death of someone one knows, in a strange newspaper (The *Scotsman*) in a strange country (Scotland). He was kind to me when I was young. I consider him a failure. He was Irish and lazy. He could have been the leading literary critic, but wouldn't bother to and has never been important.'

MacCarthy had been – among other things – drama critic of the New Statesman, *and an early English-language supporter of the works of Ibsen and Chekhov. After Eliot's dismissal of MacCarthy, there followed 'a gay dinner at the Garrick' and then*

. . . since it was a beautiful evening, a hour's drive in the City. As soon as we reached St Paul's Tom started sniffing about: 'I feel like a child returning to its old haunts' and showed me the basement where he'd worked for two years at Lloyd's. We drove along his particular King William Street to the Monument, reached the Tower and got out of the car and strolled down to the river. Tom, his hat on the back of his head, really enjoyed himself. We stood for a long time looking at the great moat, the trees and grass round the Norman towers, the Beefeaters in their splendid red and black. 'How peaceful and quiet – this is lovely.' We returned a slightly different way, Tom calling out the names of the streets, the famous City Firms (old friends) – 'go slowly, I want to show you ALL my haunts' – and then we drove gently back to Chelsea by the river. 'Thank you very much for a very nice, recuperative evening.'

*On 25 June they met after a gathering for the Braille Centenary Meeting
at the National Book League in Albemarle Street. They repaired to the
Akropolis on Percy Street, 'a small, comfortable, well-appointed restaurant concentrating on real Greek cooking at reasonable prices', as* Tatler
described it at the time. They talked

. . . of prayer (while drinking martinis). 'I have taken to praying on
the Underground – it avoids the feeling of an empty mind with
thoughts blowing about in it – but it's tiresome trying to fit in prayers
with stopping at stations. I don't know if it's good for one's prayers,
but perhaps it is good for the Underground. Lately I had a curious
experience – after a period of blankness in my mind I "came to" to
find I had been saying a prayer. I don't know if I am afraid or not.'
   20 July, Sunday: I sent T. a note a few days ago asking if he would
have any objections to me coinciding with him at Chardonne (my
particular Swiss retreat, to which I was introducing him) for two days.
No reply. After church we went for the usual drive and I enquired
if he had got my note – 'yes, but not relevant at the moment' as the
reply. When we had finished our drive he produced from his missal
an unfinished crossword and a note for me.

*Three days passed before she remarked on the note he had handed to her.
For the next week there was a peculiar back-and-forth regarding how
much he wished to see her, or anyone, or did not wish to see her, or anyone.
There is an emotional distance in the way in which she keeps track of this
exchange, though her use of the word 'frightening' seems telling.*

23 July: The letter had as its theme 'I want to be alone', but making
all sorts of plans whereby he would vacate the room at Chardonne
for me etc. and asking me to let him know what I would like. I sent
a half-sheet saying 'NONSENSE – but thanks all the same', and
this evening we discussed the matter very amiably.

On 30 July he told her, in regard to some future dates:

'Not two days running – I cannot see anyone two days in succession.'
I suggested that his 'Trade Union rules' about not seeing people were
frightening. 'No, you can take it as a compliment; it's not worth the
bother of telling most people.' And about hurting people, a propos
another matter: 'Well, I suppose we all hurt each other from time to
time and want to run away and hide.'

*On 17 August, a Sunday, he brought her the record of Robert Speaight
reading 'The Waste Land', which – despite the above exchange, and the
one that was to come – offered Mary another opportunity to note the way
in which she was special to Eliot.*

'Please listen to it alone and tell me what you think of it. I think it is
rather good and brings out unexpected dramatic qualities. I haven't
asked anyone else to hear it and would much like your view.' At the
Garrick we had a poor but restful dinner.

   1 October: Dinner at the Étoile – I wondered why – a most unusual
invitation. Then I discovered it was a special occasion, in order to break
to me that there were to be no more Sunday dinners 'because John wants
to change to Tuesdays and Thursdays OUT, instead of Sundays and
Wednesdays'. Awful for me, for week-days are always much less easy
than Sundays, much more difficult to arrange and much less peaceful.

*She would note that this change of plans didn't actually reflect the reality
of what was going on.*

John told me some time after that this change of routine suited
him . . . as little as it did me.

*Yet she went along with it, as did John. It was Eliot who remained in
control of the relationship.*

21 October: Well, anyway, though I don't like cooking after a long office day, T. certainly settles in. This evening he arrived at 6 p.m. and stayed until 10.30 p.m. Some more talk on the new play. 'The social distinctions in the different acts are tricky – and I <u>must</u> ask you about organists – inferior organists.'

He talked again of the voices he hears when he is going to sleep. 'They are very distinct – the individual voices I mean – and they say such silly things – they are never the same voices I have heard on other nights and never recognisable as the voices of people I know.' On the Sitwells: 'Edith thinks she is a great poet – I think she is a good poet in a small way. She and Osbert are embarrassing.' At 9.30 we listened to the Turpin-Angelo fight, which was very exciting.

A nice image, Mary and Tom listening to boxing on the wireless. Randy Turpin was Britain's first Black world boxing champion: the year before, he had beaten Sugar Ray Robinson to the world middleweight title. The next entertainment was more literary: the Welsh actor and playwright Emlyn Williams had begun performing a one-man show of readings from Dickens – standing at a lectern that was a reproduction of the one Dickens used for his own readings – the year before; he would carry on with the show for the next three decades. 'All the best people' were the cream of that social world: actual and literary aristocracy packed into the stalls.

30 October: Quite an adventure. Lunch at the Russell Hotel and on to the Drury Lane Theatre to the 'Private View', so to speak, of Emlyn Williams doing his Dickens Readings, with the Queen Mother present. The theatre was packed and our seats were in the middle of the stalls. All the best people were there – the David Cecils, the Duff Coopers (now Norwich!) the Fabers in a box, Lord David Hamilton, with his boxer's broken nose, Robert Lusty, David Higham, Peter Quennell, and John in a stiff collar in a box with the Crewes. E. W. was splendid – starting with the Veneerings and the

Podsnaps, on to Paul Dombey's death . . . We called on the Fabers in the interval – well, we tried in the first interval, but lost our way and had to start again in the second interval, this time with success. After the performance Tom took John home in a taxi, then returned to my flat – where we had a great deal of gin and conversation of a profound nature on hurting people – a topic he seems to have on his mind at the moment.

11 November: Sherry this evening – quite a surprise. T. brought a nasty little article from an American magazine, practically accusing him of homosexuality and mentioning John. And he told me of another, more serious, article from 'Essays in Criticism' – an article on 'The Waste Land' – hinting at the same so transparently that he is consulting his solicitor about a possible libel action. The solicitor asked for a copy of the poem and T. is much amused at the thought of the poor man trying to understand it. A very lively dinner at the Russell Hotel, then on in the car, at great speed, to the Festival Hall for a concert. We had Mozart and Brahms – very nice indeed. As we were coming out in the crowd a little man got fearfully excited at seeing Tom and, clutching his young lady, followed us for a long way, his eyes popping out.

In the July 1952 issue of Essays in Criticism, *a young academic, John Peter, published 'A New Interpretation of "The Waste Land"'. The piece suggested that the poem's speaker is in love with a young man who later died; after Eliot himself died the article was reprinted, and it was suggested that the young man in question was Jean Verdenal, to whom the poet had dedicated 'Prufrock'. Verdenal, who was just a little younger than Eliot, had met the aspiring poet in Paris in 1910; Verdenal was studying to be a doctor. A contemporary account describes him as 'a young man of extreme friendliness and of rare distinction'. The two became close; Verdenal was killed in the Dardanelles in the spring of 1915, just a few days shy of his twenty-fifth birthday. Mary's open-mindedness did not include a liberal attitude to homosexuality, then still illegal in England. But the 'accusation' was troubling not only because of its implication: its connection between the poetry and the person was uncomfortable in itself. As Peter Ackroyd has written of Eliot: 'His own horror of self-revelation has led to the assumption that there are such revelations to be made. This obscures the true nature of Eliot's life, just as it diminishes his poetry.'*

30 November, Sunday: This morning I was given a large tin of beef stew – last Sunday he had brought a small ditto, explaining that he had a larger one but didn't like to bring it as he was wearing a coat with rather shallow pockets and he was afraid it would fall out while he was collecting. He had been seeing Janet Roberts, discussing the famous article. Helen Gardner was very angry about it and had written a strong protest. 'Janet suspects that the writer is himself homosexual and thinks I am one of the fraternity. I shall send the article to my dilatory solicitor and get him to write a strong letter. After all, that does NOT happen to be my temperament.'

Janet Roberts – Janet Adam Smith – was, by 1952, literary editor of the New Statesman; *her husband was the poet Michael Roberts, who had compiled* The Faber Book of Modern Verse, *published in 1936. In 1953 she herself would publish* The Faber Book of Children's Verse. *Helen Gardner's* The Art of T. S. Eliot *had been published in 1949.*

1st December: After an agreeable evening with Tom I sent him a note to thank him for a decade of a very remarkable (to me) friendship.

4 December: No reply to my note – indeed I had told him that he needn't trouble to reply, since I would be seeing him this evening, when we were dining with Margaret Rhondda. He arrived very early at the flat and in fine spirits – I made no mention of my note but hoped (to myself) that he had liked it. We had a very good evening at Arlington House – easy talk, literary and political – no effort. On our way home we discussed many future dates.

7 December: But he did reply, two days ago – and I was astonished. It was a very hurt letter, having got mine all wrong. I must have mentioned one of our recent conversations about hurting people, for he said I was perpetually hinting that he was hurting John and me and would I give him chapter and verse and if it was true perhaps he had better 'sever his connection' with both of us. He really is most unaccountable, for he had written this, and posted it, before we dined chez Rhondda – and, as I have recorded, he was in excellent spirits and full of plans for the future. I wrote a mildly indignant note and told him not to be silly – and took it in a fog to Carlyle Mansions. Lucky I did, for the fog to-day was impenetrable and church was impossible.

10 December: When he turned up this evening I suggested he might read my letters: of course I hadn't attempted to drive, but had delivered the note by Underground. 'Oh,' said Tom, rather weakly, 'did you really?' and, after a pause, 'are you sure?' I said mildly that he was really rather odd, posting such a letter and then coming and being so amiable and friendly, knowing what was in store for me. 'Ah, but all ladies are the same – you have a terribly ingenious way of putting me in the wrong – and I don't like feeling GUILTY.' A further, and most cheerful, talk on hurting people then followed – I think we've had enough of that topic.

She closed the 'topic' by opining that they had now 'cleared away the fog' but that this was all 'most peculiar'.

She wrote him a note thanking him for his friendship, insisting she required no acknowledgement: and yet, hoping for acknowledgement. He needn't trouble to reply, she recorded carefully; yet she was also willing to set down – her parenthesis adding emphasis – her desire. What resulted over the next few days was an elliptical exchange, during which he apparently threatened to break off all contact, with both Mary and John Hayward: a few years hence they would again discuss his hurtful behaviour. The words she chose – 'unaccountable', 'mildly indignant', 'peculiar' –

are diminishing in their nature, yet insistent in number. Notably – 'I think we've had enough of that topic' – it was she who chose to end this painful discussion.

It was around this time that Martin Browne received a draft of the first two acts of The Confidential Clerk; *Eliot would complete the play by the middle of the following year.*

26 December, Boxing Day: Back to childhood this evening – sitting in front of a lovely fire. I asked if he, like I, looked for castles in the fire. 'No – but lots of other things – I was afraid of fire. Once Marian was cleaning some white gloves on her hands and she got too near the fire and was burned. The cook and the housemaid came running at her screams and they put some dough on the burns, but when the doctor came he said it was the worst thing they could have done. And we had three or four gas mantles on the same bracket and the housemaid used to go round with a taper and light them all. Some of the gas brackets were very near the muslin curtains, so if there was a breeze they caught fire. The gas was always left burning, even if there was nobody in the room. We lived in a slum for years, because it was the family place and even when the neighbourhood went down Grandmother wouldn't move, so father wouldn't leave her – "in case of emergency". Mother had a coal fire in her bedroom and the housemaid used to bring coals and paper and sticks, and light it early every morning. When I left my Dame School and was sent to a small Preparatory School my mother kept me in sailor suits and the other boys laughed. I still have a photo of myself in sailor suit, with my best friend – who is now President of the Chase National Bank. I was a little lonely at home, because all my friends had moved to other neighbourhoods.'

Certainly there is a photograph of Eliot in a sailor suit, taken when he was about ten years old, at the Downs, the family's summer home in Gloucester, Massachusetts.

He told Mary that he had just had a demand for £17,000 income tax.

The Cocktail Party made about £35,000 of which he gets, he reckons, about £4,000.

28 December, Sunday: Tom is going to sit for Epstein. 'I went to tea with him and he seemed to think my contours would be suitable.' It will be interesting to see what they make of each other.

In fact Eliot had met the sculptor Jacob Epstein the year before; Mary was not aware of that, or Eliot did not correct the impression. Both were Americans by birth who had become naturalised British subjects, though Epstein's youth on New York's Lower East Side was very different from Eliot's, to say the least. Epstein's bronze bust has 'the air of a benevolent bird of prey', as the designer and critic Richard Buckle remarked.

31 December, New Year's Eve: I drank a Happy New Year to T. and Mrs Eggerson. 'I drink to you and Mrs E.! Mrs E. never appears in the play, but I have tried to keep up her character throughout. I know about them both from my years at Lloyd's, of course. Mr McKnight lived in the suburbs and kept an allotment.' As we drove back: 'Shall I sing to you?' and off he went, rendering music hall songs of his youth in a more than usually tuneless voice.

1953

The year of THE CONFIDENTIAL CLERK – the premiere at Edinburgh and the London run from the middle of September. It was not the most successful of Tom's plays, mainly, I think, because the people in it, with the exception of Eggerson, seemed so unreal.

It is rare for Mary to make a literary judgement on Eliot's work, but the play, when it was finally produced later in the year, was a puzzle to critics, a strange, absurdist farce of mistaken identity. 'The narrative pattern is staggeringly intricate,' opined Kenneth Tynan. 'It is bizarre; it is the "wrong shape"; it has the weird whorls and intersections one might expect if one's eccentric uncle set about playing with a model railway set.' The New Statesman *was equally puzzled. 'We are never quite sure what the problems really are; and as for the solutions, they none of them seem to us to fit at all.'*

Mary was about to move from Bloomsbury to a new flat on the Chelsea Embankment.

8 January: Oh dear, the last time we'll have supper in this flat and, alas, the last coal fire. T. had been taking the chair at the half-yearly Council of the Alliance Française, of which John has just been made a member. He seemed exhausted (I'm afraid he must be a very bad chairman), but revived quickly on gin. After supper he lay back in my long chair by the fire and listened to the Mozart Oboe Quartet and the Haffner Symphony – his eyes closed – probably asleep.

11 January, Sunday: A very gay drive after church. Tom rarely laughs unrestrainedly and I was struck again by the high pitch when he does, an extraordinary contrast to his low, rather harsh voice when speaking . . . As we passed the statue of Richard Coeur de Lion

at Westminster: 'He couldn't speak a word of English and wrote poems in Provençal.' He offered me all his suitcases for my move.

On 15 January she noted that Eliot made 'the last visit to Brunswick Square – I hope he will soon feel equally at home in my Chelsea flat'. On 18 January they collected his suitcases for her move.

22 January: My birthday. T. brought a very heavy suitcase full of food – silly, we might have fetched it from Faber's in the car. Having been lunching at the Italian Embassy he was all got up in stiff collar and *chapeau melon* and looked very spruce. It seemed so odd meeting at my office instead of in Brunswick Square, but I had already partially moved. We discussed a club which occupies the ground floor of the house in which my new flat is on the top floor – said to be a centre for the Chelsea 'pansies'. 'I suppose their alliances never last – they must live a life of fear and ostracism – like souls in hell. I believe in hell, yes, I do. I live in constant fear of it myself. If there is a Heaven there must also be a Hell. But it's all OUTSIDE TIME and therefore beyond our earthly comprehension. Yet I <u>know</u>, I have always known hell – it is in my bones. I don't believe this is common – perhaps I am abnormal. Can human beings sin unredeemably – I think they can get to a stage where they don't want to be redeemed.' We dined very peacefully at the Connaught, expensively and well. 'I haven't finished the third act yet – there are many difficulties which I solve gradually: <u>squeezing</u> all the time is the hard core of the trouble which I must eventually solve. The real difficulty is to avoid a flat ending or an unresolved ending – sometimes, because I cannot express the reality I have to take refuge in <u>unrealities</u>.'

Seventy years after they were made, Eliot's remarks on homosexuality are difficult to read: but as to living a life of fear, there was something to that, for homosexuality would not be decriminalised – and then only partially – for another fourteen years.

Towards the end of the month they changed their routine, having drinks after hours at his office, as Chelsea was too far for him to go. He had finished the third act of The Confidential Clerk *and they had made 'many dates' – but these had to be cancelled as Mary fell ill with a high temperature, as she noted on 15 February, 'Quinquagesima Sunday'. He wrote to her when she was ill. 'Do eat all the sugar you can get,' he instructed her on 7 February; the following day he wrote, 'I hope your secretary has been cooking for you – I don't know how you manage: and it is peculiarly unfortunate to be stricken just after moving and without a telephone. Let me know when you are well enough to be visited.'*

He did indeed turn up on 15 February.

The Great Poet turned up in good spirits, striped trousers and stiff collar about 6.45 p.m. at the office, having been assisting to entertain the Duke of Edinburgh at his English Speaking Union.

The English Speaking Union had been founded in 1918 to foster 'a good understanding between the peoples of the USA and the British Commonwealth'. The Duke of Edinburgh had become its President in 1952, and would serve until 2013. In 1948 Eliot had chaired the 'Books Across the Sea' initiative; thousands of books were sent between the United States and Britain as part of the scheme.

He told Mary of a party at the Institut Français:

It was very dreary. I sat next to Bertie Russell – he had his new wife with him but didn't introduce me. I do find him trying – he gives me the creeps – one of the Successful Failures.

Bertrand Russell had married the New Yorker Edith Finch in December of the year before; Eliot's dismissal is blunt, considering how closely they had been involved in previous years. Eliot's reference to 'the creeps' may be making reference to Vivien's long-ago affair with Russell; there was too Eliot's objection to Russell's strong anti-Christianity. But again Mary is a recording angel only of what she observes, not privy – as far as we are aware – to that part of Eliot's history.

She wanted to read the new play and told him so: not yet, was his answer. 'There's a lot of Simenon in it – Le destin des malou and La neige était sale.' Those novels were published in 1947 and 1948 respectively.

Another talk on prayer this evening: 'It takes me one and a half hours to get to bed – prayers for twenty minutes – oh, and to-night I must finish the rosary. I say some prayers before undressing and some after. I never read in bed because I fall asleep so quickly – my insomnia is waking up too early. My voices still go on, but don't disturb me. Mostly they say ordinary things, mostly crazy things.' As we said good-night: 'I shall remember you in my prayers this week-end and remember you on Monday in a different way.' And, a propos Lent: 'Why not try, as I am doing, to get an hour quiet in the week and read a holy book?'

They arranged to meet 4 March, but he didn't turn up. 'This morning Miss Fletcher telephoned apologies that she'd forgotten to give me a message that he'd been called away.' When they do meet on 8 March they 'strolled along discussing the remissness of Miss Fletcher'.

12 March: Supper at Chelsea to-night. We were both very tired, but after a cheerful drive from Bloomsbury T. settled down in front of the fire with his gin while I cooked the supper. That was a great success, considering the strain of producing it all on a cooker with which I am not yet familiar. The rest of the evening we spent in listening to the Schubert Great C Major Symphony.

15 March, Lent IV: The day started delightfully – strolling back from the Old Church (where we have the services in the Sir Thomas More Chapel still, owing to war damage) very sunny and pleasant. And later we had a long drive. Then T. suddenly said, before bolting into his flat: 'I have no dates free until after Easter I'm afraid.' I fear he is on the verge of another Bad Turn – I see squalls approaching.

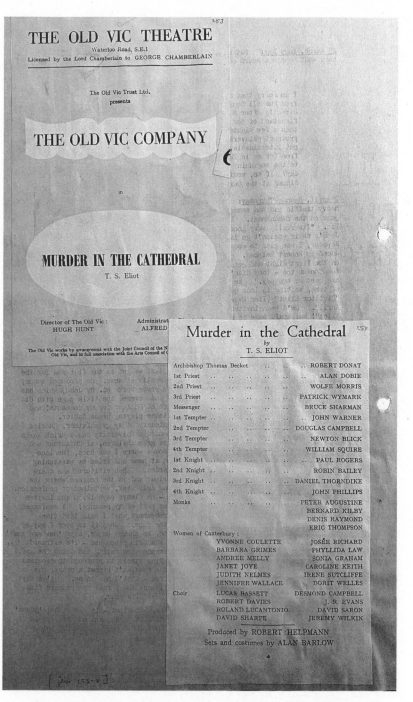

Programme for the Old Vic production of *Murder in the Cathedral*.

He advances and then retreats; she makes light of his threatened with-drawal, once again.

22 March, Passion Sunday: In the course of the week I sent a note round, so I did, saying we had better make no plans for the present, owing to his great busy-ness and received in reply a serious note thanking me for my magnanimous thought, saying he hoped to 'look round' on Wednesday and we must arrange which day we would go to Tenebrae next week! After church to-day we took our usual drive and I was told that my note was 'generous, like a man, not a woman' . . . and we'd meet on Wednesday . . . quite dotty.

The ellipses above are Mary's. They met on 2 April, Maundy Thursday, and she recorded a long entry as they drove from Bloomsbury to church via her flat through heavy traffic. He praised the new Murder at the Old Vic, starring Robert Donat and directed by Robert Helpmann; he was quite excited about it, she wrote. He had been invited to the Abbey for the Queen's Coronation: 'Mr and Mrs T. Eliot,' she noted. In the section below, she mishears – perhaps – the reference to his grandfather; he is speaking of his great-grandfather, William Greenleaf Eliot (1781–1853), whose centenary fell that year.

At long last we got to the flat and for the first time Tom settled in as though he were really at home. He produced a copy of the famous Penguin (Anthology of T.S.E.'s prose works ed. by John) which has been so severely dealt with by Ifor Evans and covered the title page with Old Possum inscriptions; and a book on the Church of England for my comments, and tins of meat and the records of Eva Le Gallienne playing Hedda Gabler. Over gin: 'I am going to St Louis for the Centenary of my grandfather, Charles Norton Eliot – a very important man. He founded a University and a Brick Works and lived to be 93. I remember the queue of grandchildren, at Christmas and Easter, to be <u>kissed</u>. And I remember the house where I was born, the lace curtains tied with ribbon – they were washed at home and dried by stretching them across special wooden frames in the garden. When visitors came there were always fresh curtains put up in the parlour and in the bedroom where the ladies put their things.'

'The younger generation must be very timid or Mr Eliot would not have remained in office for so long,' began Benjamin Ifor Evans's dissection of Eliot's Selected Prose; the 'narrowing of literary taste' he called Eliot's 'greatest disservice to our time'. Nevertheless, Mary pasted his review into her manuscript. Eva Le Gallienne was a remarkable theatrical impresario of the early and mid-twentieth century, a driving force behind New York's off-Broadway scene and an acclaimed translator of Ibsen.

Over supper they spoke of Confession, as it was Holy Week, and then they headed out to St Stephen's, 'to our annual "jaunt" of Tenebrae', she wrote, 'that great, dark, magnificent service'. The Night Watch, or Gethsemane Watch, is a vigil to mark Jesus' Agony in the Garden, when he invited his disciples to watch and pray with him: 'And he cometh, and findeth them sleeping, and saith unto Peter, Simon, sleepest thou? couldest not thou watch one hour? Watch ye and pray, lest ye enter into temptation. The spirit truly is ready, but the flesh is weak.'

3 April, Good Friday: Tom has given up the Night Watch at the Blessed Sacrament, which he did for so many years, at the insistence of the Vicar. The <u>very</u> long Liturgy began at 10.30 a.m. and after two hours we came out again into the sunshine. 'So many women taking the Watch, I much prefer the men's Night Watch, but it's a token. I feel a little nostalgia all the same. But perhaps it was just self-righteousness, taking the most difficult time (2–3 a.m.) that nobody liked doing.'

They went for a long drive; he wanted to take her to Epping Forest, and to see Victoria Park.

As we drove through Regent's Park: 'Would you like to go for a sail? Let's go one day! What headlines! and we must go to the Zoo.'

*On 5 April, Easter Day, they met at church – though only she made it to the 7 a.m. service and saw him come at 8.*oo, *with 'cloth cap, fur coat and rather bleary-eyed, saying he'd decided 6 a.m. was too early to get up – it takes him so long to shave'.*
  Afterwards:

'Oh bother,' says Tom suddenly, 'I've forgotten the periodicals and the books I said I would give you and the Hedda Gabler book – those records will take at least two hours to hear and we must do our prep beforehand.'

Two days later, Easter Tuesday, they met for dinner at the Garrick and discussed the progress of The Confidential Clerk: *it was fascinating to work to a framework, he told her. 'One is not free, writing in this medium, but that is part of the fascination.'*

We arranged to go and see *Murder* at the Old Vic 'in the gallery' on 30 April. After dinner, at his request, we came back to my flat to hear some music. We had the Schubert Trio – and Tom lay back in his chair, eyes closed and silent. But he was grey and all tensed up. He was worried about the strain I had been through and, when I thanked him for a good evening, said: 'Well I am glad if a dismal person like myself can help.'

It is telling that she does not record the nature of the 'strain': what was significant to her was Eliot's apparent empathy, not – it would appear – the events which had affected her. They had changed the date for their planned theatre visit because of his commitments; in the end they saw Murder in the Cathedral *on 2 May.*

Tom arrived at my flat about 5.30 p.m., fell over the step, picked himself [up] and came in beaming – threw his hat and coat down, placed the latest song (of the Jellicles) open on the piano and said: 'I give you a great deal of music, most of which you return to me without comment. You can play and sing this one . . .' A hurried supper, then off to the Old Vic, which started at 7.15 p.m. It was the Last Night and a great crowd. We wedged ourselves into the Upper Circle – people eating ices and sweets already. As the curtain went up Tom whispered: 'You'll see a splendid spectacle, but the words are VERY boring!' Certainly the play was very well put on by Robert Helpmann, but I thought Robert Donat was a v. melodramatic Becket and much of it was over-played. The chorus was interesting – much done by solo speakers (but I can hardly sit through it now). In the interval we went out, unrecognised, through the crowd and investigated a tattoo shop and a valentine shop. The second half was worse than the first. The knights brought the house down, and Tom buried his face in his hands. The end was very funny. All the actors, looking like a Football Group, bowed repeatedly and then Donat made a speech. 'I want to thank you all on behalf of Mr Robert Helpmann (indicating the wings) – this splendid cast (indicating the Football Group and bowing low to them) and for myself I thank you (with a tremble in his voice) from the bottom of my heart (indicating that organ) and last but not least – Mr T. S. EL-I-OT.' Tom laughed helplessly. We struggled out and were piloted to the Stage Door and, after a wait, Mr Donat's dressingroom. Tom looked round the door, then called to me: 'Come on Mary, he's quite respectable.'

We sat down and had a very cosy chat with Donat and Helpmann, cigarettes all round. As we reached the street again Tom was bombarded by autograph hunters. On the way home we discussed the three Beckets – Speaight, Groser and Donat. I said I thought the three rolled together might be effective. Tom said: 'Speaight is an actor being an Archbishop – Groser a priest trying to be an actor – Donat an actor failing to be an Archbishop, yet Donat was the only one who gave some idea – too much perhaps – of what the Archbishop and Chancellor had been like.'

17 May, Sunday: A gloomy Poet – full of fears about his coming journey to the U.S.A. He is anxious to get off, so that he can start coming home again, and was very poor company indeed.

He dropped her a brief but chatty postcard on 19 May, remarking that he owed her tuppence, and there was more talk of boxing, and the last bout that Jersey Joe Walcott had fought against Rocky Marciano: 'I am sorry about Joe Walcott; but one of these days I shall just sit down in the ring myself.'

He would send these cards when they didn't see each other for a few days, she noted on 26 May: '"to keep in touch" as he says'. She recorded a long dinner at the Garrick, and some of their conversation.

A propos someone who knows him well and has no interest in his religious life: 'Yes, it is indeed the whole of me, yet too many people think it is irrelevant.' And of his early discipleship to Ezra Pound: 'I always felt myself to be a protégé of Pound – at least, that's how it looked to me – perhaps, I think now, I ought not to have glossed over the things he said and changed the subject. Perhaps I ought to have said he was talking damned nonsense and that he would never know anything about politics. I might have saved him.'

Eliot left for the United States at the end of May, and returned in early July. The trip took him to St Louis, to Cambridge and to Connecticut and New York. At Washington University in St Louis he delivered a lecture, 'American Literature and the American Language', in which he spoke a little of his own artistic journey:

Some of my strongest impulse to original development, in early years, has come from thinking: 'here is a man who has said something, long ago or in another language, which somehow corresponds to what I want to say now; let me see if I can't do what he has done, in my own language – in the language of my own place and time.'

Mary saw him upon his return – they met at church, on 6 July, and he was 'in splendid spirits'. He brought her back nylons from America, and went to visit his White Russian, Tereshchenko, in Wandsworth: 'I believe he finds some sense of "atonement" in his assiduous attentions to sick people.'

On 27 July Eliot dropped Mary a line after he missed seeing her at church the day before; he said he wanted to meet her brother Humphrey, but he must visit Tereshchenko. He told her that it would be hard to see her in August: an American friend would be arriving, and staying at the Basil Street Hotel. He did not say that the friend was Emily Hale.

The Confidential Clerk *opened at the Lyceum Theatre, Edinburgh, as part of the festival, with Paul Rogers as Sir Claude Mulhammer and Margaret Leighton as Lucasta Angel. Overall, it was not received as well as* Murder in the Cathedral *or* The Cocktail Party, *though some critics thought to hedge their bets. 'It is likely to be found brilliantly entertaining even by those who are left wondering what it is all really about,' was the verdict of* The Times. *It would open in September at the Lyric Theatre, Shaftesbury Avenue, and ran until April 1954; it then went to the Duke of York's for another four weeks.*

4 August: A telephone message awaited me this morning: 'Mr Eliot will be calling on you between 6–6:30 this evening' – rather like Royalty. And so he did and accepted 'two for the road' with alacrity. It was late when we drove to Chelsea, having discussed Archbishops' biographies, Free-Masonry (which he hates), Cathedrals and other burning topics. On a more delicate matter: 'Its a relief that, with understanding, we can both say what we really mean to each other. I wouldn't say what I say to anyone but you, nor would I allow anyone else to say what you say to me!'

To be able to say what one really means to someone is certainly significant, and it is no wonder Mary recorded this emphatic statement. Yet there is a difference between speaking one's mind and revealing the truth of one's heart. Mary believed their relationship to be free and frank, but, as the entry below shows, she had accepted – so it seemed – the role of bluff good friend, able to take whatever he threw at her. The entry also shows that he had clearly at some point told her a little of what had passed between himself and Miss Hale.

On 9 August, he told her the play was going well – they looked at a church in Marylebone, passed the zoo and decided again they must visit.

Suddenly: 'I may not be able to go to Windsor next Sunday – there's an American friend coming, and I'm not sure when and I shall have to meet the train.' This is, undoubtedly, Miss Emily Hale – to whom T. was engaged for so long – his conscience about her and the way he 'jilted' her must be very bad – he hardly ever meets trains!

11 August: T. very uneasy this evening – probably the imminent arrival of Miss Hale. However, he climbed up the stairs to my office, banged on the door, and arrived announcing 'Enter B. Kagan!' He can't discover if Miss H.'s boat (he hasn't mentioned her by name yet!) has a boat train. He is also, naturally, nervous about the play and talked of the 'failure' of *Family Reunion* – 'but it was put on first at the Westminster – almost a provincial theatre'.

15 August, the Assumption: Three minutes late I was, having promised to collect Tom at 7.40 a.m. and there he was rushing along, tense and agitated, trying to hurry for a bus in case I didn't turn up. Later to-day T. telephoned (which, these days, he only manages to do himself in great emergencies, except from home) to say that Miss Hale (still anonymous) was arriving at 2.45 to-morrow, so he wouldn't be able to go to Windsor. I, a little unkindly, asked him to telephone to the Morsheads himself.

16 August, Sunday: I was still feeling a little unkind and, after church, drove in the direction of home, saying I supposed he

wouldn't have time for a drive to-day. 'On the contrary,' said Tom, pleadingly, 'I have too much time and too little. I shall lunch at the Garrick at 1 p.m. and would prefer to spend the time until then in your company.' So I gave in, weakly, and we went on a tour of the City – got out and looked at St Benet's, newly painted – walked down Paul's Wharf and returned via Hatton Garden. 'See you at the Dress Rehearsal in Edinburgh next Monday,' says the Playwright.

They both went off to Edinburgh to the Festival for the opening of The Confidential Clerk. *On 24 August she gave his niece Theodora lunch in Edinburgh; she and Eliot were staying in 'a dim little pension'. She left a cutting for Eliot from the* Sunday Express *entitled 'The Mysterious Mr Eliot'. They went on to the dress rehearsal and he was in good spirits.*

As to the play itself, well, for me it was difficult – there was so much in it that we had talked about so often. There was very little poetry in it – it is clever and rather tiresome and, in parts, hard to sit through with attention. I am sometimes afraid these days that Tom, with his curious, rather malicious humour, may be laughing at his public – and they won't know it, though they may suspect it. And I am also afraid that his public may laugh at him – and he <u>will</u> know it – and that will drive him further and further into his 'prison'. Now I must read the play.

How complex her feelings are, acknowledged and unacknowledged. Her admission to feeling 'unkind' is revealing, as is her idea that there is mockery in his work. That 'prison' is perhaps one she had hoped – and continued to hope – to free him from.

25 August: FIRST NIGHT & WORLD PREMIERE OF 'THE CONFIDENTIAL CLERK'.

In the course of the afternoon, via niece Theodora, I sent Tom a dark red carnation and was glad to observe that he wore it. The play

EDINBURGH
INTERNATIONAL
FESTIVAL
OF MUSIC & DRAMA

IN ASSOCIATION WITH THE ARTS COUNCIL OF GREAT BRITAIN, THE
BRITISH COUNCIL AND THE CORPORATION OF THE CITY OF EDINBURGH

ROYAL LYCEUM THEATRE

EDINBURGH

24th August — 12th September

1953

THE CONFIDENTIAL CLERK

Characters in order of their appearance

Sir Claude Mulhammer	PAUL ROGERS
Eggerson	ALAN WEBB
Colby Simpkins	DENHOLM ELLIOTT
B. Kaghan	PETER JONES
Lucasta Angel	MARGARET LEIGHTON
Lady Elizabeth Mulhammer	ISABEL JEANS
Mrs. Guzzard	ALISON LEGGATT

Directed by E. MARTIN BROWNE

Settings by HUTCHINSON SCOTT

The Confidential Clerk: programme from the Edinburgh International
Festival of Music and Drama, 24 August–12 September 1953.

was a GREAT SUCCESS I think – crammed, of course – and buzzing with excitement – nervous excitement. Tom is, indeed, 'The critics' nightmare'.

She had a bad seat, under the dress circle, 'surrounded by young gum-chewing Americans'.

Still we had a good view of the Royal Box – Tom, the Shereks and Theodora. In the first interval someone went into their box (it was, I learned later, Miss E. Hale!), in the second I went with Martin to see them. Tom looked white, but seemed quite pleased and we made arrangements for meeting on Friday. I didn't see him again, but watched him slink out of the box before the last curtain.

28 August: The critics uniformly laudatory – too good to be true. I lunched again with Theodora, who had been agonised throughout and told me that poor Miss E. Hale was a shadow of her former self and ought to have kept away.

Her pity for Emily Hale – 'poor Miss E. Hale' – is a place of safety for her. How carefully Eliot kept them apart, so much so that she barely seems to register a woman she might have regarded as a rival.

His moods swung back and forth, according to Mary – cross and morose, but he invited her to see a play she referred to as 'Hosea' by Norman Nicholson; it is called A Match for the Devil *and is based on the biblical book of Hosea. Nicholson, a Cumbrian poet, had been a contributor to* The Criterion, *and Eliot had accepted his first book of poems,* Five Rivers, *for publication by Faber and Faber in 1944. On 29 August Mary wrote that they went to see the play in a church hall in a 'slummy little street'.*

As we arrived Tom said, 'Well, one relief, Nicholson will not be here – so embarrassing if he was, and I might not recognise him if he was. Please poke me if I go to sleep.' But Nicholson was waiting for us and claimed me as an old friend. We all sat together, I sand-wiched between them, throughout. A somewhat dreamy and, at times, naïve and embarrassing play. Afterwards we met a group of unwashed Scottish poets led by Hugh MacDiarmid, who is a Communist and dislikes Tom – and then went behind the scenes to meet the players. At last we extracted ourselves and walked, exhausted and aimless, over Waverley Bridge towards Calton Hill. He said he would dine in his pension to-night and, when I asked what his niece was doing, said he hadn't asked her. In the taxi in which he took me back to my hostess he said: 'There are times when I wish I could get right away from POETS – they quarrel so. I only like Edwin Muir of this lot. Hugh MacDiarmid is a nasty fellow and mischievous.'

And to-morrow he goes off to Geneva.

Theodora, Tom's niece, begs me not to leave him, however trying he is and tells me that both his dear sister Marian and she herself have hoped for some time that I will marry him. Not much of a hope, I guess.

Not much of a hope, although she records it, using the word itself twice. Muir was the Scottish poet whose translations of Kafka first brought that writer's work to an English-speaking audience; MacDiarmid was indeed a Communist, though not always formally a member of the party.

Eliot went off to Geneva with his friends. On his return, on 20 September they drove out to Windsor for their postponed visit to the Morsheads. The mosaic to which he refers was one of a sequence created by Boris Anrep, a Russian émigré artist who had been befriended by the likes of Augustus John and Clive Bell, and inspired in his creations by the pavement artists outside the National Gallery.

We went through the latest press cuttings en route. 'I am glad there are two bad ones – they were all so good I began to be afraid the play was mediocre. But nobody seems to know the proper meaning of the word "Changeling" – it is a <u>fairy</u> child.'

He tells her of visiting the National Gallery to see Boris Anrep's mosaic 'with a dreadful picture of him in it'. She writes:

He says: 'Nobody asked my permission. I went to see it lately, with Theodora or Emily – I forget which' – the first time he had mentioned Miss Hale to me; no doubt he knew that I knew who the mysterious friend was all the time!

There follows a brief farce of making dinner arrangements.

4 October: Tom is upset, because I suggested that we shouldn't bother about making dates, but go back to Sunday dinners, so much more peaceful for both of us.

6 October: A characteristic note saying: 'Nothing, it has been said, is irreparable except Death' and went on to say that I was to remember that he is an old man with an uneasy conscience and bad dreams.

8 October: A note, very cross, saying 'I understand from Miss Fletcher that you are dining with me on Thursday next week.' This really made me rather angry – I supposed he'd told Miss Fletcher to fix up with my secretary. I wrote an indignant denial, but didn't send it.

9 October: My secretary says Miss F. has not telephoned and that she (my secretary) would not dream of making an engagement for me without telling me.

11 October: I've been getting tired of this, but couldn't think of anything I could do. To my surprise Tom was in church at 8 a.m. After the service he really was very funny. I let him leave first and gave him plenty of time to sneak off home before I appeared. But there he was, strolling along and pretending to examine the tombs

and monuments in the churchyard, in a nonchalant kind of way. I came up behind him and asked if he would like to have the key of his suitcase (which he had lent me for my holiday). He was round in a flash and produced from his pocket a battered little tin of BREAKFAST SAUSAGE, which he held out with a shy smile – just like a small boy, who wants to apologise, but can't. We were, indeed, glad to see each other.

After the High Mass it looked as though he'd 'got away with it' again. He chatted away, rather self-consciously, and, on getting out of the car, asked me whether I would like to dine on Thursday. I said I had not yet had an invitation to dine with him and didn't know if I was free, but perhaps he'd like to come round to tea with me this afternoon. At this he slammed the door of the car, saying: 'NO – you don't understand, I am an old man – I shall NOT go out again to-day.'

Cicely Courtneidge, mentioned below, was an actress and comedienne who was appearing in London in a revue, Over the Moon *– a different style of theatrical experience from* The Confidential Clerk.

15 October: Well, an accidental meeting between our respective secretaries elucidated the fact that Miss Fletcher was still clinging to a postcard I'd sent her a long time ago booking to-night for Cicely Courtneidge – she had failed to observe that we had altered the date and had been to the show some weeks ago. Perhaps it was Providence, for the muddle was a great help in breaking the tension. Having said, severely, that he'd call at 7 p.m., he arrived at 6 p.m. I remarked on the reproving tone of his note and he replied: 'Ah, but when I am serious you laugh and when I joke you take me seriously.' I agreed. After which we settled down to gin and reasonable talk. He brought papers and books for me and more reviews of the play. At dinner at the Connaught: 'It seems the highbrows are massing against me now . . . Sometimes I think the theatre is too exciting. I was nervous

at Edinburgh, but not in London.' After dinner we went and sat in the lounge, where it was very quiet. In the car driving home I tried to clear up the misunderstandings of these last days. I begged him never to be so cross again and added that I could only be myself with him and I should probably often offend again, but surely he knew me well enough to explain without 'taking umbrage' and going off into a gloom. 'Oh yes,' said Tom, 'but I expect I shall do it again – and if we both realise that, well it's not anything to worry about. You know I have no grievance, but I thought you were rather too dramatic.' We both agreed that it had been very exhausting. On arrival at Carlyle Mansions we were both a trifle *émotionné* and held hands – then Tom said: 'Oh, my attaché case is in the boot – rather an anti-climax, as Lucasta says!' – and laughed as he waved good-bye.

18 October: Dedication Festival and St Luke: I have had, in the past, to be very careful how I behaved after 'an upset', but this morning Tom was in good spirits and we had a wonderful conversation about CREMATION. He has left instructions that he is to be buried (unless he dies of some infectious disease, when he will be cremated) in the St Stephen's plot at Brookwood Cemetery – that dreary place. 'I feel it an obligation to fertilise the earth'! What a man.

Their South Kensington church, St Stephen's, had a plot in Brookwood Cemetery in Woking; Eliot was not, however, buried there, but in the church of St Michael's in East Coker – from where his ancestors had emigrated. And he was, contrary to his conversation with Mary, cremated.

Things quieted down later in the autumn. On 26 October he told Mary that his sister Marian would be coming the following summer: 'I am fonder of her than of anyone else in the world, of my own kin', though he was apprehensive about her being in London for nearly three months. He wanted to take her out of the city for a few weeks. On 2 November, All Souls', he had been to All Saints, Margaret Street, in the morning. She wrote of him saying:

'But they didn't pray for <u>my</u> dead – they only pray for Christians. My dead are Unitarians and therefore, in my opinion, they are NOT Christians – but don't tell those who are living – they would be hurt and think me very bigoted.' After which he relapsed into gloom. He sat by the fire in the flat and we had some music, and a conference on where he could take his sister in the summer. But he was very tensed up and only really became cheerful en route for home, like a donkey with carrots in front of his nose. On getting out of the car he said: 'I am sorry I shall not see you again this week, but we'll meet on Sunday.'

On 9 November he wrote a note of apology; he was rude, he said, 'unintentionally'. She did not reply, but on 12 November they had an agreeable evening, though he looked, by her account, white and tired. Ten days later she got the flu again; Mary makes sure to note that he telephoned her 'himself'.

By the end of December things are back on an even keel between them.

20 December: A lovely drive to-day after church – in the purlieu of Paddington, finding all sorts of extraordinary places. T. sang a great deal – 'I don't like it when you're cross with me', and 'Come on my Houseboat with me', were two specialities. He says he goes out and does his Christmas shopping at 8.45 a.m. 'You want a rosary and someone else wants a cocktail shaker – but I've no vitality.' We stopped at a Pedestrian Crossing for a nice man and two children. 'Perhaps he's taken them to church at the Abbey. I hope so. I expect mummy has gone home to cook the lunch and he's taking them for a walk. Yes, I hope that's so.'

22 December: We dined at the Garrick after office drinks. He talked of the Ottoline Morrell days: 'I was in the middle twenties and very young for my age.' He was first taken there by Bertie Russell. He talked of David Cecil, Eddie Sackville-West and the Huxleys – all clever young Oxford men of the time – and how they

had bewildered him – but looking back he believes his judgement of them to have been sound. Then on relationships with people: 'The people whom one likes up to a certain point – the people with whom one had something in common only in the presence of a third person.'

27 December, Sunday: Collected Tom at 10.30 and we drove to church discussing the important topic of Baggage Insurance . . . Tom goes off with the Fabers to South Africa on the 31st and returns alone by sea. I go to West and East Africa – and he will be back before me. We went through addresses again and he is actually looking forward immensely to getting on board ship: 'those few days of complete negation, which is the height of enjoyment – before I begin to think of the things I may have to do'. He also asked anxiously about nylon bathing dresses. 'Is it true that nylon doesn't photograph AT ALL?!'

29 December: A very late telephone call and a husky voice saying: 'I just rang up to say good-night.'

1954

In February 1954 The Confidential Clerk *opened at the Morosco Theatre on Broadway; it ran until the summer.* Brooks Atkinson, writing in the New York Times, *was unimpressed with Eliot's latest drama:*

> The Confidential Clerk *is the logical result of his long attempt to shake off the shackles of his own genius. A gifted man has written a commonplace play. He has learned technique and lost art . . . [The verse] sounds like a kind of rhythmic prose that acts like an anodyne. It does not awaken the play . . . From the practical point of view the style is not good theatre.*

Meanwhile, Mary travelled to Africa on behalf of the British Council on a lecture tour. She was gone from 3 January until 12 April: 'It was, probably, unwise to attempt to "cover" West and East Africa in three months,' she would write in her report of her remarkable journey – it might have been unwise, but she certainly gave it a go. She travelled all over Nigeria, the Gold Coast and Togoland, Sierra Leone, the Gambia, East Africa and Johannesburg, Tanganyika and Zanzibar, Kenya and Uganda. She recorded the total distance she travelled: 17,200 miles. She gave fifty lectures, made fifteen broadcasts, and attended twenty-six conferences or committees, forty-eight official dinners or lunches and fourteen cocktail parties. Her report is marvellously detailed, and in the handwritten diary she kept she made notes on every country or region, on their populations, languages, exports, their governments and politicians. She was, as ever, indefatigable, interested in everything she saw. Her account is of its time, but no less vivid for that.

Here she is in Kano, in the Northern Region of Nigeria:

1954

It seems that this is the Old Testament come to life – naked children everywhere, dogs, goats (and little brown kids), sheep (picturesque, but insanitary). On further inspection, however, the picture is brought a little up to date – camels and donkeys tread warily on the sandy, narrow streets, for fear of bicycles – of which there are many, including children's machines for hire – and the occasional disturbance of the late Raleigh motorcycle (the modern ass). A perpetual background music is supplied by countless tinny little 'radio boxes' crooning cheap American dance tunes.

She was there to visit schools, and to assess prospective student visitors to Britain. She gave lectures on the 'life of a student in Britain' and spoke at women's training centres. She lectured too on universities in Britain. Very little could put her off. On 19 January, in Lagos, after a visit to the British Council offices, she reported feeling 'rather unwell'. She then noted that at 3.30 she was 'removed, dramatically, in an ambulance, to Creek Hospital, with food poisoning. Spent three days, not altogether unpleasantly, recovering.' When she was let out of hospital she drove 100 miles to Ibadan, on 'the "suicide road" – very dangerous, many accidents. Stopped at Abeokuta for a sandwich lunch.'

It is hard to imagine how – had Eliot truly reciprocated her feelings for him, and accepted her suggestion that they marry – their styles of living would have meshed. For in this period he too was on the African continent, in South Africa, but this was for a rest cure in the warmth. Immediately upon his return, he suffered heart palpitations and was assessed at the London Clinic; no organic origin was found for his troubles, which seemed to spring from anxiety and overwork.

Mary's diary picks up on 4 April, Monday in Holy Week, just as she returned to England.

On my return to London I dropped a note at Carlyle Mansions to report my arrival, as promised and, greatly to my surprise, had no reply. I had not only expected some greeting, but also some arrangements for Holy Week. Miss Fletcher then rang up to say that: 'Mr Hayward has forwarded your note to Mr Eliot to the office and asked me to let you know that he is in the London Clinic with a racing pulse, but is very bright in himself'! John, whom I rang up immediately, sounded really worried – it seems that Tom had had this pulse for a fortnight and was now in the Clinic for observation. He promised to keep me in touch – but no visitors or letters were allowed. The Press got wind of the illness and gave out that he had angina. Marian (Tom's sister) cabled to me and John and I concocted a reply. After Easter Tom was much better and was reported to be sitting up and reading many newspapers. I thought he might have managed to send me a postcard – but he revels in his illnesses as excuses for not doing anything at all unless he feels inclined.

He came home on 5 May and they were finally able to go for a drive on 9 May, Sunday. She had sent him another novel by Georges Simenon. 'He was waiting with his arms full of cigarettes and periodicals – thin in the face, but cheerful.' He told her that he had been writing a letter to her when he 'fell into a syncope', as he said – fainted, she thinks.

The next thing he knew was the following morning, when a nurse was standing by his bedside! On his return from the Clinic he found the letter he had been writing to me, which had never got sent. He talked a great deal about his illness and a little about Africa and says he must consult his confessor about non-fasting communion when ill.

He went back to the office that week, and they headed out to Kew on 12 May.

The weather was kind and we had a glorious walk in Kew – chestnuts, azaleas, lilies, cherries all in bloom. T. talked away: 'Did I first introduce you to Simenon, or you to me?' The Jane Austen houses on Kew Green led us to Miss Charlotte Yonge (whom he has never read) and then to Mrs Gaskell who, so I was assured, went to a Mardi Gras Festival in Italy and, in a moment of abandon, threw some flowers at a strange young man – Charles Eliot Norton – thereby starting a romance. We sat among the lilacs and talked of the Hotsons! and of people who set Tom's poems to music; of Goethe because T. will have to give a lecture in German on Goethe (whom he doesn't like); and we sat among the azaleas and discussed the Changing World, the Isle of Wight visit and Jacquetta Hawkes! On the way back we talked of a plan whereby I might go to Sussex for the week-end when he is there recuperating, so that we could drive on the downs – 'that would be very pleasant and comical' says Tom.

19 May: This morning I had three letters from T.: one a request for a book of stamps which I was to bring to Littlehampton, another asking for the Ferry Time-Table for the Isle of Wight, a third giving instructions for reaching Clymping – so complicated that nobody could understand them. And he also rang the office to make sure that I was coming.

Leslie Hotson was a Canadian Shakespeare scholar of Eliot's acquaintance. The novelist Elizabeth Gaskell met the critic and future Harvard professor of art Charles Eliot Norton in Rome, in 1857; Gaskell had travelled there with her daughters and formed an important relationship with Norton, who was seventeen years her junior. Eliot had reviewed a volume of their letters, decades before; Mary's 'so I was assured' is another reminder of her place at the outskirts of his writing life. Their frames of reference were different, which was clearly refreshing for him.

In late May she went to Sussex to stay with friends; Eliot was near Littlehampton. She found him in what she described as a dark little room of a medieval-looking hotel.

Poor Tom, in shabby tweed coat with leather patches, ragged cuffs and very baggy flannel trousers – looking, I must say, old and ill. He was so pleased to see me that I think he must have been getting rather bored. Lunch in a low-ceilinged dining room, very antique, next door to the Shereks. After coffee he went and slept on his bed for half an hour, while I did the crossword next door. We had a lovely drive, after I had, by request, taken his pulse and found it perfectly normal! We prowled round Chichester Cathedral and had a good tea in the city – returning him to his antiquity at 6.30 p.m. – after which I went off to the friends I was staying with.

23 May, Sunday: I returned to Clymping to find Tom huddled and muddled, after having had the Fabers to lunch. We went for a stroll by the sea, I took his pulse again, which was again quite normal, but, as he saw me off for London I thought he looked 'faded'.

On Sunday 6 June, after attending church, they drove round Trafalgar Square and the Park; he was anxious about taking his sister Marian to the Isle of Wight when she arrived. 'What a worrier he is!'

He has decided that he will meet his sister and niece at the airport on Sunday 20th. 'Unless I collapse, then I will ask you to do so.' He brought a dozen books for me (clearing out his shelves) and his watch to be mended while I loaned him one of mine.

13 June, Trinity Sunday: This afternoon we went to Wandsworth to call on Mrs Tereshchenko – widow of Tom's friend whom he had visited so faithfully and so often through his illness. The lady was a typical White-Russian, T. very familiar with the horrid little flat and the rather nice children (grand-children) and so kind. We listened at length to the lady's troubles, and there was obviously very little that I could do to help. We returned to tea at the flat.

On 20 June Marian, 'now 77 and frail' as Mary wrote the next day, arrived as planned.

28 June: T. telephoned the office to ask if he could come round this afternoon to consult me 'about the journey' [to the Isle of Wight,

with Marian] – yet again. We drove to Chelsea and observed various bearded gents, young and old, which prompted T. to inveigh against the present fashion: 'They are all trying to imitate D. H. Lawrence or Lytton Strachey. Lytton Strachey was the most loathsome man I've ever known. I am fond of his sisters and until they die I won't say anything about their brother. He was evil – AND good, for he did kind things for people.' We drove along the Mall, decorated with much bunting etc. for the visit of the King and Queen of Sweden. 'I wonder what they do with the flags afterwards. Store them in the cellars of Buckingham Palace?' We got the journey all taped (I hope) and chose some books for them to take to the Isle of Wight. And there was a long story about his visit to the widow Tereshchenko. I pointed out some detail. 'Oh yes – I would never have seen that if I hadn't talked it all over with you in such detail. How muddled I do get these days.'

On 12 July Mary arrived at the Farringford Hotel, Freshwater Bay on the Isle of Wight; Eliot and his sister Marian had been there since the beginning of the month. The hotel had once been the home of Alfred, Lord Tennyson; it was later sold by Hallam Tennyson, the poet's eldest son, in 1945 to British Holiday Estates, and opened as a Thomas Cook hotel the following year. The hotel, Mary wrote, was 'a strikingly ugly building, literally bedewed with portraits of the late Poet Laureate. Marian delighted to see me – no doubt she had been enduring one of Tom's apprehensive periods. He, in grey tweeds, nervous and awkward.' Eliot and Marian were staying at the nearby 'old-world' cottage. Once there, 'I said I would like a stroll and Tom said he would come with me – very pleasant, skirting "Tennyson's Down", looking at his bridge (a fragile, rustic affair which he had had constructed so that he could walk undisturbed by prying eyes – just like Tom – and then was rather annoyed because nobody noticed him).'

The next week was wholly delightful, she wrote. They drove along the coast and walked together; there was gin and tonic in the evening, and

Mary's postcard of Farringford House, Isle of Wight.

huge meals, as she wrote on 13 July. It is hardly surprising that she felt absolutely part of the family – not least because Marian wrote a letter to her mother. Eliot had been ordered to give up cigarettes after his heart attack: he continued, however, to smoke one cigar a day, and from a later entry it seemed he still struggled to give up the cigarettes.

Tea is at 4 p.m., no sooner, no later – the time-table of meals is very strict. I sometimes wonder if this brother and sister have ever really let themselves go! After tea I announced my intention of climbing Tennyson's Down, Marian said she would come with me to the foot of the down and Tom remarked 'then we can wave to you from the top' – so I concluded he was coming too. When we reached the top we found a heavy sea mist descending on us, so we came down again in case we got lost and walked through the fields instead, to Freshwater Bay. There we walked along the beach and explored the little village more thoroughly. By 6.30 the mists caught up with us and rain threatened, so we hurried back – and found Marian writing to my mother which, I hope, will give pleasure. After an enormous dinner and coffee in the drawing room (plus Tom's daily cigar) we returned to the Chalet, where Marian read and Tom taught me 'Petunia' – his favourite patience. After Marian had gone to bed we opened the windows, played another game and then went to bed.

14 July: Oh dear, pouring rain – and breakfast a trifle on the solemn side – but I suggested we should go to Osborne – which we did and the rain cleared so all was well. We joined the crowds and toured the State Apartments – an incredible array of Victorian objets d'art and paintings of Albert, Viccy and family. The Durbar Hall was really incredible – the most splendid affair and so completely out of place like the Pavilion at Brighton, only Indian and not Chinese. Marian found all the walking rather tiring, so we found her a chair wherever possible and decided to give the Swiss Cottage a miss. A really lovely drive back, with splendid views of sea and countryside, racing white clouds and a very blue sky. We were actually a little late for lunch. After lunch my host and hostess rested and the sun was so good that we then had tea in the garden. Tom and I had another very good walk, collecting innumerable wild flowers and we walked two miles beyond Tennyson's Monument to look at the Needles. On the way back we lay on the grass on top of the down (not too near the edge, for Tom can't do with heights) and talked and talked. Then, very reluctantly – 'we mustn't be late for Marian' – we made for home. More patiences after dinner. A lovely day.

The next day, while waiting to take Marian and Eliot 'to their respective hairdressers' Mary tripped on the hotel stairs and injured her ankle and arm; without saying a word she drove them to their appointments but then found a doctor to make sure nothing was broken. Her ankle had to be bandaged, and Eliot cut up her food for her.

16 July: After lunch, when Marian had gone to rest, Tom and I sat in the garden and he talked of his childhood: 'Of course I was much the youngest, but I don't think I was spoiled – on the contrary, I always

T. S. Eliot in front of the Tennyson Monument
on the Isle of Wight.

felt I was ignored, because my brother and sisters were so much more important – but this feeling has NOT survived my childhood – I am always conscious of arrogance!' He called his parents Ma'am and Sir – or Mama and Papa – and he had 'no sentimental or silly affection for them, but only a proper awe and respect' – and he added 'a child who doesn't know his parents is fortunate' – which perhaps explains a great deal of his later writing and not least *The Confidential Clerk*.

The weather worsened rather on Sunday 18 July; they went to church,
Marian to a local Unitarian church. Afterwards:

Tom lay flat on his back in the sitting room 'to see what it is like
sleeping without a pillow' and I read him the crossword clues.

It was a beautiful evening, she recorded, and the next day was lovely too,
with 'a last and lovely drive in the morning'. She wrote on 19 July:

I think the week was a great success, all the same, but I felt very sad
at leaving – feeling I should probably never see Tom like that again.

Yet Marian's visit wore on Eliot. He was gloomy when he and Mary met
at church on 8 August and he expressed his concern for his sister: 'I shan't
really breathe freely again until I get a cable announcing her safe arrival
home.'

10 August: We were both tired. Tom came in for an hour and drank
tonic water, as he was going on to a dinner he didn't want to go to. So
we sat and talked uncomfortably with our eyes on the clock . . . On
his own reception into the Church of England: 'It was much worse
than getting naturalised. I was baptised by an American clergyman
– he became a Roman Catholic later on and is now a layman. My
sponsors were Canon Streeter and an Oxford don called Somerset. I
was confirmed next day by Bishop Strong – he hurried so much that
I felt he was determined I should "pass".'

The Anglican clergyman was William Force Stead, like Eliot an American
who spent many years in England; he was chaplain of Worcester College,
Oxford, from 1926 to 1933 and later, as Eliot says, converted to Roman
Catholicism. In the mid-1960s Stead recalled the experience of Eliot's
baptism into the Anglican church, which took place at Finstock, in the
Cotswolds, where Stead was living at the time:

Eliot with his sister Marian on the Isle of Wight.

'Eliot came down from London for a day or two, and I summoned
from Oxford Canon B. H. Streeter, Fellow and later Provost of
Queen's College, and Vere Somerset, History Tutor and Fellow of
Worcester College. These were his Godfathers. It seemed odd to have
such a large though infant Christian at the baptismal font, so, to avoid
embarrassment, we locked the front door of the little parish church and
posted the verger on guard in the vestry.'

On 16 August there was quite an 'episode', as Mary wrote when they ventured to the Prospect of Whitby, an historic pub in Wapping: he had phoned her that morning saying Marian and Theodora were taken with her suggestion of a visit, though John had said it was 'not a nice place' to take them. At the beginning of the evening he was very cross, in one of his 'towering rages' as she put it; but the evening, in the end, was a great success.

As we drove to the docks I noticed that Tom was gradually thawing and interpolating a word in the conversation here and there. By the time we reached the Prospect of Whitby and got the party upstairs (through an empty bar and a practically empty restaurant!) he was obviously pulling himself together and became fairly normal. Marian was enchanted with everything, which was a great help – we went out on the balcony and observed the river and then had dinner. After dinner we started for home and Tom was in excellent spirits. He guided Marian through the Bar, her eyes popping out of her head, and then took a tour of the floodlighting – over Tower Bridge and through the City. Marian was quite blissfully happy and so grateful. After depositing them at the hotel, Tom sprang into the car again exclaiming: 'Well! I did you an injustice! I was very much annoyed with you because I thought you had arranged this party, on a MONDAY, without consulting me! I didn't realise it was Theodora's idea.' Well, I didn't say much – but I really was rather annoyed with him – and suggested he might have told me earlier.

The next day, as she noted, marked the date of the Battle of Bosworth Field: the last battle of the Wars of the Roses in 1485, at which Richard III was killed. P. G. Wodehouse, referred to below, was captured by German forces in the early years of the Second World War and tricked into making a series of broadcasts to America from Berlin. The response to the broadcasts, in both Britain and the United States, was vitriolic: Wodehouse was widely condemned as a traitor and a coward, and although an MI5 investigation into his wartime actions found no evidence of treachery, he was certainly naive. Eliot's opinion of him hints at this naiveté, but Wodehouse's reputation has proved far more durable than Eliot predicted.

22 August, Sunday, Bosworth Field: I had been away, so had not seen Tom since that remarkable evening. He was waiting for me outside church after the early service, looking rather nervous. 'Did you remember to pray for Richard III?' I said I had not, but I had told Theodora to do so! An odd way of saying good morning! Later in the morning he was in fine form and I asked him what he really thought of P. G. Wodehouse's behaviour in Germany in the war – adding that Theodora says she cannot possibly read him now. Tom laughed: 'That's VERY American of her – how annoyed she would be to hear me say so – P.G.W. has, I think, never grown up – he's a boy, who wrote very good stories for boys – mainly read by older boys – and in Germany he was a boy – quite ready to broadcast and say he was comfortable in his hotel. Nobody can read him now, because his particular kind of joke is played out and so is the world he wrote about – like Angela Thirkell.'

26 August: Much comings and goings in the week, before the family departure – Marian spent an evening with me – she does so want me for a sister-in-law and thinks Tom completely blind (but she doesn't really know him). She considers that I spoil him – and she is right and thinks I ought, for my own sake, to leave him. I didn't say so to her, but I fear it is too late. The two ladies left this afternoon and I waved to them as they passed Tite Street, Chelsea, on their way to New York and Boston (in the airport bus).

Five minutes after I returned to the flat Tom turned up – a much relieved and exhausted man. Of course he talked of the family: 'My brother Henry (said to be an insignificant likeness of myself, but much better looking and better tempered) was an archaeologist, who married later in life and had no children.' I settled my guest

in with gin and reading matter and went to cook the supper. After
a few minutes he came strolling into the kitchen and stood about
talking – very distracting. He mixed the salad, cooked the bacon,
got in the way and enjoyed himself very much. We had an extremely
messy meal. T. got covered in pear and washed in the kitchen sink –
carried trays and made himself generally useful.

*The inclusion here of a description of Eliot's seemingly contented domes-
ticity – even of her own casual irritation with him – is telling, following
as it does another familial urging that the pair should marry. Yet there
is Mary's parenthesis: 'but she doesn't really know him' – as if she cannot
hide the truth from herself.*

On 27 August she wrote that she had at last read the copy of The
Confidential Clerk *he loaned her, after she had seen a dress rehearsal
of the play, knowing nothing of the play except from snippets of their
conversation:*

You said you wished to know my reaction . . . I do not think the
results are likely to be of much value to you, for I consider myself
very unrepresentative – I can't pretend to be 'the man in the street'
and I've still less pretence to being a literary critic! In between these
two poles I should, no doubt, be an ardent member of a Poetry and
Drama Club or the 6th Form Literature Mistress – but I am none of
these things – just an uneducated Musician who knows more (tho'
very little) about the Author of this play than most people.

She was determined to be HONEST: the capitals are hers.

My first reaction was summed up by a French lady for the First
Night yesterday. She said 'With the exception of the old Clerk, I
found I could not care <u>what</u> happened to <u>any</u> of the people in the
play – they were not real people at all, they were puppets who spoke
when the author pulled a string. I do not think the author cares

about them either.' She went on: 'Is he inhuman? Does he dislike
and fear people? Is he afraid of knowing, and caring, too much about
human beings?' I said to myself: 'for the first time Tom has created a
character who is alive and who matters to him' – and I guess I meant
the same thing as the French lady.

It's not a comedy at all – even though it is very funny in parts –
it's a sad and depressing play. You are putting, only too clearly, the
rootlessness of this younger generation and the irresponsibility of
their elders who are to blame.

*Yet she softened a bit, too – if only, perhaps, to draw attention again to
their close relationship. She was, she wrote, left with a 'desire to follow
some fascinating signposts . . . I wonder if I shall be able to spot how it
ties up with* The Cocktail Party *– probably that's too difficult for me and
I may have to have your help.'*

*On 1 September Eliot showed up at her office just as she was leaving;
he looked tired and bedraggled, but improved, she wrote, after he stretched
out on her sofa with a sherry. He had been to see a production of* The
Confidential Clerk *in Golders Green: 'a good mediocre performance',
he said. Meanwhile, across the Atlantic, Hurricane Edna had struck the
North-East, causing great devastation.*

The U.S.A. hurricane was front page news and Marian had written of it. 'And it caused the wreck of my great-great-grandfather's
steeple in Boston. I last remember being in a really bad hurricane
in 1896 – it's terrifying.' I talked of going to a difficult situation in
Oxford to-morrow and the tension there, and he said, as he has
often said before – born out of his own experience – 'It's the most
completely lonely feeling – somebody might write about that – you
feel your friends have not just deserted you – they have completely
disappeared – there's nobody to tell about it and nobody to hold
your hand.'

She keeps herself out of her own tale – the difficult situation is alluded to but not described. And she notes in him what seems like both an attempt at connection and yet, at the same time, a complete refusal of connection. He acknowledges only loneliness, disappearance, desertion.

5 September, Sunday: I was rather cross with Tom – a few days ago he had asked me to send him a list of any books I wanted, out of the new Faber catalogue. I did so, and received a note from his secretary to say: 'Mr Eliot regrets that he has no spare copies of the books you list.' I asked why the rocket, this morning. 'Well,' said Tom, with a mischievous smile, 'you said you only wanted the books if I had spare copies, but you are having them all the same!' He goes to-morrow to Geneva – and this evening I took him a very nice Georgian snuff box for his birthday.

He wrote to her on 7 September in gratitude for the gift, saying he was deeply touched, and thanking her too for her company and help during Marian's stay, and 'enlivening the visit by your presence'.

19 October: This evening Tom brought more books and a tin of beef and drank half a bottle of sherry. He had been present at the unveiling of a plaque in Tite Street to Oscar Wilde, who had lived there. 'Compton Mackenzie did it very well – a very neat speech and the wording on the plaque is just right – OSCAR WILDE – WIT AND DRAMATIST – no mention of his prose and poetry. Compton Mackenzie had a good story of him. Someone asked, the day before the First Night of *The Importance of Being Ernest*, if he thought the play would be a success. "Of course the play will be a success," said Wilde, "the question is, will the audience be a success!" It's a pity,' said Tom thoughtfully, 'that he said that – I might have thought of it! Whistler was unkind to him. One day Wilde in a melancholy fit said: "last night I dreamed that I was among the dead." "Well," said Whistler, "I'm sure you were the life and soul of the party."'

28 October: For the first time for years Tom talked this evening about his married life – 'the dreadful nights when she would say – "I ought never to have married you" or, " I am useless and better dead" – and then my disclaimers and her floods of tears – but the next morning that would be quite forgotten. I think it was nine years altogether that I knew her mind was deranged. She used to go about a great deal with me and I was afraid of the dreadfully untrue things she said of me and afraid that my friends believed her. I couldn't say anything – a kind of loyalty perhaps and partly a terror that they would show me that they believed her and not me. We were married for seventeen years – I mean, we lived in the same houses. Happy? NO I was never happy – but I don't think I have ever been happy.'

The last, for Mary, a hedge against disappointment.

31 October, Sunday: In view of the forthcoming religious orgy we neither of us went to church early. At 10.30 Tom appeared burdened with many small packages – lighter fuel, cigarette lighter, cigarette holders and filters for me – a grand gesture to mark his determination to give up smoking cigarettes. I am quite sure he will succeed.

On 1 November, All Saints' Day, Eliot had a copy of William Golding's new novel Lord of the Flies *in one pocket and a pipe cleaner in the other. They agreed to meet very early the next day for the requiem at St Stephen's; they were so early they went for a drive and discussed praying for the dead. 'I pray for certain people daily – thinking of each of them for about a second – the others I take as representatives of greater numbers.' He then observed cheerfully: 'This time next year you and I may be dead and we'll be needing the prayers of the faithful!'*

Lord of the Flies *had – famously – been sent to Faber and Faber by Golding in the autumn of 1953; the title at the time was* Strangers from Within. *The author described it as 'an allegorical interpretation of a stock situation'. A reader for the publishing house looked it over and wrote on the covering letter: 'Absurd & uninteresting fantasy about the explosion of an atom bomb on the colonies. A group of children who land in jungle country near New Guinea. Rubbish & dull. Pointless. Reject.' It was rescued from the slush pile by the great Faber editor Charles Monteith.*

21 November, Sunday: Every Sunday lately we have been for immense drives – 'Sunday Constitutionals' Tom calls them. One day we went to Parsons Green: 'I've been here before. Many years ago Geoffrey Faber and I were driving to Cambridge for a conference. We got stuck in a fog here, so we telephoned from the house of a taxidermist – a little man in a back room. He was stuffing a FISH – no, it wasn't a dream!'

28 November, Sunday: This morning before church we drove 'into Surrey', i.e. over Battersea Bridge – we got out of the car and examined Battersea Church – charming, on a beautiful morning, with seagulls (probably sheltering from the storms at sea) whirling around and swans racing down-stream on a very strong tide.

These drives would carry on into the late months of winter: on 19 December Mary wrote of a 'wild drive' to Putney, and getting terribly lost; after church they struck out for Bunhill Fields, the Dissenters' burial ground in which lie the remains of William Blake and John Bunyan. It was 'a delightful expedition which took us an hour'. 'T. loves pointing out all of his old haunts in the City.'

On 30 November they had supper at her flat, which Eliot cooked 'most methodically, with sleeves rolled up'.

I asked if he was chewing the cud of the next play. 'Oh no, there is plenty of time for that – it will be my last effort and mustn't come too soon. As for poetry – well it doesn't come. I've never wanted to write a poem – but when something begins to take shape in my mind, then I have to get it into some form of expression.' As for

Christmas: 'By the way, you won't get an old rosary. I've hunted everywhere, but it seems they are not to be had. It will have to be one of those stream-lined modern things.'

And indeed on 15 December, Sunday, he brought her 'a lovely rosary'.

He'd taken a great deal of trouble about it but 'couldn't find a nice enough one' though he had tried many shops. 'So this must do until I can find a better one. I thought of Asprey's, but only after I had purchased this. I hadn't thought of going to a non-religious shop.'

He came to supper on Boxing Day and stayed till 11 p.m. 'The Cultivation of Christmas Trees' was one of his last poems; it had been published in the autumn as part of a Faber series.

He seems disappointed at the reception of his Christmas Poem – the first 'straight' poetry he has published for five years. He is maliciously amused at his choice of Books of the Year for the *Sunday Times* – absurdly highbrow. 'One must keep the flag flying! . . . But I was horrified that so many distinguished people included Betjeman's "Late Chrysanthemums" in their lists – it just goes to prove that people dislike poetry.' After supper he demonstrated his latest Patience – 'Dress Parade' – very difficult.

He told her that on Wednesday he wished to go to St Stephen's at 8 a.m. in honour of St Thomas of Canterbury: 'and I have little doubt that I shall take him,' she wrote.

29 December, St Thomas of Canterbury: Pacing up and down Cheyne Walk, looking like a funny old bear, was T.S.E. in his brother's old brown tweed coat with fur collar – he must have been very hot, for it was a warm morning. It was still dark as we drove

1954

The Cultivation
of Christmas Trees

by

T. S. ELIOT

illustrated by

DAVID JONES

to Mary Trevelyan
Christmas greetings
from T.S. Eliot
1954

FABER AND FABER

24 Russell Square London WC1

Mary's inscribed copy of 'The Cultivation of Christmas Trees'.

along to church. The congregation numbered five, including ourselves – the service was taken by a white-haired old priest who was
served by a white-haired old server. The lights were dim and the
church was festooned with holly – very Christmassy. I thought of
Canterbury and that horrible murder so soon after the Christmas

sermon. Driving home Tom said: 'I must say that the Archbishop's murderers showed a fiendish ingenuity in their choice of date – one of the hardest to observe in the whole calendar.' But we were both glad we had made it – 'to rejoice and mourn' with Tom's special St Thomas.

1955

2 January. Sunday, Christmas 1. We both skipped the 8 a.m. service this morning having celebrated the New Year yesterday, very early and very cold. This morning I was half a minute late for our 10.30 assignation and Tom was already in the street looking at his watch. We drove round Chelsea and I gave him a New Year present of a thing to clean spectacles with – all new gadgets delight him. He spoke at length of a letter to *The Times*, signed by C. Day-Lewis, Naomi Mitchison and Herbert Read, protesting at the refusal of the Home Office to grant visas for Iron Curtain countries' representatives to attend a Conference of the Authors' World Peace Appeal. 'It's always people who have a lower-middle class background who sign letters like that – they aren't gentlemen and don't know how to behave. But it's annoying that they assume that they represent all the literary men. I have a private slogan, which I do not broadcast, SUSPECT ALL POETS.' After the service, as we were driving round quiet squares, T. suddenly burst out with: 'WHY should I have been cursed with such mediocre contemporaries?' I remarked that it was a good thing I didn't keep a hidden microphone in the car.

The Authors' World Peace Appeal was set up in 1951 as a response to Cold War political tension by a group of British writers, including Compton Mackenzie, Naomi Mitchison, Enid Starkie and Alex Comfort: the latter would go on to publish The Joy of Sex *in 1972. Later in the month, questions were asked in Parliament regarding the refusal of the visas; the Home Secretary replied that 'foreigners cannot be admitted to this country to attend meetings organised by bodies which are, consciously or unconsciously, serving the purposes of the Communist-dominated World Peace Movement.'*

On 5 January Eliot recommended to Mary the work of writers he did admire: W. H. Auden, for instance. William Empson, he told her, had written 'three good poems'. He had a new poet up his sleeve, a Canadian – 'name of Watson – not a good name for publicity purposes'. Faber and Faber published Wilfred Watson's first book, Friday's Child, that year, and it won the Governor General's Award in Canada. Eliot thought him 'first rate'.

On 14 January she went briefly into hospital and was 'greeted with some lovely white freesias, chosen by himself and dispatched with a note – clever Poet'. He telephoned when she arrived home to wish her 'God speed'. When she returned to London on 21 January she found a message from Miss Fletcher that Eliot had been taken into hospital with a very high pulse. The next entry in her account does not appear until 25 February; she had no direct news of him for six weeks. He sent her a note on 26 February, anxious to see her – and noting that while he has been at home recuperating Miss Fletcher comes four days a week at 5 p.m. to see him.

5 March: This morning I went for a walk – and saw an old man on Chelsea Bridge trying to pick up his walking stick. I thought of helping him, but decided it would embarrass him, looked back to see how he was getting on – and saw it was Tom. It was quite a shock. I didn't call to him – I thought it best not to. This evening he telephoned, quite briskly, no mention of the liver chill, and said he thought he would go to church at 11 a.m. to-morrow 'if you happen to be passing'.

They met on 6 March. She made no comment on his long silence, but thought 'the Great Man looked a bit sheepish'. When they met again on 10 March she picked him up at the Faber and Faber offices and noted that he walked 'slowly and deliberately, and still talks a great deal about his pulse, how nervous he is still and how difficult it is to get back to normal'. They had supper at her flat; he was able to climb the stairs, as the lift was out of order.

In the course of the evening and after some music, we talked again of the Clinic and his failure to send me a message. 'Next time I shall send you a message and leave some money for you for incidental expenses – what do I owe you for calls to America?' We planned a concert, a theatre, a visit to Billy Graham etc. and through the evening he kept suggesting presents – a sign, I suspect, of contrition. I took him home about 9.30 p.m., not too tired after the Great Adventure.

The American evangelist Billy Graham had first come to Britain the year before, when he had preached to a total of nearly two million people; he returned in 1955, and, after appearing in Scotland, preached for a week at Wembley Stadium in May.

An entry dated 10 March shows that Eliot made good on his promise of gifts.

At 6 p.m. the Great Man, straightening the knee on every stair, arrived triumphantly with books, papers AND a small portable wireless, a lovely little thing, which he had purchased himself this morning – 'it is said to be the best thing on the market'. He brought a few problems for me, including an invitation to be Vice-President of a rather dubious-looking Italian Cultural Society. He is seeing his doctor again this week and may go to Sussex for a few days – 'will you come and see me again there?' – I said, of course, that I would.

She dropped him at the Athenaeum for what she called 'his lonely meal', and noted a conversation with John Hayward about finding another close friend to help him recover more quickly. John replied that he has no close friends except us two.'

On 26 March they had one of their 'eccentric drives', paying a visit 'to our favourite little houses in Launceston Place and Victoria Grove – with their painted doorways and iron balconies'. They spoke of Billy Graham, who had just arrived in Glasgow. 'T. declared that the excitement over him was "symptomatic mass hysteria, caused, perhaps, by people at the dawn of a nuclear age wanting to be made to believe, being past making the effort themselves".'

22 March: Rather a notable evening. I drove to Faber's and found Tom waiting in the hall, reading the *Church Times*. 'It has', he said, without preamble, 'a very interesting article about the Jamaican immigrants and the Colour Problem. What people don't seem to realise is that we can't afford a colour problem on an island of this size. It is all very well to talk of Christian Love, but what we need is tighter immigration laws.' We sat in the car in Garrick Street for some time, talking. As we got out and proceeded along the street to the Club I noticed how very slowly Tom walked – like a really old man.

The Empire Windrush, bringing migrants from the Caribbean, had arrived in Britain in 1948, bringing the workers needed to restore post–war Britain, and staff the new National Health Service. Thousands of immigrants of colour began to arrive each year, until the 1962 Commonwealth Immigrants Act restricted opportunities for entry. Eliot's attitude was not uncommon; Christian love, for him, clearly had its limits. Mary, as ever, does not – at least in this record – comment or argue, despite the fact that her experience of travel across the world, among many different people, as well as her work with students from abroad, meant that her own attitudes were far more open-minded. Perhaps her casting him as an old man is a kind of acknowledgement that his attitudes are outdated and offensive.

The dismay she does record is their mutual dislike of the redecoration of the Garrick Club. Old chairs had been removed from 'the big room' 'and a lot of cheap-looking Parker Knolls had taken their places'. He told her about the first time he had to give an after-dinner speech, in 1921; he was to be one of the speakers at a dinner of the Poetry Circle of the Lyceum Club. He had prepared a topic, only to find that an earlier speaker had prepared the very same one! Aldous Huxley spoke before him, and Eliot described the scene.

'He looked very tall and thin and young – which he was – and rather unwisely had fortified himself with a powerful cigar. It was evidently going to be a long speech – but he only got as far as Athens when he suddenly fell flat, right over the table. He got faint, I believe – a mixture of the cigar and the close atmosphere. He was carried out to lie on a sofa and I was asked at once to make my speech. I can remember nothing of what I said at all. I only remember my vast relief at sitting down again and finding it was all over. Yes, I know now, it was in 1921, because one of the ladies, who must have been in her late fifties, asked me later to dine with her. I went to Hampstead or Primrose Hill I believe – and I think that her husband and others were there, and she showed me her Tarot pack of cards – the only time I've seen one. And she asked me to give her my signet ring – not this one, but one which belonged to my father and grandfather. She said, after holding it for some time, "it's curious, I can only feel one thing – the wearers of this ring have always been in a state of ANXIETY" – she certainly guessed right!'

Madame Sosostris, the 'famous clairvoyante' with her 'wicked pack of cards', would appear in 'The Waste Land' the following year.

We talked of Ezra Pound. 'Perhaps he was never really sane. Oh yes, as a young man I swallowed him whole, and a lot of other people too. I think he has become gradually, increasingly, insane, through a long period of years. He only liked good poets and had no compassion for, or interest in anyone else. He could never laugh at himself – nor could he be laughed at – he has always been egocentric.' I talked of Ezra Pound's early letters – especially those referring to his attempt to raise money for Tom so that he could stop being a Bank Clerk at Lloyds and devote himself to writing, 'For a long time I knew nothing about it, or I would have stopped it. When I did know, it was too late – but in the end it never came to anything. He never realised that it would have put me in a very embarrassing position in my relationship to him and the others – not that I, at any rate, have ever been able to write to order. His wife was always a very negative person, wearing draperies and reclining on sofas. When they lived in London it was he that did the cooking – and very well too.' He went on: 'There seems nothing in his ancestry to account for his insanity – his father was in the American Mint and his grandfather was Governor of Wisconsin.'

He had referred to this collection of money on his behalf a few years before, speaking to Mary in 1951, and is emphatic, as he was four years previously, that nothing came of it.

26 March: Late this evening he telephoned. He never announces himself, just starts to talk. 'Well, I ought to have explained that I picked up a cold on Thursday, from Miss Fletcher, I suppose, who says she's had two days of influenza. I wish she'd kept away from the office. So I thought it better not to come out. But if you are passing at 10.30 to-morrow . . .'

This curious obsession of never letting anybody do anything for him is growing, even to the extent of this kind of childish pretence . . . 'If you are passing . . .' is intended to convey that I would be going out of my way to pick him up because I happened to be passing that way anyway. And he probably makes himself believe this.

The next day, 27 March, was Passion Sunday, as she noted, the fifth Sunday in Lent; she volunteered to bring him some 'Huskoids' – a throat lozenge – after church. And so she did. He had taken a French posset – a confection made with cream, nutmeg and sweetened wine – but it had been too strong and stopped him sleeping. It was Miss Fletcher, he insisted, who had made him ill. If there was any hint of attraction between himself and Valerie Fletcher, he gave absolutely no sign of it to Mary. Rather the reverse.

'I am annoyed with Miss Fletcher, I must have caught her cold. She has a strong sense of duty, too strong, and is very obstinate. I can't get to know her – she shuts up like a clam – though of course that suits me very well really.' He gave me a variety of books and we looked at his picture gallery (reproductions of portraits) of his ancestors and a charming picture of his father.

Eliot appears to continually disparage 'Miss Fletcher', despite that strong sense of duty. Mary will not reflect later on what Eliot's deflections might have meant.

When she saw him again on 31 March at the 8 a.m. service at St Stephen's she remarked that he was looking 'terrifyingly old'. But on 7 April, Maundy Thursday, he made his way to Mary's in a cab.

In the sitting room, pouring out sherry, eating biscuits and remarking: 'Good – that's what I need – cosseting!' He looked remarkably well. We made a nice plan that, at the end of his visit to Sussex, I would go for the week-end and drive him back to London. Rather gloomy about his speaking engagements – 'all made before I was ill – and now I shall have to keep them' – the Authors' Club Dinner – and a luncheon meeting of the Conservative Union with Anthony Eden in the Chair, at which he is to speak on 'Literature and Politics' – 'and I am ending with a question they won't be able to answer – "what is man, that Thou art mindful of him?"'

He had been to a substitute Confessor, his own being in hospital. 'Rather useful, as I could confess the old sins without feeling too embarrassed, and I said: "For these and all my other sins which were very limited owing to my illness . . ." which I thought rather neat.' During the Austerity Meal which he had requested we discussed Americans, then started to get ready to go to Tenebrae – T. singing loudly, in the bathroom, 'Say gel, I'm certainly glad to know you' – and some tuneless portions of Tenebrae. We had a bet on the length of the service, which I won. We sat together – I shall always connect the 'Have mercy . . .' psalm with Tom kneeling beside me in the darkness. I waited for him afterwards while he collected. As he got into the car he asked: 'Did I smell strongly of T.C.P.?' On the way home: 'St Peter's failure does make one feel less desperate.' We arranged to meet at 10.10 a.m. precisely to-morrow – "for the Mass of the Pre-Sanctified".'

Their familiarity with the language and rituals of the church bring them together; Psalm 51, 'Have mercy upon me, O God, according to thy lovingkindness: according unto the multitude of thy tender mercies blot out my transgressions,' is often sung at the Tenebrae service. The mass of the pre-sanctified takes place on Good Friday; the Host has already been consecrated, hence the name.

8 April, Good Friday: But at 9 a.m. he telephoned to say he thought it wiser not to go to church this morning, as he'd had a heavy cold for a fortnight and would have a heavy day next Tuesday!! I was SO astonished that I was quite speechless! There is nothing wrong with him except a little catarrh. I telephoned John after half an hour who said that both he and Madame A. were extremely irritated with him – and that he had shut himself up in his room and was playing patiences . . . This is disturbing, for he really minds a great deal about Good Friday. I suppose it may be the result of a fluctuating pulse on an already highly-strung subject. He needs, as J. and I agreed, fresh air and sun – in every way. And it's a most wonderful heat-wave day.

Mary and Eliot met at church on Easter Day, 10 April; she had been to the 7 a.m. service and he was coming into the next one, looking 'gloomy and pasty'. Suddenly:

'How much would you get for this car if you sold it in part exchange for a new one? £100? Then you'd have another £650 I suppose to expend. I might advance you the money.' 'Oh dear no,' I said, 'though it's a very kind thought, but I wouldn't like to be in your debt – though in fact I am much in your debt already!' 'That', said Tom with a laugh, 'is a play upon words.'

That evening she got an agitated phone call from John Hayward, saying Tom had not been in to see him – not since Good Friday, and hadn't wished him a happy Easter, 'which seems unchristian', said John. She responded carefully to Hayward.

I said I thought Tom really couldn't help hurting us sometimes – and John agreed that he has a streak of sadism which he fights against.

Tom and John made it up the next day, and on Easter Monday Eliot came to Mary's for 'a pleasant, idle evening'. She would write to John of the importance of him speaking his mind to Eliot: the letter, dated 21 April, was marked 'Oh VERY PRIVATE!'

I've been meditating on your comment that perhaps you'll have to be a bit careful in future to 'cover' any hint of criticism to him. I am sure the <u>opposite</u> is right. ONLY YOU (& perhaps I, to a much more limited extent) can say things to him that must sometimes be said – nobody else would dare. I have noticed of late his immense <u>indignation</u> with anyone who disagrees with <u>him</u> (never <u>you</u>) – and that is a bad state to get into. So I consider it's practically your mission to tell him what you really think!

It is a terrible strain on any human being to be made to feel he is a Classic in his lifetime & Tom needs, more than he will ever know, honesty from his closest friends. Besides, he doesn't admit criticism from anyone else, because he refuses to admit their views have any importance.

That's <u>my</u> view – anyway.

24 April they spent in Sussex – 'A very happy day by the seaside!' She stayed in Littlehampton, and they drove all around, including to Arundel, attending sung Eucharist at St Nicholas.

An attractive 14th century church nestling in the great walls of the castle. As we walked up to it the bells were pealing and the daffodils and flag of S. George were waving gaily in the wind.

In the afternoon we had a delightful tour of West Sussex, Tom doing the map reading. The country was looking wonderful – we got lost several times and turned the car right under the nose of an enquiring bull on finding ourselves in a thick forest instead of on a down. We found a dreadful place for tea at Pulborough, with a completely batty little maid, very dirty – and nobody else there. So awful that I took a strong line and we walked out. T. said: 'That was frightening – really awful' – then another place that was no good and finally a very pleasant little tea-room looking onto an old walled garden, where we had a peaceful half hour. Very difficult getting into the main road again. Tom insisted on crossing to the opposite side of the road (v. dangerous) in order to direct me – waving me on and then changing his mind several times. After tea we visited Storrington and wandered in a very peaceful and ancient graveyard sheltered by a down. As we drove back in the evening the downs and forests looked wonderful in the sunset. T. was full of stories all day – including one of a hoax telegram sent to Mauriac after Gide's death purporting to come from Gide from the Next World: 'Viens d'apprendre que l'enfer n'existe pas. Previens Claudel.'

'Just learned that hell doesn't exist. Warn Claudel.' André Gide, winner of the Nobel Prize in Literature in 1947, had died in 1951; he, along with François Mauriac and Paul Claudel, were significant figures in French literature in the early twentieth century. Claudel had died in February of that year and Eliot had written a tribute to him published in Le Figaro Littéraire *in March.*

We left the next day. A perfect morning and we drove slowly until we got into Surrey. T. still in holiday mood but as we got nearer London a weight of depression began to fall. As we were driving through Esher a small car passed us and a woman waved. 'Your lady friend?' I asked – but no, so we thought she must have been waving to the car behind. But it slowed down and we saw it was the Huxleys! We had to stop and get out and chat for a few minutes. Juliette, who is nothing if not direct, asked: 'Where have you two been?' 'Sussex' we replied. As we got into the car again we both collapsed with laughter – the Huxleys were evidently very much intrigued and they will have a happy time THINKING THE WORST and spreading it round. I said: 'The Huxleys of all people.' Tom, helplessly laughing, said: 'I know – give them a few months and they'll have a fine story buzzing round'. We talked later of how careful he and other famous people have to be in expressing their views on people and things in public. 'It's so difficult to remember how seriously my most casual remarks are or may be taken.'

How forthright she is, accepting the Huxleys' misapprehension of their relationship cheerfully; and yet, perhaps revelling in it too, a glimpse of what her life might have been with Eliot. Five years before he had instructed her to arrive at a dinner party a careful ten minutes after him, lest anyone believe – perhaps – that they were a couple. What her real feelings were about these fluctuations of action and emotion she leaves the reader to guess, but her silence, indeed her denial, is affecting.

On 28 April she noted that she had 'given way' on the new car, willing to accept his offer because he used her car such a great deal. He was worried about forthcoming trips to Germany to collect the Hanseatic Goethe Prize in Hamburg, and to the United States, and shared his worries with Mary.

'I'm really frightened – not only about health, but that a strike or something will prevent my coming back. I wish I was going by sea and coming back by air. My pulse seems all right and I've got my doctor to write out what is the matter with me and what to do if anything goes wrong!'

On 8 May, Easter IV, however, Mary reported that Germany had been a success.

He will now have far more courage for the more arduous visit to U.S.A. After church he was low at having to give lunch to two cousins. I offered to help, since he doesn't like them! 'No, I think better not – they might think I didn't want to have them alone. If I liked them better I'd like to have you.' A lovely drive in Hyde Park. On the Serpentine bridge we stopped and Tom wrote me a cheque for £650, saying as he wrote it: 'One of my strongest principles in life is never to lend money with any expectation of its being returned' – a remark I should have taken strong exception to if it hadn't been entirely his suggestion. We arranged to meet if possible to-morrow, his last day before he leaves for America.

They did meet on 9 May.

We drove very slowly home through Hyde Park, discussing the technique of saying the Rosary – and I wrote down his 'plan'. He said: 'I am always afraid of it becoming automatic. By the way, my Confessor once told me that it is a mistake to keep repeating a prayer, once you've found your thoughts have wandered and you've actually not prayed it at all – it's best then to make an act of penitence.' As to his cheque: 'I forgot to say you should pay it in at once – one never knows, when making air journeys, if one will survive.' He always has this fear of air travel.

On prayer: 'I shall pray for you daily, as I always do and have done for a long time. I do think it helps to know that one's friends are praying for one.' I remarked that, as he knew, he was permanently on my 'short' list. 'My short list is getting too long. I keep meaning to remove some names, but it seems discourteous and unfriendly.' We said 'Bless you' and 'God be with you' to each other – and I told him that I so often prayed the *Cocktail Party* prayer for him. 'Do you really? I am glad to know that. It's a rune – like a Gaelic rune.' Then he disappeared, a trifle abruptly, grasping a small present I was sending by him to Marian.

He informed her that he was due to return on 20 or 21 June, depending on when his ship, RMS Queen Elizabeth, *berthed. He was travelling to see his two sisters in Boston, and stayed with his friend and publisher Robert Giroux in New York; he also went down to Washington DC to see Ezra Pound, who remained in St Elizabeth's Hospital. While he was gone, Mary's new car arrived, as she noted in her diary on 1 June. 'My new car – a Wolseley 4/44 – is very smart. I drove it to the United Services Club for lunch.' It was indeed a handsome, modern car; no wonder she was pleased with it.*

In June she would write: 'Nice to get back to our routine.'

22 June: A firm voice on the telephone after breakfast – no greetings, no preamble, said: 'Well, you kept very late hours last night. I could get no reply and what about the Albert Hall to-night?' I agreed to pick him up at the office and he must look out for a SMASHING car. There he was, on the doorstep of Faber's, very spruce in his middle-weight grey and with three packages of lovely nylons for me. The car was inspected with great approval and off we went to Chelsea. So pleased is he to be back.

The *Queen Elizabeth* was a nightmare of people wanting his auto-graph and wanting to talk to him and somebody sent him flowers for the journey and somebody else sent champagne which he shared with Paul Gallico and others.

At the flat he settled down as usual with the *Manchester Guardian*. I went to cook supper, but he was soon in the kitchen, distracting me with stories of his adventures, like a small boy, just back from school. At supper full details of the health of his family and a few hints of the ovations he had received at his readings.

On Sunday 26 June they took a stroll after early service.

After the High Mass we went for a walk in Holland Park and talked further of America. 'I went to see Ezra Pound, but his conversation is now so disconnected that I couldn't remember any of it.' He unpacked a number of small presents he had purchased for me on the boat. When discussing further dates for this week he remarked: 'Oh but that wouldn't do, that would mean two evenings running.' I nearly said why the . . . not? Very peculiar.

She continues to seek an emotional intimacy, to press him in ways he does not – quite – wish to be pressed.

10 July, Trinity IV: T. in a great flap this morning because I was two minutes late arriving to pick him up at 10.30. A very hot morning, against which he was oddly protected by a raincoat and umbrella. He remarked, on getting his diary out of his pocket: 'Well, we'll be going to the theatre on the 20th and I suppose we'll have to have some supper at Prunier's first at 6 p.m.' I suggested, mildly, that he should tell me what all this was about and he replied, rather sulkily: 'I supposed Theodora had told you.' I was slightly annoyed at being taken for granted like this, but had to admit I was free, as I'd been keeping the evening for Theodora – and therefore said I thought his niece would prefer to go with him without me. 'Well, I've got the tickets – and anyway, I don't see why.' He was very disgruntled and added, fiercely: 'I am taking Hope Mirrlees out to lunch and I shall pick her up at the Basil Street Hotel. I shall go by Tube, I wouldn't like to take you out of your way.' Silly old boy. As he was getting out of the car he said, very ungraciously: 'Well, Wednesday is the

only day I could look round this week.' He banged the door as I was saying I could see if I was free and let him know, and stalked into church without waiting for me. Almost a tiff!

This storm in a teacup blew over; they went to see Terrence Rattigan's Separate Tables, *which was playing at St James's Theatre, on 20 July: 'a stirring and sordid piece', she wrote.*

After the first act Tom turned to me and said peevishly: 'Well, no doubt it is all very remarkable, but I have NO idea what he is getting at!' which is exactly what people say after his own First Acts.

3 August: Collected the Poet at 12.30 in order to assist him to entertain the Hotsons at lunch at the Ecu de France. He read me a postcard from Mrs H. saying she would be there early 'in order to book a table'. He had forgotten, as I discovered later, that they had suggested the lunch – they must have got a shock when he proposed the Ecu de France, one of the most expensive restaurants in London. We arrived very early, put the car in a garage and went for a stroll. We visited the newly-repaired St James's Piccadilly, met the Rector (known to me) outside by chance – pink with pleasure when I introduced him to T., and he took us round. After he had gone off we looked at the memorial tablets to departed R.A.'s – 'the surest way to oblivion' remarked Tom smugly. On entering the smart restaurant we were discussing the Reserved Sacrament, and whether St James's had it or not. 'Well now, as you'll have observed, I didn't genuflect. The light was so very bright I decided it was electric light.' The Hotsons enjoyed the lunch very much (and must have been relieved to find that Tom was paying for it) – but it was rather exhausting. Now T. goes, to-morrow, to Switzerland for four weeks.

À l'Ecu de France was on Jermyn Street, and a very grand restaurant in its day.

While he was in Switzerland, Eliot sent Mary eight postcards over the course of four weeks, she recorded. The little exchange that follows is perhaps the most poignant of her account.

8 September: This evening he was waiting on the steps of Faber's with: 'Well, I looked out of the bathroom window and you weren't there' – and bringing a large parcel of books. A beautiful evening, so we went for a drive in the City, to the Tower and over Tower Bridge – with a great red sun sinking behind the cargo ships. T. at first rather sombre, relaxed and quoted Shelley and enjoyed prowling about in by-ways. A splendid and leisurely dinner at the Ecu de France, where the Head Waiter bowed like corn in the wind and Tom burst into French. (The Head Waiter's son, at school in England, played Becket in *Murder* and got an autographed copy of the play.) As well as consuming lovely food we talked for two hours and made plans for the reception of T.'s grand-niece Priscilla, age 21, who comes on Wednesday for a week. I asked: 'May I arrange your life for you' – 'That is exactly what I want you to do' – and we plotted out the week. A fine Silver Match cigarette lighter for me. He feels very superior having given up smoking. He hopes to settle down to some work now.

12 September: T. in excellent spirits and a bowler hat when I collected him this evening. 'Let us take a cup of sherry at your river residence,' and brought a signed copy of his speech at Hamburg – very grand.

15 September: Meeting after the 8 a.m. service, T. looked me firmly in the eye and said (He never says good-morning – just the first remark that is upper-most in his mind) 'Have always been worried about the gospel – ONE leper only but where were the nine? and what happened to them?' The niece had arrived yesterday, 'a little slip of a thing and very thin. I offered to present her with an overcoat – perhaps you could advise her. I sent her some flowers and looked in on her on the way back from the office.' (Poor child – never alone before, plunged into the Basil St. Hotel!)

In the Gospel of St Luke, Jesus cleanses ten lepers; only one returns to
thank him. Eliot, like Jesus himself, asks, 'where are the nine?' Eliot's
niece was Priscilla Stearns Talcott, later Talcott Spahn. In the evening
they took her to dinner at the Prospect of Whitby: when they went to pick
her up at the hotel Eliot told Mary of her history.

As we approached the Basil Street Hotel he said: 'Don't let's go in
yet – there is no need to be punctual and I must tell you all about
the child. My sister Charlotte, as I've told you, married beneath her
– a tiresome man. They had two daughters, 'Shardy' and Theodora.
Shardy married a very nice, dull man called Talcott. I liked him. He
was a gentleman and a good fellow. But she got tired of him and ran
away with a photographer, when this child was very small. After she
died Talcott married again – a nice woman and they had a boy. Now
he's gone and died very suddenly three months ago – so this girl is
left with a step-mother and a half-brother.'

It is further evidence of the grandeur of his family's lineage that Eliot says
his sister Charlotte married beneath her; her husband, George Lawrence
Smith, was the son of the Dean of the Faculty of Arts and Sciences at
Harvard. He was an architect, having studied at the Massachusetts
Institute of Technology.
   They had a fine evening, Mary reported.

We returned her to her hotel. 'Thank you VERY much Mary – you
have been angelic – I really couldn't have managed without you.'

In the next days Eliot brought Priscilla to tea with Mary, and asked
Mary's advice regarding such matters as what Priscilla should tip the
hotel staff, and what gift he should give her. Mary seems indispensable
to him. At the end of the month she reminded him that they were due a
trip to Windsor in a few days' time; he said he might not be able to go –
because his athlete's foot might land him in the London Clinic.

4 October: 8.30 a.m. telephone: 'This is Bunsen Nehemiah speaking'
– Tom, from the LONDON CLINIC! Where are you speaking
from? I asked. 'From BED' says Tom, very happily. It seemed that
his doctor ordered him to bed for a week, so instead of going to
Midhurst he'd returned to the flat, re-packed and trotted off to
the Clinic. But he talks of Windsor next Sunday, all the same. It's
becoming a danger to him, this Clinic.

*He would remain at the Clinic until 14 October; while he was there they
continued to joke about imagined names. She calls herself the Bailiff's
Daughter of Islington, she wrote on 9 October. Eliot picked up the game.*

'Ah then, you must be the mother-in-law of Bonsir. He wants
to change his name to Goodchild while he is in England, but he
wouldn't be recognised by that name in Nigeria, so he'll revert to
calling himself Badboy when he returns home . . .'

*Eliot remained, Mary wrote, in a light mood in the next days; there was
much talk of Bonsir Goodchild, and he sang old music hall songs. There
was a 'a nice, easy evening' at Margaret Rhondda's.*

23 Oct. Trinity XX: The Poet is very mercurial. After 8 a.m. he
quoted poetry in the street, which I suspect him of having composed in the Service. At 10.30 he was glum and yawning. After the
High Mass he was in terrific high spirits. This is 'Education Sunday'
and our Evangelical Vicar at the Old Church has instructed us to
pray for the educational system of this country. 'I cannot pray for a
framework,' said Tom, peevishly. We agreed to start for Windsor at
3.15. 'I have given deep thought to the matter of what I should wear
this afternoon. As I told you, I intended to wear my country tweed,
but I think it is better to wear my Sunday Best – and my new F.O.
hat – not this one, and not a bowler, which I used to wear for our
expeditions to Windsor. I think that is too formal.'

But by 2.45 p.m. London was yellow with fog and the A.A. said it would thicken and become dense. When Tom appeared (in his BOWLER) I told him the weather report and he was extremely pleased. 'Good, let's go back to your flat and telephone. My doctor told me to avoid FOG!' So then we explored Islington and had a happy afternoon around Canonbury Square, returned to the flat, had a large tea with toast made by Tom and the Schubert Great C Major Symphony.

They planned tea the following Sunday but he wrote to say he had caught cold and would have to cancel. But when they met on 30 October for church he was recovered. 'We talked, like everybody else, of Princess Margaret and Captain Townsend.' Princess Margaret, the Queen's younger sister, had fallen in love with Group Captain Peter Townsend, who had been the late King's equerry and deputy master of the household; he was fifteen years older than Margaret, and divorced. Their relationship was the subject of feverish speculation in the press, and on 31 October Margaret announced her final intention to renounce the match as incompatible with the teachings of the Church of England; she would not have been able to contract a church marriage with Townsend, as he had a spouse still living. Mary does not preserve the matter of her conversation with Eliot on the subject, which was front page news all over the world. As for the Book of Revelation, an angel seals the servants of God in chapter seven; the verses scroll through the tribes of Israel, in rhythmic repetition. Mary gets the title of Eliot's poem mentioned below slightly wrong: 'A Song for Simeon' was first published in 1928.

1 November, All Saints' Day: Cold and foggy. Tom, after church, had his annual indignation meeting at the Vicar's omission of the 'sealing of the twelve tribes' from the Revelation [Revelation 7:4]. 'Oh dear . . . but I remember he left them out last year. I always look forward to Issachar. People are so afraid of repetition – they don't seem to realise that it is the essence of poetry.' We talked of his own

lines on the Saints in his 'Song of Simeon' – 'they shall praise Thee and suffer in every generation – with glory and derision'. 'Yes, the word derision came very easily, no trouble at all.' He thinks he won't go early to-morrow, for All Souls. 'If you go, take a cup of tea first and don't communicate.'

On Remembrance Sunday, 6 November, they had tea at Mary's flat and listened to Elsa Lanchester's recording of the 'Cat Poems', as she called them, set to a score: an attempt at musical adaptation long predating Andrew Lloyd Webber's Cats. *Since the early 1940s, Lanchester – now best remembered as the Bride of Frankenstein from the 1935 film of the same name – had been performing successfully in cabaret.*

Dreadfully cheap and vulgar. T. was horrified and will NOT allow them to be published. I said he must have had fun writing the poems. 'Oh I DID – they gave me less pain and more pleasure than anything I've ever written.' Then he begged for some music to forget Miss Lanchester with – and we had an hour of Haydn and Mozart.

8 November: A characteristic telephone call: 'Well, I'm dining at the Garrick, where I shall drink wine, so I shan't want a drink before, but I thought you might come round to my office.' It had not, obviously, occurred to him that I might like a drink. I was given: MURDER in Greek – *The Cocktail Party* in German, the ESSAYS and *The Confidential Clerk* (*Der Privat Sekretar*) also in German. And his address to the Conservative Association. I asked if he would like to sign all these – 'not now, but we'll have a grand signing session at your flat'. Again on the Cat Poems – 'I have quite decided, I shall NOT give permission for them to be published – they are vulgarly, cheaply and archly done. I thought I had invented the name 'Growltiger', but when the poems came out my uncle Christopher (the only surviving brother of my father) said: "Tom must have got the name from the game my father, his grandfather, used to play

with us as children. We got under the grand piano, which was covered with a tablecloth and came out and growled like tigers" . . . I think there must be quite a lot of things I think I've invented, when I'd known them all the time – that's very odd. It is said we never forget anything – a terrifying thought.'

On 23 November he told her he was writing: 'I've started to get something down – but it is very bad so far.' On 27 November, at the Garrick, he said, 'very suddenly':

'I think they are coming again – 7 imaginary characters – still seven – but I can always add a nurse or a servant, because they can be understudies. It's rather an odd experience – like being in a railway carriage in a dark tunnel with 7 people – you can't see them, but very gradually they become apparent as the light grows. They take on their own characters – not what you think they are, quite often. And the good people have some bad strains which come out and the bad people have some disconcertingly good points – they fit themselves, not into a situation I make for them, but into an old play. Oh yes, they are beginning to move.' On the way home I said again what a blessing my Wolseley car is. 'I am very glad, because that gives me a great deal of pleasure too.'

Eliot's final play – with eight characters, not seven – was The Elder Statesman, *which would be first produced in the summer of 1958.*

7 December: T. was waiting for me with two tins of shortbread and several books. At the flat he talked of his wife, for the first time for many months. 'It took me a very long time before I realised that she was unbalanced. For so long, shut in with her; I was a different person – only gradually did I realise that, with her, I was slightly unbalanced. I'd always thought it was my fault. The worst was when she would say: "Oh I am such a trouble to you, I ought to die" – then

I would promise anything and the tears followed. But the next morning it was just as bad.'

On Sunday 11 December, 'a very wet morning', they climbed into the Wolseley and headed off to church for a seasonal party.

On arriving at church: 'I'm glad I didn't give away this hat – it's very useful in this weather and nobody notices how old it is except me. But I like to dress well and I don't care who knows it – right is right – that's what I say!'

We talked of sins of the tongue: 'I say things I ought not to say about people sometimes to complete strangers, in a sort of desperate attempt to keep the party going and I only realise afterwards what I have done.' The party was hot and noisy and we escaped before long and settled down to tea and music in the flat. He asked for an obscure Bartok Quartet, which, said I, was as difficult as some of his poetry. 'It's very odd – I really do feel my poetry to be so very simple and straightforward.'

14 December: 'I have two books for you for Christmas – and the rules of the game are that as soon as you've read them you'll get some more. I suppose I'll have to take your word for it – or examine you on some of the minor characters.' This was the new Oxford Edition of Dickens to which, in *Pickwick*, he appended an enormous inscription. We struggled through the traffic – 'oh that's VERY clever' said Tom when we did a successful short-circuit. I reminded him of a short cut we'd made one Maundy Thursday evening and never managed to find again. 'Like that lovely picture of the village green and church that we once found right in London. I do hope we come across it again one day.'

On Roger Fry: 'A bad man – no, I mean an evil man – they were a queer lot, that Bloomsbury lot – silly, unintelligent and malicious, but they were cosy. They were kind to me and I found that gratifying – only one of them was able – Maynard Keynes – (I think Lydia was very good for him – a Russian peasant of Scottish ancestry!) – but the rest were really a bad lot – and quite a-moral.' On the new play: 'It's moving a bit – I have done one Act – now my seven imaginary characters are having a rest – it's quite a business embarking on a new character in a new scene. I think about them as people a good deal – on the Underground, in taxis and so on. I don't put words into their mouths, but I try to think inside them and their characters.' 'See you on Sunday' . . .

His dismissal of the 'Bloomsbury lot' is a repudiation of the connections of his past. His friendship with Leonard and Virginia Woolf had been crucial to his development; their Hogarth Press had published his second book of poems in 1919 – and it was the critic and painter Roger Fry who had mentioned Eliot's work to them: certainly, gratifying kindness. And it is perhaps unfair to describe the economist John Maynard Keynes's wife, born Lydia Vasilievna Lopokova in St Petersburg, as 'a peasant'. A dancer with Serge Diaghilev's Ballets Russes, she had trained at the Imperial Ballet School. Her father worked in a theatre, and her mother was the daughter of a clerk – though her mother was, indeed, of Scottish ancestry.

26 December: I got influenza and lay in bed reading *Pickwick* throughout Christmas. T. telephoned and, although terrified of infection rushed in once with flowers, fruit and whiskey. To-day he was quite put out because I was going away to recover. A note from him reached me in the country which ended:

Yours respful
nephew (adoptive)
Bunsir.

1956–1957

In the first days of 1956 Mary and Eliot had a quiet supper at her flat; her brother Humphrey joined them. Again, she noted Eliot's domesticity, serving the soup while she answered the telephone.

He had been to the Fabers' for the week-end. 'No, I didn't enjoy it – I was bored – but then I expected to be bored – and it passed!' What a jolly man he is!

He and Mary agreed that Tom looked 'very old', she says. The seven imaginary characters had got stuck again, Eliot said. 'I find I've got one of them on the stage through the whole play. I'll have to give him an afternoon off somehow.'

18 January: As arranged I swept up to Fabers at 4.59 p.m. and Tom swept into the car. I told him (to my view) a fascinating story, which he constantly interrupted – one of his comic moods. He apologised and I (being the original 'Julia') said: 'Oh well, I can always interrupt your interruptions!' On alighting from the car at Chelsea, T., with his hat on the back of his head, sang loudly: 'I've a date with you in Harlem'. Unless one happens to want to talk seriously, T. in these absurd moods is the greatest fun – but he won't be interrupted – it seems he has to work his mood out of his system.

A few days before he had brought her another recording of the 'cat poems'; this time Robert Donat was reading the poems, which had been set to music by Alan Rawsthorne. One side of one record was apparently enough: 'I can't hear the music and the words simultaneously, I don't think it works – it seems to me that children would be bored.'

On the new play: 'Some of the 7 are turning out to be horrible people – oh not all – one of them is a peach of a girl – my difficulty is that she is too good to be true. I've got temporary names for them all, but they may be changed. What matters most in a verse play is that their names have the same number of syllables.' I said, not for the first time, 'Well, do make them human beings this time.' 'Don't I always? They seem to me human – but perhaps I don't know much about human beings.' I said: 'How can you? You dislike them so much!' 'Well, I'm sorry for them – they seem to me pathetic.' I added: 'You only like them at a distance – so long as they don't come near you – so how can you know them? But the odd thing is that you do seem to know a lot about them, one way and another – you've got an eye for their little failings!' This was all taken in very good part – but I don't think T. listened to the Mozart he asked for on the gramophone.

She notes that he doesn't listen: but his deaf ear, she believes, is turned only to Mozart, not to her critique. Her freedom to speak her mind she sees as evidence of their closeness: but she must also, somehow, understand that he will not hear her.

On 19 January he attended a supper party at hers; he brought a good bottle of burgundy and cigars for the gents: 'I meant to give you some cigars for them – but I think I'd better offer them myself – men usually suspect cigars offered by a lady!' Guests included Robert Ford, a radio engineer who had been working to set up a radio network in Tibet and been imprisoned by the Chinese; and Lord John Hope, a Scottish politician. Tom enjoyed himself but began to falter.

At 10.30 I rescued Tom, who suddenly looked very tired and old and ran him home in the car. Then I returned to give my other guests whiskey. 'That was VERY well worth while,' said Tom 'and thank you for bringing me into it.'

At the end of the month, however, Eliot was back in the London Clinic with an irregular heartbeat and a bad cough; he was very weak. But Mary wrote briskly on 24 January that 'in John's view he's suffering from nothing worse than a cold in the head.' She heard nothing until 15 February, when she and John expressed hope they would be allowed to visit at the weekend. Eliot's pulse had been racing, 'probably caused by bronchitis developing'. He called her on 17 February.

He feels very weak, has had a bath, unaided, in a tub in his room, gets up for lunch and tea, which is very exhausting, but doesn't enjoy going back to bed as his behind and his heels are sore and the Night Nurse who rubbed him with eau-de-cologne had left.

19 February, Lent I: A very heavy snow blizzard which rapidly became covered with ice gave me a most perilous drive to the Clinic, where, however, I arrived intact. We had a long and cosy talk, not only about his symptoms. I explained that it was difficult for me to obtain first-hand information about his progress, to report to his family and Tom suddenly had the idea that he would instruct his doctor to keep me informed should he fall ill again. That would be a great help. He expressed his thanks for the flowers and books I had sent him and even said how glad he was to see me. I promised to look in to-morrow evening with his prayerbooks, which I did – but the doctor was with him so I didn't stay.

He was in the hospital for five weeks with bronchitis and cardiac trouble; he was at work on the lecture he would deliver on 30 April at the University of Minnesota. The Gideon D. Seymour memorial lecture, 'The Frontiers of Criticism', would be delivered over loudspeakers in a vast college arena: more than 16,000 free tickets had been mailed to those who requested them. He continued, too, to work on The Elder Statesman. *When he went home at last on 25 February he rang Mary the next day, 'very gloomy', saying 'I feel very weak and stupid.'*

4 March, Lent III: At 3.30 p.m. he turned up to tea, having walked along the Embankment – restless but spry – came to help make the tea, sitting in the kitchen, superintending the toasting of buns, carrying the tray and setting the table. He was in a flap about his prospects and I suggested he should take his doctor's advice and go away from this country in January and February: 'Where can I go? I don't want to twiddle my thumbs, at great expense, in a rich hotel – where I will run short of books and shan't be able to get at the papers I want. And it would mean two months away then, two months in America and a month in Geneva. As it is, I've managed to get the first two acts of the Play in draft before I fell ill – now I must do my lecture on Criticism for America – I don't see how I can get back to the Play until September. I sometimes think I might live in the country – but I can't find a house by myself and run servants.' But he cheered up and signed his Christmas present of Dickens at great length and remarked: 'There! well perhaps I am not quite as stupid to-day as I thought.'

The next day Mary said he was in good cheer, 'agreeable and sunny'; and the day after that made short work of her own elevation. For as the London Gazette *had reported at the very end of 1955, Mary had been awarded an OBE for her services to overseas students; yet she barely remarks on the honour at all. This seems more than natural modesty: the focus remains on Eliot.*

6 March: After a strenuous morning at Buckingham Palace getting an OBE from the Queen and a lunch-party afterwards and a short and useless afternoon at the office – I was thankful to slip round to Fabers and collect Tom. We did a little shopping for supper on the way home and drove back by the river. He interfered much in the cooking of supper, but then we settled in to some music for the rest of the evening. He looks v. tired still and he accepted thankfully my offer to drive him home again to-morrow evening.

On 15 March, they had dinner at the Oxford and Cambridge Club.

At dinner we discussed the doctor business again: 'I've not forgotten this and I shall write you a note of authorisation and write and tell Marian what I have done. I want you to be free to ring up the doctor when you feel you should and I have already explained to him that you will now represent the family should I fall ill.' As we drove home, suddenly: 'Oh, these night buses. I have a nightmare sometimes that I get on one, the last bus for Leytonstone perhaps, and when I get there it is strange to me and I don't know where to go or what to do. But then, I'm a neurotic – it's absurd when people say to me that I am behaving neurotically – of course I am – I'm a neurotic!'

21 March: We had, for some weeks past, been discussing his next visit to Sussex and whether I could fit in another call on him there. This morning, a propos of nothing, I received an odd, stuffy note saying: 'I can't have you or anyone coming down to the country solely on my account' – silly old boy. I thought of taking him seriously for once and nearly sent a message to say I wouldn't be looking round this evening – but it was really rather funny, so I didn't, and awaited events. Sure enough, the telephone rang in the afternoon: 'Can I count on you for 6 p.m.? . . .' I remarked that I wasn't sure I was speaking to him for writing me such a stuffy note, at which he laughed and said I must take him as a comic. Over drinks at the Russell we talked of his note. 'Women always get me in the wrong,' he said. 'That's what you always say,' I replied – 'I knew that would come!' But really he was quite unhappy at his odd little spurt and added, rather pathetically: 'you must make allowances for a neurotic' and added that he hoped very much that I would come to Sussex. He also gave me the name and address of a priest to summon to his death-bed!

She did visit him in Sussex the following week; these accounts of their conversations make it seem absolutely evident that the pair were drawing closer and closer.

29 March, Maundy Thursday: A very homey supper at the flat – T. boiling the eggs and making the soup. Then off to the annual Tenebrae – and back again to the flat for cocoa and biscuits. T. insists on paying for a hired car while mine is being mended.

The Wolseley had had a knock from a van while Mary was driving back from Sussex.

2 April, Easter Monday: T. had volunteered to come round and advise me on some papers I had to write. I picked him up at the flat at 5 p.m. – a very grim and tousled poet, in remarkably bad form, with a terrible air of 'I must do my duty' about him – white and tense and in no mood for giving advice. But he did his best and I poured sherry down him with excellent results. I hope it lasts. As we drove back through Bank Holiday crowds, he remarked: 'How very ill-favoured these people are!'

3 April: No, still in bad form. Much worried about going to church next Sunday – would there be a draught?

5 April: The skies seem much clearer – but I am no 'weather prophet' these days. I took him to a meeting: 'Don't go too fast – we have plenty of time and it is so much nicer driving with you than looking at the depressing faces in buses.' On arrival – 'let's do the crossword puzzle – I needn't go in yet.'

11 April: T. has made a good speech to the Poetry Book Society – 'I was much thanked – I think really sincerely' – retired from being President and superintended the election of Stephen Spender to succeed him, at his own suggestion. 'Stephen seemed very pleased. I can't think why. I suggested him so as not to have Day-Lewis. I object to him on three grounds (a) political (b) moral (c) that he is not a good poet. And I can't forget the way he wangled himself into the Oxford Professorship a few days before the announcement of his divorce. I am not sure about Auden – it is all Enid Starkie's doing – I dislike her.'

Starkie was an Irish-born literary critic at Oxford who was believed to have had a hand in the appointment of W. H. Auden as Professor of Poetry at Oxford; his five-year stint in the post began that year.

12 April: In pouring rain we collected each other at Fabers and dined at the Oxford & Cambridge, starting with an hour on Tio Pepe. T. gave me a passport photo of himself, with his ears unusually protuberant. 'Yes, my ears do stick out. I have always been very sensitive about them since a terrible episode in my childhood. I sat between two little girls at a party. I was very hot. And one of the little girls leaned across me to the other and whispered loudly: "Look at his ears!" So one night I tied some rope round them when I went to bed, but my mother came and took it off and told me they would fold themselves in, so I needn't worry.' He had been to see his doctor and fixed up with him that he was to answer all my questions freely – and was about to send him a note of authority in case I needed it. After dinner, in an almost empty lounge, we read, of all things, the *Sketch* and *Tatler*. T. fascinated by the pictures of the debutantes and their very nouveau-riche names – especially the parents of one girl – Sir H. and Lady Fysh. After dropping Tom at his flat I thought how very odd that I should now be his 'next of kin' in this country.

On 15 April she joined him for a dinner at the Garrick with some American friends, Mr and Mrs Leon M. Little – Mr Little had been at Harvard with Eliot and was a retired bank president.

A most pleasant evening – and then he will be leaving for the United States.

I said: 'Pray for me – I shall say the Hail Mary and your Rune for you every day.' 'Of course' said Tom 'I shall pray for you every day, as I always do.' As he got out of the car he held my hand and said: 'God bless you – take care of yourself – que Dieu te protège.' Nice and cosy. I hope he will be all right.

He sailed for the United States on 19 April for a six-week visit. As to the stadium-sized crowd he drew in Minneapolis, Peter Ackroyd notes that Eliot had, by this time, become a symbolic figure in Western culture: 'He had become a kind of totem; his extraordinary authority was based on that sense of a cultural order which he had once sought and which, by the strange alchemy of his career, he now embodied. He had become the representative of a tradition which, without his presence, might finally disappear, and the fact that he now had very little left to say only heightened the almost ritualistic sense of occasion which that presence provided.' This sense of him as totemic makes the contrast with those quiet bacon-and-egg suppers at Mary's all the more intimate.

He suffered another attack of tachycardia on the voyage home.

Mary met him on 24 June, after he had returned from the United States; on 15 June she had reported seeing a horror-comic photograph of Eliot in a wheeled chair being taken off the RMS Queen Mary to the French Hospital in the middle of the night. When they met he told her that he'd felt well all this last week in America, but was unwell during the voyage; when the ship berthed at 2 a.m. an ambulance was waiting. Mary relays his account.

'Two sailors wheeled me off the ship and then the PRESS began – they were like <u>vultures</u> – they gave me an appalling feeling of nausea, but at the same time, of pity – that they should have such a dreadful job to do. One even put his camera through the window of the ambulance close to my face and flashed – not speaking to me at all. We got to the French Hospital at 5 a.m. – just light it was – and there I saw a miserable, shivering little man, running up with his camera – he must have been hanging about for <u>hours</u>.'

And indeed, Eliot's arrival and illness were broadcast around the world: 'Mr T. S. Eliot, the poet and playwright, who was taken off the liner Queen Mary in a wheelchair when the ship docked at Southampton early yesterday, was at the French Hospital, London, to-day stated to have "had a good night, and to be getting on all right".' This was the Coventry

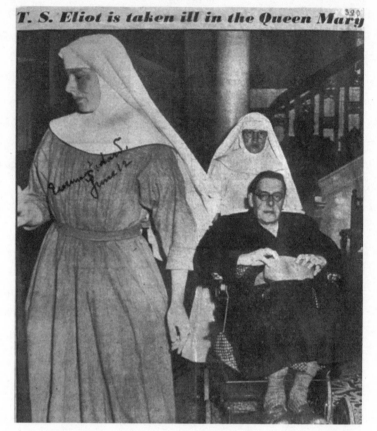

Mary's clipping of Eliot being taken off the *Queen Mary* in a
wheelchair – which made headlines around the world.

Evening Telegraph; *the news was also reported in the* Aberdeen
Evening Express *and as far away as the* Daily Independent Journal
of San Rafael, California, and the Berkshire Eagle *in Massachusetts.
This degree of fame was, certainly, not new. A cartoon in the* New York
Times *run in April 1950 showed people in a tattoo parlour asking to
be inked with the poet's lines; he was plagued by autograph-hunters.
At a New York party the writer Katherine Anne Porter wrote of guests
'swarming around him, grabbing him, patting him, owning him'.*

*Eliot's sister Margaret had died suddenly the week before, which had
upset him. 'Marian's cable gave no details – but I am afraid she may have*

died alone and not been found for some time.' Unsurprisingly, he seemed distracted when he and Mary met.

He asked often about me, but every time I started to tell him he interrupted immediately to ask a question which usually produced a train of thought in another direction . . . Walter de la Mare had died: 'He wasn't my kind of poet, but I am sure he was a nice old man – just not my cup of tea. I thought his *Memoirs of a Midget* a creepy, unpleasant book.'

De la Mare – now perhaps most famous as the author of the poem 'The Listeners' – had died two days previously. Memoirs of a Midget, published in 1921, is a strange, surreal novel, its protagonist dreamy and diminutive. It would not have been Eliot's cup of tea.

26 June: This morning I went to fetch Tom again and drove him to Bloomsbury. We sat in the sun in the car while Tom read Marian's letter to me about his sister Margaret's death – how she had died alone and been found by the Rent Collector and Marian had been rung up by the police, then Cousin Frederick had come and taken charge and was the greatest help. Marian had had their sister cremated and put in a little box in a vault 'store' with her name on it and a place to put flowers. She had left instructions that she wished to be buried at St Louis – 'I am sure she did,' said Tom, 'she never really lived after she left there.'

In the afternoon I went to see Tom's doctor, to discover, at the request of Marian, the real state of his health. There is, he said, an organic cause of this disturbance – in a lesion between the left and right compartments of the heart. Should this lesion get slightly out of hand it causes heart beats to increase from 80 to 120/40. 'The sensation of the patient is as of the imminence of death.' However, it seems that Tom's heart and arteries are in excellent condition and there is nothing wrong with him 'except the normal minor ailments of an old bachelor of 67'. It is not known what brings on these heart attacks, though the condition is not rare, but it is clear that strains, worries, tensions are contributing factors. 'Mr Eliot has few real worries. He has very few enjoyments – a good meal, a good cigar, an Honour. Why would he not enjoy the dramas of ambulances etc., it is harmless and if people laugh – well, let them.' The doctor again assured me that he would ring up the moment anything was amiss and added: 'I don't <u>know</u> Mr Eliot – we never talk of anything but his health – he seems to have a nervous dread of disclosing anything concerning himself. He likes to do his bit of writing – so I let him.' It is evident that this doctor, though sensible and with a sense of humour, does not know his 'illustrious patient' – he doesn't, for instance, know that Tom has an abnormal fear of death.

Soon after 5.30 this evening, long before I was expecting him, Tom arrived for supper and he immediately set to preparing the easier part of supper, drinking sherry to give him confidence in his own ability as a cook. A most agreeable evening listening to music.

How intensely personal, for Mary to visit Eliot's physician for herself. How notable, her inclusion of the doctor's remark that Eliot is an 'old bachelor'.

29 June, SS. Peter & Paul: After the service, in a voice loud enough to be heard by several people coming out of church: 'I have got a nice book about the puberty laws of Africa for you'! Then, 'I went to old de la Mare's funeral yesterday at St Paul's – it was dreadful – a man got up and conducted the music with his back to the altar – and, would you believe it, we had "Crossing the Bar". He is going to be buried there – I will NOT be buried there – don't you forget. I've given my solicitor all instructions and John knows. I have got a plot in St Stephen's burying-ground at Brookwood, as you know, but I think Somerset (East Coker) would be a much nicer idea.' T. had left his engagement book in his room, so after breakfast he rang up

to make various dates – and 'God bless you!' he said, abruptly – and rang off.

De la Mare had been a chorister at St Paul's Cathedral as a boy; his ashes are interred in the crypt. 'Crossing the Bar' is a poem by Tennyson.

On 4 July Eliot went to Peter Brook's production of The Family Reunion *at the Phoenix Theatre – and enjoyed himself, according to Mary.*

'A lady sitting next to me in the stalls looked at me piercingly for some time, then said: "You <u>are</u> Mr Richard Church, aren't you?" I said I was not, but I knew him, and we had a happy little chat. I went on to the stage after the performance and met all the cast. I thought it pretty good and well cast, with one or two exceptions. But I shan't say any more until we've seen it next week.'

They would indeed go together on 10 July. 'Luckily I thought all the "right" things about the casting,' Mary noted after their outing. Three days before that, however, on 7 July they met at her flat with the Bishop of Kensington, to discuss the issue of finding a new vicar for St Stephen's. Eric Cheetham had retired in spring; Eliot had contributed a piece to the Church Times *to mark his departure, writing that Cheetham had made the church 'a centre of Evangelical Catholicism: truly Catholic and truly wholly Anglican'.*

T. and the Bishop of Kensington met 'accidentally on purpose' for tea at my flat to discuss privately the question of the new Vicar. T. arrived very early. 'Well, I managed to go for a walk, but it was so hot that I thought I would come straight here. I think I'll take my waistcoat off' – which he proceeded to do in my bedroom. When the Bishop arrived they both sat in their shirt-sleeves and had 'choc ices' for tea in the kitchen, which they greatly enjoyed . . . After tea they got down to business. I was sad to observe Tom's slowness – halting

PHŒNIX THEATRE

CHARING CROSS ROAD, W.C.2

Licensed by the Lord Chamberlain to PRINCE LITTLER
General Manager   ...   ...   FREDERICK CARTER

TENNENT PRODUCTIONS LTD.

present

PAUL SCOFIELD—PETER BROOK SEASON

THE FAMILY REUNION

by

T. S. ELIOT

Directed and Designed by PETER BROOK

First Performance: Thursday, 7th June, 1956

Characters in order of speaking

Amy, Dowager Lady Monchensey ...	**SYBIL THORNDIKE**
Agatha ⎱ *her* ⎰	**GWEN FFRANGCON-DAVIES**
Ivy ⎱ *younger* ⎰	**NORA NICHOLSON**
Violet ⎱ *sisters* ⎰	**PATIENCE COLLIER**

The Hon. Charles Piper ⎱ *brothers of* ⎰	**DAVID HORNE**
	her deceased
Col. The Hon. Gerald Piper ⎰ *husband*	**CYRIL LUCKHAM**

Mary, *daughter of a deceased cousin of Lady Monchensey* **OLIVE GREGG**

Denman, *a parlourmaid*   ...   ...   **CATHERINE WILLMER**

Harry, Lord Monchensey, *Amy's eldest son*   **PAUL SCOFIELD**

Downing, *his servant and chauffeur*   ...   **HARRY H. CORBETT**

Dr. Warburton   ...   .   **LEWIS CASSON**

Sergeant Winchell   ...   .   **NORMAN SCACE**

NOTE

The Furies (Erinyes) of Greek mythology, the avengers of crime against kinship, who appear during Act One, were propitiated, according to the Orestes legend, by the expiation of crime, and became transformed into the Kindly Ones (Eumenides)—the "bright angels" of Act Two.

First Nights   345

ELIOT REVIVAL WELL DONE

POWERFUL CAST IN "FAMILY REUNION"

By W. A. DARLINGTON

In the days when T. S. Eliot was feeling his way towards a workable form of modern verse-play, "The Family Reunion" was an elaborate experimental attempt to graft a present-day theme on to ancient Greek tragedy.

That the attempt was not capable of full success nobody has said with more downright force than Mr. Eliot himself. That it had, and still has, more than ordinary interest was proved by its revival at the Phœnix last night.

This revival is very much better than the original production; but there are obvious reasons why it should be. The director and the cast know a lot more to-day about Eliot plays than anybody did then.

Peter Brook as director gives tremendous atmosphere to the house whose young master is (so oddly) pursued by the Greek Furies and compelled to expiate his own and his father's sin of wanting to murder their wives; and he handles the Furies themselves with eerie effect.

FINE TRANSITION

Paul Scofield plays the hero, with a fine transition from the haunted creature of the first act to the free man, master of his fate, in the second.

Sybil Thorndike, back from Australia at last, is perfect as his mother. Gwen Ffrangcon-Davies is fine as the aunt upon whom most of the family troubles seem to centre. Lewis Casson is incisive as the doctor.

With players of the calibre of David Horne, Cyril Luckham and Nora Nicholson acting as chorus the cast is an immensely strong one, and some of the speaking is a joy to hear. If only it were the fashion to speak all modern plays like this, the pleasure of playgoing would increase by fifty per cent.

Programme for Peter Brook's production of *The Family Reunion*, Phœnix Theatre, 1956.

and hesitating as he tried to make his points, but very confused. Still maybe, the position is slightly clarified. T. outstayed the Bishop for a long time.

20 July: I had told Tom of my visit to his doctor. 'Well, now you know all about my fell disease – I hope you don't think I am a hypochondriac?' I reported, over drinks at the Russell Hotel, that I was much reassured by the doctor, because I know now that the only real harm that could come to him, damage to his heart, has not happened and the doctor says that his heart is in excellent condition. I insisted that I did not think him to be a hypochondriac, because the doctor had told me how dreadful patients feel when they have these attacks. T. was immensely cheered and said: 'I am very glad you went to see him – a great help to me. I know I fuss – but my special fear is that I am planning my life on the supposition of frequent attacks.'

Random remarks: 'When I write a piece of prose I always re-write it three times – even a letter to *The Times*. When I see what I have written in the past I always want to re-write it. Public speaking is the art of speaking second-best words slowly, but NOT stopping.' We discussed holidays and plans for niece Theodora's visit. 'I shall be leaving for Switzerland on 14 August – so I must make my confession. I always do before the Feast of the Assumption.' And, on liking people: 'When I was young I didn't like people because I was afraid they would be kind to me – now I suspect almost everyone of liking me because they want to get something out of me. What a dreadful time millionaires must have! For me, it started after the success of *Family Reunion* – now I believe I have a reputation I shall never lose, of being very rich and very miserly. Or I am thought neurotic.'

23 July: We lunched at the Russell Hotel as Tom was coming with me to choose a typewriter in a shop in Southampton Row. He was in bad form. He had meant to return from Cambridge this morning, all carefully planned – but it seems he came back last night – and was very secretive about it. I guess that something or somebody had upset him – or he wanted to avoid something or somebody and so

he ran away. He is also in a great state about his London Library speech and about the wedding of his god-daughter at Beaconsfield on Saturday, when he has to motor there with the Fabers, have a picnic lunch and propose the health of the bride.

Eliot had joined the London Library – a private library established in 1841 under the auspices of Thomas Carlyle – in 1918; he became its president in 1952 and remained in that post until his death in 1965. As to Eliot's 'secretive' behaviour – was she troubled by it? It is difficult to ascertain. But Mary had, by now, shown that she was willing to accept him for what he was, even when she found his actions difficult or challenging. But she continued to believe she was in a special relationship with Eliot: 'You are different,' as he told her.

2 August: Met T. at the 8 a.m. service and suggested a drink this evening, after which I would propel him to the Royal Court Hotel, where he is dining, on my way home – 'If you'd <u>like</u> to see me.' 'You know quite well' said Tom 'that I never <u>want</u> to see <u>anybody</u>.' 'Proposal cancelled,' I said cheerfully. 'Oh no – I didn't say I didn't want to see <u>anybody</u> – and you are different – and anyway I want to discuss arrangements for Theodora's visit.' So we drank Tio Pepe and talked for two hours – and were very low, naturally, about Suez in particular and the world in general. 'I suppose it is absurd really, but I spend much time assuring myself that the correct version of anything I write is safely deposited both sides of the Atlantic.'

The Egyptian president, Gamal Abdel Nasser, had nationalised the Suez Canal – previously controlled by British and French interests – on 26 July. But Mary gives no indication here, or anywhere in the manuscript, of her close connection to the crisis: for her brother Humphrey had been appointed Ambassador to Cairo in August 1955. Yet Prime Minister Anthony Eden's direct involvement in the crisis meant that his ability to influence events was curtailed: 'Tell him to cheer up!' Eden wrote on a telegram Trevelyan had sent, warning of the grave difficulties that surely lay ahead.

5 August, Trinity X: A heavy GLOOM – due to Egypt in the first place and accentuated by the sight of a number of ladies cleaning their cars outside the flats, in slacks. This afternoon we picked up Theodora after lunch and drove to Osterley Park – a very pleasant expedition, though Tom 'on duty' can be very heavy going. To top up we had tea very late at the Oxford & Cambridge. On the Transfiguration, to-morrow: 'I think you ought NOT to go to church to-morrow morning' – because he wanted an excuse for not going himself!

6 August, Bank Holiday: From 4 p.m. I played the piano, waiting for Tom to come to tea. He was, I thought, taking an unusually long walk. About 4.45 he strolled in, having been sitting in the kitchen for some time, listening to me playing.

On 9 August they took Theodora to see a farce, Hotel Paradiso, *with Alec Guinness and Irene Worth, at the Winter Garden; they had dinner before at À l'Ecu de France, a firm favourite. Everyone enjoyed themselves, Mary reported – noting also that she drove them all there and back with great efficiency.*

12 August, Trinity XI: On our early morning visit to St Stephen's Tom talked of the psychology of the apparently devout people who, when he collects, 'refuse the bag'. When we got into church I realised, too late to borrow from him, that I had left my money behind. When he came round with his bag I was kneeling devoutly – and trying not to laugh. There was much mocking when he rejoined me in the car after the service.

Eliot went off in August for a month's holiday in Switzerland; on 7 September Mary wrote of her holiday in Hertfordshire, during which 'Tom sent me a postcard from Geneva almost every day'. But when he came home he was straight back to the London Clinic with an abscess on his hip and some tachycardia: she spoke to his doctor again, who advised her to take him out for lunch and a drive, 'but without telling him it was the doctor's idea'.

Tom was delighted to come out – he was in good spirits and enjoyed his jaunt. We lunched in the anonymity of Russell Hotel and had a sunny drive in Regent's Park. All the story, of course, of his illness – and we talked of dreams, for he had been sleeping badly, and of friends: 'I find, as I grow older, that I have hardly any <u>real</u> friends – most of those I thought were friends are not the people I thought they were. The Bloomsbury Set, of course, were very kind to me and I didn't see through them – but then, I was still in my twenties and <u>very</u> unhappy.'

9 September, Trinity XVI: Took tea at the Clinic this afternoon and we then went out for another drive – Hatton Garden, S. Paul's, Tower Bridge, Tooley St., Southwards and back by the river. 'I had an idea this evening that I'd be driving through a tunnel in Bermondsey – it certainly does make my life much more varied – these absurd things we do so suddenly.' He showed me a letter of protest sent to the British Council with regard to a lecture given by one F. Bateson in Oxford – in which he stated that Mr Eliot had ill-treated his wife, hated women, referred to them always in a perverted way and suggested that after his death obscene poems will be found among his papers. It seems that, some years ago, Bateson published a journal of literary criticism and included an article suggesting that T. was a homosexual. T. put his solicitor on to it, who extracted a very grovelling apology from the author, but a v. unsatisfactory one from Mr Bateson. One reason for the attack may be that Tom is writing slightingly of Bateson's kind of literary criticism.

Mary had referred to this event before – as had Eliot – at the end of 1952, when it had occurred (see p. 148). F. W. Bateson was the editor of the journal in which John Peter's piece, claiming that Eliot had a romantic attachment to Jean Verdenal, had appeared.

When they met on 10 September, Eliot mentioned his friend, the poet Hope Mirrlees; he said that John was afraid of her. Mary replied – 'in a light-hearted way' – that she was not surprised, as she herself thought Mirrlees appeared formidable. Eliot was, apparently, not best pleased at this.

11 September: T. went home yesterday. This morning I received a note from him at which, after reading, I exclaimed to myself 'Strike me pink!' He accused me of impertinence and forbade me to sneer at his friends! By the afternoon another note arrived, saying he had written the first after a very restless night, but still thought he was justified – that he would not refer to the matter again, but 'a lapse of a few days would be best and he hoped to go to High Mass on Sunday'! I couldn't stand for that, so I wrote a very terse note, though slightly frivolous, saying I refused to be put in the corner for something I had not done, asked him what he had had for supper at the Clinic and ordered him to telephone at once and come to tea on Sunday. Which he did, rather sheepishly. I asked how he was. 'I think my stomach is a little disordered' – 'I should think it IS' I said, told him to go to bed early and come to tea on Saturday. He said of course he would come to tea and I only just refrained from saying 'jolly d. . . of me to ask you.'

When they had their tea on 15 September he seemed nervous.

After tea I said that he really must try not to go off pop like that – it was bad for his pulse AND mine – that I had only, as he knew, met Miss M. once and that my remark was of the most usual and light-hearted and he had been quite ridiculous. But I really believe he thinks that to say someone looks formidable is quite an insult. He was laughing by the end of my sermon, and so was I – but I was really sad that he could go and do this kind of thing to one of his most intimate friends.

Some might say that Mary herself was quite formidable; perhaps her sense of her own character played a part in this exchange. Perhaps too it is an indication of Eliot's desire to keep certain relationships absolutely sep- arated: Mary's remark about Mirrlees – however gently meant – crossed a boundary. Things relaxed when they met next, and she continued to collect Eliot's gossipy judgements on his contemporaries.

The poet and critic Herbert Read – who had been one of the signatories to the letter to The Times, *sent the year before, regarding the refusal of visas for the Conference of the Authors' World Peace Appeal – had been a regular contributor to* The Criterion; *Eliot, however, disliked his use of psychoanalytic theory. Malcolm Muggeridge was an eminent journalist who would go on to be a household name as a broadcaster; the Garrick has always been the haunt of journalists as well as actors and artists.*

18 September: Oh well, he was much better this evening and we had an most agreeable three hours – dining at the Garrick. A propos Herbert Read: 'How can he talk such nonsense? The man really is an ass. But he has written some good poems.' On *The Criterion*: 'I think it was the last literary periodical to publish long reviews. At one time it was monthly – and 2/6 instead of quarterly 7/6 – but I was not a good monthly editor. It's quite a different technique, short reviews and articles. I was a good quarterly editor – there was time to collect the right people to write on subjects on which they specialised. I could give them more than two months and they would produce something really worth reading.' I love these Garrick evenings – sitting in that huge quiet room, surrounded by Zoffany pictures and others of David Garrick, Mrs Siddons and so on. And the long dining room table lit by candles. To-night Malcolm Muggeridge and Mr Casey (former Ed. of the *Times*) were dining. Even at dinner T. was very outspoken on his favourite

(alas) topic of his health. 'I have had no diarrhoea to-day – last night my temperature was 99 – that is unusual for me – I must take my digitalis this evening. I don't feel very well and I am still not sleeping properly.'

Of Ottoline Morrell: 'She was a very domineering woman who, when she found a good doctor or dentist, was determined that all her friends should go to her "find". She made me go to a German psychologist – a nice man – but he asked me my dreams and gave me the most extraordinary reasons for the things I dreamed. I soon began to dream things I thought would interest him – so I stopped going to him.'

30 September, Trinity XVIII: Agitation yesterday, because I didn't turn up at the 8 a.m. service for Michaelmas Day – having gone to Hertfordshire without telling him. T. seems edgy these days and cannot bear being disagreed with. He snapped out at me: 'My dear lady . . .' but I laughed so much at being thus addressed that he laughed too. This afternoon we took a walk in Bushey Park, in delightful sunshine, and watched herds of deer – discussing angels, archangels and saints.

We got back to the flat for tea and drinks about 6 p.m. He is sleeping better again. 'I think I have got my nerve back a bit now – it is so difficult feeling one may go off pop at any moment and nobody understands.' For the last few months I have noticed at intervals a nervous spasm or twitching in his leg, which he seems unable to control. I wonder if I should mention this to the doctor.

4 October: A very private and confidential story about Herbert Read. Then on D. H. Lawrence: 'I only met him once – at a party given by the Aldingtons. I was very uneasy – there was electricity in the air. I didn't know until afterwards that Richard Aldington and his wife had just decided to part and were throwing a last party together. Lawrence sat on a sofa and looked acutely miserable. Frieda looked venomous! Lawrence had done some good things extraordinarily well – but he was a sex maniac and sadist combined.

He couldn't do (nobody could) what he tried to do ON PAPER –
but he was in some respects a remarkably good writer – he had the
heart of the matter in him.' As to the new play, it doesn't look as if he
would get it done for Edinburgh next year – 'but I must get it done
for 1958 – I shall need the money!'

*Aldington was a literary polymath, a poet who was one of the founders
of the Imagist movement, a novelist and a critic. He was also the author
of the first serious biography of D. H. Lawrence, published in 1950. That
'private and confidential story' is another example of Mary's wish to both
reveal and conceal: reveal her closeness to Eliot, and demonstrate that his
trust in her was justified.*

*On 8 October he was in a 'grey mood', Mary wrote. He had received a
list of his late sister Margaret's possessions and it had upset him. 'I very
nearly cried when I read the list – such a poor, mean little list of small
worthless things.' But after church they had a pleasant outing to Hyde
Park, and then she took him to his dinner.*

This evening, because I like him to have as much use of the car he
gave me as possible, I drove him to the International Sportsmens'
Club where he was dining with Lady Wavell. We were much too
early, so we parked in Berkeley Square and T. told me stories of false
teeth. 'By the way, surely there is something in *The Cocktail Party* – at
the beginning – about false teeth? We must look that up. But it is
too easy to get a laugh like that.'

16 October: We had arranged supper chez moi, but I fell ill with
a feverish cold. T. telephoned at some length and announced his
intention of bringing me his bottle of whiskey to-morrow morning,
en route for his office – most kind.

17 October: And so he did, having walked in pouring rain – bringing his bottle and talking to me through my bedroom door. In the
course of the day he telephoned three times.

It would seem, from her account, that their intimacy was growing ever greater, as he spoke to her through her bedroom door and brought her whiskey to warm her. And yet she could not know how far she was from her heart's desire. On 26 October they groaned over the 'State of the World'; on 1 November she remarked that her family was just starting to get out of Cairo after 'the Suez catastrophe'.

We dined at the Oxford & Cambridge and, in order to get away from Egypt, fell into talk of poets in general and English poets in particular. 'I like David Cecil – he's an odd and likeable man and I have a soft spot for him as he is the only literary <u>gentleman</u> we have to-day. Off the record, on the whole I would say that the best English poet to-day is Edwin Muir – plodding, plebeian, but <u>sound</u>. Auden? Well, he's no longer English – he is the opposite of what I am – but I certainly think him to be far the best poet of his generation. Day-Lewis, Spender, Herbert Read – all mediocre poets, mediocre politicians – and Day-Lewis is a mediocre ADULTERER. Edith Sitwell is not nearly as good as she thinks she is – too much of an exhibitionist – she is jealous of other women poetesses, particularly of Kathleen Raine and Anne Ridler. Both are very domestic, good at husbands and children. I think Anne Ridler is the better, though she is not a good playwright. Marianne Moore is quite outstanding and way above most of the men of her generation. She has invented a new medium, hitherto unused.'

Cecil Day-Lewis – who would be appointed Poet Laureate in 1968 – certainly had a tumultuous love life: for a decade he carried on a dual relationship with his wife Mary and the novelist Rosamond Lehmann, and in 1950 left both women for the actress Jill Balcon. Anne Ridler had been Eliot's secretary – she had begun work at Faber and Faber in 1935, under Richard de la Mare. But she was an accomplished writer too, publishing ten volumes of poetry in her lifetime. Mary, recording Eliot's speech, puts the word 'poetess' into his mouth: he may not, in fact, have used this term, but all the same there is a sense that the female poet remains the other, not in the same category as her male contemporaries. Even his praise of Moore here is cast in terms of the masculine ideal.

He is working himself into a panic about Sister Marian's visit next summer in honour of her eightieth birthday. 'Supposing one of us gets ill? I'm not sure I can stand the strain of having her alone.' I reassured him that either I or Theodora would be on duty throughout the visit.

They spent a great deal of time together in November and December; they were together every few days in these last two months of the year, and all seemed very companionable. And yet Eliot's life was about to change entirely: and Mary knew nothing of it. Margaret Behrens, who had stayed in Shamley Green during the war, was a friend to both Eliot and Valerie Fletcher; she had invited them to spend the winter at her home in Mentone. Valerie – Miss Fletcher, as she is always referred to here – had begun looking after more and more of Eliot's affairs, even as Mary believed (as she made all those visits to Eliot's doctor) that she was the most significant woman in his life at this point.

Mary would also introduce him to one of her great post-war achievements: the 'Goats' Club', launched this year at the University of London. As she would later write:

It was started in an attempt to bring a few more students together with a few more students than they would meet and get to know in their every-day lives, to help them get to know each other by doing things together, to give them a feeling of belonging to a group which would look on each one of them as an integral part of the whole. This year, fifty different countries are represented in the membership, including all Commonwealth countries. Members meet and make friends with other members from countries with which, diplomatically-speaking, they are hardly on friendly speaking terms!

She came by the name after bumping into a student who said to her:
'Without people like you we should all be lost goats!'

22 November: Ah well, winter draws on and there was a NARSTY
fog and raw East Wind as I walked up the river to church. I hardly
expected to see Tom, but he was there, come wind come weather, and
we discussed the collect for the Sunday and Lady Cynthia Colville.
Another long 'drink' at the Russell this evening and then on to dine
with the Rhondda/Bosanquet friends at Arlington House. All right
– pleasant and easy in spite of the International Situation. T. at his
kindly best and we all tried to concentrate on NOT talking politics.
We left at 10 p.m. – all having enjoyed a respite from every-day
struggles.

27 November: T. visited the University of London Goats Club
this evening. I met him by arrangement in the Russell Hotel –
where I found him sitting on a highbacked chair in the hall, looking extremely miserable. He is really QUITE AWFUL before he
has to do anything and to-night was no exception. He hardly
spoke through dinner and appeared to take absolutely NO interest
in the programme he'd insisted I should arrange for him. Very ungra-
cious in fact. But the moment I took him upstairs in the kitchen
lift at U.L.U. [University of London Union] he was amused and he
got a tremendous reception from the students. He read well, entertained them with the story of S. Lucy's Day in Sweden, was photographed with them and agreed to be their President, as well as signing
many membership cards. He really enjoyed it and was, I think,
quite touchingly pleased that he is still such a success with the
student generation. It is many years since he has read to a student
audience.

In attendance was a young Adu Boahen – a Ghanaian 'goat' who would
in later years come to be known as one of the greatest historians of the
African continent. As Boahen would write:

My most vivid memory is that of the visit of T. S. Eliot, one of the very first visits as far as I can recall. As usual, we did not know who the speaker was going to be but enough hints had been dropped on this occasion to convey the impression that he was a really big man. After the usual waiting and humorous introductory remarks by Mary, we were asked to guess who the guest speaker was. Many suggestions came and I remember shouting that he was a banker for the simple reason that the rather detached and cautious look about him reminded me of my then bank manager. Can you imagine my pleasure when he said my guess was not too far off the marks since he in fact started life as a bank clerk? He read some of his poems to us, and what an evening it was!

It was Mary's practice not to reveal who her guest speakers were going to be: the secrecy ensured that her charges showed up, enticed by mystery. A British goat, Robert Watson, painted a vivid pen-portrait of Mary in those days:

She – Nanny Goat – the one and only M. T. – made it, and made us. We turned up at U.L.U, PROMPT – 8 pm (might get a spanking or threat of from the Boss if we were late), put on our labels, had coffee and biscuits, and excitedly waited to discover who this Tuesday's guest was going to be. One might recognise him, her, them, etc. Embarrassing if one should have and didn't, and it was always that week that Mary Trevelyan would ask you who our guest was. 'Are you saying you don't recognise him?' You hid, if you could find any space in the crowded room.

Watson went on to say of Mary: 'She was always available, always had sensible, not necessarily comforting, advice – but the right advice nonetheless.'

3 December: Picked up the Poet and drove him home. Very gay at first, but a striking change into silence. Perhaps he'd remembered

something someone had said in the course of the day which had annoyed him or, just as likely, I had caused the offence. We had been talking of advertising and I said I wondered if Fabers advertised enough – I often looked for them and failed to find them among the others. 'Oh well,' said Tom 'it's a question how far it pays – anyway there are FAR too many books and FAR too many publishers.' I wouldn't put it past him to be writing me a note this evening and accusing me of sneering and impertinence in referring to Fabers at all. Poor Tom – but at least I realise how very little I understand of what is going on in that very disturbed brain of his.

Humphrey Trevelyan and his wife Peggy – as she is usually referred to, though Mary spells her name differently – had been expelled from Egypt in November; his next post would be at the United Nations in New York. He went on to be Ambassador in Baghdad, Moscow – arriving just after the Cuban Missile Crisis – and Aden.

6 December: This evening Tom came to supper to meet Humphrey and Peggie, just emerged from Cairo. He listened avidly to their description of their adventures in their flight from Egypt.

12 December: Splendid form this evening for a change. For some reason he talked of his christening and confirmation. 'All in one day I was done – christened at Finstock and confirmed at Cuddesdon, with my two sponsors, Streeter and Somerset, both of whom I barely knew. Nobody really "prepared" me – it was all a bit hole and corner, but there was a general idea about that I'd read some difficult theological works! After the christening I was driven to Cuddesdon. I sat by Thomas Oxon. for twenty minutes, on a sofa, then I was "done".' We talked of Christmas plans and T. asked to come to tea the next two Sundays. I've a feeling something is 'up' at home, for he was in no hurry to get back. I said I had a present for him that I thought he would like. 'Bless your heart!' said Tom. It must have been the Tio Pepe.

16 December: T. turned up at 3.30 and stayed until after 7 p.m.

Talking of Christmas presents: 'I always give Miss Swan a present – it started years ago, when she was very kind to Vivien. But I
don't give Miss Fletcher anything – I don't think it suitable to give
one's secretary presents.' Muscular spasms again, which he seems to
try desperately to control. He picked up *Bleak House*, which he had
given me, and read to me for an hour – all his favourite bits.

*Where does one draw the line between privacy and deception? At this
point it's difficult not to believe that Eliot, in regard to what he shared
with his friend Mary – who had stood by him through thick and thin
for nearly two decades – was tilting towards the latter. For by this point
he had declared himself to Valerie, and had given her a ring: she wore a
finger-guard over it to conceal it, but, as Lyndall Gordon has written,
was 'noticeably radiant to Hope Mirrlees when she visited the office. The
situation offered Eliot another opportunity to indulge his taste for secrecy
– he and his fiancée would meet behind a pillar in the Russell Hotel across
the square from Faber and Faber.'*

He continued to work on The Elder Statesman, *too: the final act was
written after his marriage to Valerie, to whom he would dedicate the
play. In it, the Lord Claverton – the 'elder statesman' of the title – is
redeemed by confronting the sins of his past, and by confessing them to
a much younger woman: Monica, his daughter. 'I've only just now had
the illumination / Of knowing what love is,' he tells her at the end of the
play's final act. Eliot commented in January 1958: 'I can only say that it is
a very different play (and I believe a better one) for so much of it having
been written during this last year, than it would have been if I had finished it before our marriage.'*

27 December: T. telephoned on my return from Oxford. Still kept
indoors by the doctor – most upset at not getting to church at
Christmas. 'All sorts of childish fears seem to come back – I can't
remember with what actual incidents they were connected, but the
fears are still there.'

29 December: A further telephone call inviting me to tea – much better, but Madame A. is hors de combat, so he'll be collecting the tea himself. He looks much better – not so many medicines as usual – had been for a walk in the sun. And he is planning three weeks with Margaret Behrens at Mentone.

And so, the year turns.

2 January 1957: It is sad to start this New Year by saying good-bye to Tom for at least three weeks, probably longer. But I must go away tomorrow and on the day I return he will have gone off to the South of France. However, although selfishly I find this exceedingly trying, anything that contributes towards keeping him out of the London Clinic is, I suppose, a good thing. We spent the best part of two hours in the Russell Hotel drinking Tio Pepe. We talked for some time about 'the awful privacy of the insane mind'. 'Vivien ran away from her nurse once, in London, but they found her again. I used to find that, once I got out of the atmosphere, I recovered normality surprisingly quickly. But at the time it seemed as though it would never end.' We drank each other's health for the New Year and regretted that we had to Box and Cox so much this month. We drove back to Carlyle Mansions. Before we said good-bye Tom dictated his address to me. Then he suddenly said: 'I am so thankful I shan't have to go to Paris – there are too many ghosts there – I never want to see it again – there are too many who have died.' Then he held my hand for a moment and said: 'As you know, I always mention you in my prayers' and bolted, embarrassed, into the flats.

POSTSCRIPT

I look back on the last entry in my diary: 'It is sad to start this New Year by saying good-bye to Tom for at least three weeks, probably longer . . .'

On January 9th I returned to London, supposing Tom to be in France, for I should have heard had he been delayed. I was slightly surprised that he had not even written a postcard in the last week before he left but there was, as usual, a letter waiting for me in London. I was very tired and decided to leave it until the morning – something, I thought, to look forward to before starting work again. I opened it at breakfast.

And so, she found the note he had written to her, dated 9 January and addressed 'My dear Mary'. She had no inkling, clearly, of what it would contain. 'On Thursday the 10th January I am being married to Valerie Fletcher,' Eliot wrote.

He told her that decision was not sudden; it has been 'coming upon us for a long time'. It was important, he said, to keep the news private thanks to the prurience of the press; he had only just told John Hayward. He and Valerie were going off to the South of France for privacy and would return to look for a place to live. He expressed himself simply and clearly to Mary:

We love each other very much and are both sure that we are doing the right thing. I do hope, my dear Mary, that you will be a friend to both of us, for I have always prized your friendship and I should be very loth to lose it. But I do believe it is too firmly based for that.

> *With warm affection,*
> *Tom.*

Before I had read this letter they were already married, in a curiously furtive way, at 6 a.m. in a strange church – and had flown off to the South of France.

Valerie Fletcher had been Tom's secretary for eight years. I knew her very slightly. She is 38 years younger than he. I knew that she did not like me and I learned, after they had married, that she had boasted latterly of opening notes I had sent to Tom at his office (marked Private and Confidential), read them herself and destroyed the envelopes before giving him the notes. She has, says someone who knew her well, a strange power. And in his letter I noticed that he said: 'I am being married to . . .', not, 'I am marrying . . .' – perhaps true.

T. S. Eliot and Valerie Fletcher were married on 10 January 1957, at 6.15 am, in St Barnabas's Church in Addison Road, Kensington. She was thirty, he was sixty-eight. The priest who married them was a friend of Eliot's solicitor, Mr Higginson, who also served as best man.

The marriage was a shock to those who thought themselves closest to Eliot – Mary, John Hayward, Geoffrey Faber. But secrecy was in his nature. There was the swift recklessness of his first marriage; his conversion in 1927 was also conducted completely privately. When Eliot did not return to Carlyle Mansions on the morning of his wedding, John Hayward wrote to Helen Gardner: 'The Bard's elopement was a stunning surprise. I knew nothing and suspected nothing until he handed me a letter to read as he was leaving – literally leaving – the flat, to spend the night with his lawyer before the 6.15 am 25 guineas ceremony.' Years later Hayward told Anne Ridler: 'I am still, like Othello, puzzled in the extreme. I feel, after eleven years, as if Tom had suddenly died – at least to me; and I can only hope and pray he has done wisely and well and found the happiness life has hitherto denied him.' The friendship between the two men immediately began to thin and falter; in putting together the 1963 edition of his Collected Poems, *Eliot removed the dedication to Hayward which had originally been placed before* Four Quartets.

A few months before the marriage Hayward had told the American author John Malcolm Brinnin that he felt Eliot needed a nurse for his increasing ill health: 'I have an informed suspicion that the ever-adoring Miss Fletcher is ready to assume the role . . . There's somewhat more to that flower of the Yorkshire marches than meets the eye. The perfect secretary has begun to see herself as the lady with the lamp.'

Eliot wrote apologetically to Geoffrey Faber in a letter dated the day before the wedding:

I am sorry to have had to leave you, like nearly every one else, in the dark until the last moment. But there were three good reasons for concealing my plans from everyone except those who, like Higginson, to whom I propose tŏ hand this letter for you, have been instrumental in their execution.

By the time you get this I and my wife should be well on our way to the Côte d'Azur for three weeks. I am marrying Valerie Fletcher, whom you know only as my secretary for nearly eight years. We are utterly devoted to each other, and I know that I am very fortunate.

Valerie Fletcher's devotion to her husband had begun in her girlhood. That first encounter with his words, when she heard John Gielgud's recording of 'The Journey of the Magi', changed her: 'After that I tried to find out everything I could about him. It was something very sympathetic. His confessor once said of him in old age that he had a childlike heart. I think that was very true.' Valerie's dedication to Eliot opened his heart in a way, it seemed, he could never have expected. He would say that 'This last part of my life is the best, in excess of anything I could have deserved.'

What, then, of Mary? Her friendship was clearly a necessary support to him during the years after the final disintegration of his first marriage, and the failure of his relationship with Emily Hale. Her own account, below, gives an indication that she was aware of this. But despite her forthright demeanour, her apparent willingness to be a stalwart, platonic friend, Eliot's marriage hurt her profoundly: his secrecy; what she came to

see – surely not incorrectly – as his deception. Now she accepts his decep-
tiveness as a character trait; now she condemns, in the strongest terms,
what she would not condemn before.

I recalled Tom saying to me in the past: 'Miss Fletcher is an odd
girl. I don't understand her, she gives me the creeps – but she is
an efficient secretary.' On another occasion: 'I hid in the lavatory
this evening to avoid walking down the street with Miss Fletcher.'
Again, before leaving for America: 'Do ask Miss Fletcher in while I
am away and see what you make of her. Such a tiresome girl, she will
keep on working late. I do wish she wasn't so devoted.'

Naturally I thought Tom had gone out of his mind. He had given
me a false address in France (as I learned in the press) and, anyway, people don't want letters when on honeymoon. So I wrote to
the office a few days before their return. It was just a note of good
wishes and as kind as I could make it. I realised very clearly that it
was most unlikely that our friendship could continue under these
circumstances. When they returned to London I heard nothing at
all and, at the insistence of a mutual friend (anxious that I should not
sever connection with Tom, as one of his closest friends, whom he
might need one day) I wrote again, more warmly, assuring Tom that,
in spite of the initial shock, my affection for him would not change.
This produced a very angry reply, accusing me of 'gross impertinence'. So, once again, I was urged to write and did so, apparently
with more success.

His powerful reaction – their correspondence is reproduced below – is
notable: overblown, even. Perhaps it was influenced by Valerie; it is dif-
ficult for the reader to see just what so appalled him, though clearly he
took issue with Mary addressing him directly, and not writing jointly to
both husband and wife. But he must have known – surely he must have
known – that his secrecy would have hurt Mary. His outrage could well
be the product of a guilty conscience.

He replied on 24 March, apologising for letting so much time elapse; he had been ill with bronchitis, he told her, and been busy with getting into a new flat – he and Valerie planned to move in shortly. 'As soon as we are settled we intend to ask friends, a few at a time, for tea or sherry, and hope that you will be one of them.' He signed the note, 'Yours ever'.

After another long silence Tom wrote, at the end of July, to ask me, at two days' notice, to dine to meet his sister and niece whom, as he well knew, I had been seeing almost daily since their arrival in London a month previously. I pleaded a previous engagement and added that, after so long an interval, I thought it better that we should now wait for a time before meeting. At Christmas I sent them a card – and found I had been cut out of the famous Christmas Card list (though my Mother was still included, so Tom knew that I should see this) and received a non-Faber card, signed by them both, in reply. And that is the last contact I have had with them myself.

Most of Tom's old friends have been 'sent to Coventry' – (Geoffrey Faber, his friend and colleague of fifty years, received a letter, brought him by Tom's solicitor on the morning of the marriage, in which he learned, incidentally, that he had been deprived of a secretary) – but what is hardest to understand is Tom's treatment of John Hayward, his Literary Executor, Adviser and friend with whom he had lived for eight years. Except for two visits to the flat to collect Tom's possessions after their return from France, no attempt was made to keep up the friendship for six months. John was then invited to lunch – when Robert Frost and Rosamond Lehmann were also present. Out of politeness John said: 'You must come to tea one day' – but had no heart to press politeness further. Months later Tom's wife telephoned to say that they were still waiting for their invitation, and they duly came – an occasion which John found both embarrassing and distressing. Since then, except at rare intervals when they have been present at the same function and Tom has done his best to avoid him, John has not seen them or had any contact with them.

Although for many years he has 'vetted' every line of Tom's plays and had already worked on the first act of the new one, he has not been consulted any more, nor has he been shown the play at any stage.

We glean our news of Tom now from the 'obnoxious press', who appear to be welcomed. After the first publicity on their return from their honeymoon, we read of Tom dancing, on two successive nights, at Charity Balls and of his intention to take dancing lessons. Every mention of him seems to indicate a startling change of personality.

Many old men marry girls young enough to be their daughters, but few marry girls nearly forty years younger than themselves. I can understand very little, but there are certain possible factors which seem to stand out clearly, which might partly account for this change. Tom was becoming more and more hypochondriac, had always had a great fear of death and therefore was probably in a panic about the future. Also, of late years, he has found it less and less possible to 'take' criticism of his work and, indeed, any contradiction of his own opinion on any subject. He needed, maybe, someone who would always tell him he was right and everyone else was wrong. Valerie Fletcher (as she informed the press frequently) had 'hero-worshipped' him from the age of fourteen.

It is also possible, I am inclined to think, that Tom is a man whose strong sexual impulses have been deliberately frustrated for many years – some of his early (unpublished) poems give some indication of this. He has married again almost exactly ten years after the death of his first wife and it is possible to suppose that he may have set himself a period of 'expiation' (see *Family Reunion*) of ten years for his real, or imagined, part in the mental derangement which befell her.

But his behaviour to his friends, combined with his continued church-going (and his retaining of the church-wardenship which he had been so determined to relinquish) remains inexplicable. In fact, everything in his present 'goings-on' seems exactly contrary to his own rigid standards and his own 'way of life' for so many years. If any of his friends had, a few years ago, behaved as he has behaved, he would have been the first to express horror, distaste and condemnation.

Tom has always been a great 'runner-away' – he is extremely deceitful when it suits him and he would willingly sacrifice anybody and anything to get himself out of something which he doesn't want to face up to. I used to wonder sometimes how far he was aware of this.

It has been said of Carlyle: 'A writer, a painter, any creative artist must in his personal relationships be without ruth. His individuality is his all; it is his most precious possession not to be parted with by compromise; he dilutes it at his peril.' Perhaps Tom is a genius. Raymond Mortimer, reviewing a book in the *Observer* soon after Tom's marriage, wrote (under the heading of MEN OF GENIUS):

> Their work is noble and expresses the highest ideals; their behaviour was often deceitful, mean, malicious and disgustingly selfish. If men of genius sometimes seem to be nastier than the rest of us, it may be partly because they are less integrated and all their virtue is canalised into the art they produce. If we accept this view, we shall be less tempted to talk about hypocrisy which I believe to be the rarest of vices. Few of us can deceive ourselves continuously and sincerely: our right hand knows what our left has done; but we have a remarkable capacity for overlooking what is inconsistent or discreditable in our desires and behaviour.

An 'expert', who knows him well, says: 'Be sad for him, but not angry. He is not the man you knew – if you saw him you would realise this. He is not himself at present and, remember, he is not a free agent. He will become himself again, I am sure. He could not end like this. He will come back to being himself.' I don't know. In some ways I would like to believe this, yet I don't know if I could wish for him to come back to being himself – that might indeed be the greatest tragedy. I am sure he is not the person I knew – but have I known the real person? Have John and I known and loved the real man?

I am sorry that I have now finished my story and I am conscious of its many limitations. It has been written in all the spare moments I could find in the last year. No there is 'no to-morrow' – but I have had my years and I wouldn't have missed them. I have not yet become accustomed to there being 'nobody to hold one's hand and nobody to tell about it' – as Tom said of the period of his first wife's illness. And I still find myself turning, in moments of perplexity or amusement, to thinking of what Tom's reactions would be. I would like to be able to say to him: 'Fare Well, Fare Further and Come Back' – a good-bye which several times sent me off on long journeys abroad. But he has gone into a strange world, into which I cannot follow him and I doubt if he will be able to find his way back to the world which he has left so deliberately, a world in which he has left so great a sadness in the hearts of his friends. Even if he does return to himself, his pride is such that he might find it impossible to return to his old friends. If he does come back, I think it will be 'without warning and without explanation'.

I can only continue a practice of many years, in saying a nightly prayer for him in his own words:

> Protector of travellers
> Bless the road.
> Watch over him in the desert.
> Watch over him in the mountain.
> Watch over him in the labyrinth.
> Watch over him by the quicksand.
> Protect him from the Voices
> Protect him from the Visions
> Protect him in the tumult
> Protect him in the silence.

Chelsea
August 1958

Mary's final quotation is from The Cocktail Party, *the play in which she saw herself reflected: the last four lines here are Julia's. Below are their final exchanges; Mary, at least, had the final word. As far as the evidence reveals, Mary Trevelyan and T. S. Eliot never met again.*

FINAL CORRESPONDENCE

Typed letter from Mary, embossed with Embankment Gardens address. Dated Epiphany 1, 13 January, 1957

Dear Tom,

I must send a note to convey my good wishes for your happiness in your new life. Your letter was awaiting me when I returned from Oxford on Thursday evening, after a week of nightmare such as you only, of all my friends, could really understand.

Chelsea must now seem very satisfactorily far away to you. But the barges are still chugging up and down the river, the swans are still flying into the sunrise and there is a quiet, grey, Whistler mist over everything. The bulbs you bought at St Stephens's bazaar are just coming out.

Perhaps you and I mean rather different things by friendship. I sometimes think I have too simple a faith in very simple things. But musicians are always said to be uneducated. And I cannot change, as I have told you before.

God bless you always,

Yours ever, Mary

p.s. The clock in the car stopped on Thursday and shows no inclination to start again.

She writes again, by hand, on Thursday 14 February, a letter marked PRIVATE please.

My dear Tom,

I fear – I hope not impertinently – that you may be a little concerned about me – & that my note, in answer to your letter, may have seemed bitter, although it was not really so. I think it was the shock – I felt quite helpless & it was all I could do at the time.

Now more than a month has passed I am, as you will know, quite lost without you. I don't know if I am right to send you this letter, but I feel I must assure you that my feelings towards you have not changed. As you said yourself, our friendship over this last fifteen years is too firmly rooted now to be destroyed, and if ever you want to, and feel you can see me, I shall be glad. But I think I shall understand if it is not possible. What matters most to me is that you should know that my deep affection for you remains, that I have you constantly in mind & pray for you daily, as always.

Very dear Tom, I look on our long friendship, with all its ups and downs, as a very deeply valued possession – please understand this – & nobody can take it away from me. If you need me at any time, I hope to be at hand – & to understand if you don't.

If this note is all wrong, please forgive. I shall feel happier for having written it – & might now even think of beginning to read BLEAK HOUSE – which I haven't had the heart to do until now.

Yours ever, Mary

p.s. I hope to go on going to St Stephen's on Sunday mornings – in my usual place. I slip out quickly at this end – to catch a bus! – & to save embarrassment.

He writes back, 17 February, 1957, typed.

Dear Mary,

I received your letter of Thursday the 14th. In your previous note you suggested that your idea of friendship and mine might differ. I think that you are right on this point, for your letter of the 14th seems to me not only superfluous but a very gross breach of good manners. There should have been no need for me to remind you that I cannot accept your profession of friendship which ignores my wife and the fact that I am married. You say that you propose to continue to go to St Stephen's, but to slip out quickly in order to save embarrassment. I cannot understand why there should be the slightest embarrassment: there is certainly no reason for embarrassment on my side.

He signed off, 'Yours sincerely'. She replied, again on embossed stationery and typed, 23 February 1957:

My dear Tom,
I would have answered your letter of last Sunday sooner, but I was a little puzzled by it – perhaps you were a little puzzled by mine? Let me try to explain.

My 'profession of friendship' was in answer to your letter to me on the day before you were married. I didn't think of referring to your marriage, nor to Valerie, for I had already sent you my good wishes. It was a private letter to you, attempting to express my regret at not responding more immediately to your professions of friendship in your letter – and I did very much want to assure you that I both appreciated and reciprocated all you said.

As to the embarrassment – it was careless of me not to make clear that the embarrassment was mine. Since you both returned to England you have not got in touch with me, nor let me know where you were staying, and it seemed that you did not wish to see me.

I do hope that you are being successful in finding a pleasant flat and that you will let me know when I may see you both. I never give my friends wedding presents without enquiring what they would like – perhaps something for the flat?

And now, bien sûr, I send my greetings to you BOTH.
                              Yours ever,
                              Mary

24 March, 1957

Dear Mary,

I am sorry that I have had to let so much time elapse before acknowledging your letter of the 23rd February; but I was taken ill with
bronchitis at the Induction of the new vicar and have only been out
and about during the last few days.

We have at the same time been occupied with all that is involved
in taking a flat and furnishing it. We hope to move in within a fortnight or so, and as soon as we are settled intend to ask friends, a few
at a time, for tea or sherry, and hope that you will be one of them.

This letter he signed off with 'Yours ever'. Mary's final reply follows.

30 July, 1957

Dear Tom,

I do apologise for the delay in writing, but your letter has only just
reached me.

It is very kind of you both to invite me to dinner on Thursday
to meet Marian and Theodora. As I expect you know, I have been
seeing a good deal of them since they have been here & I think they
particularly enjoyed an expedition we made to see the Morsheads.

Actually I have another dinner engagement on Thursday, so I
couldn't accept your invitation. But in any case, after this long interval, perhaps it would be best to leave the question of our meeting
until a little later on.

I hope you are both well.

Yours ever,

Mary

AFTERWORD

Mary Trevelyan was devastated by the end of her friendship – her relationship – with T. S. Eliot. Anstice Goodman – later Lady Goodman, and, like Mary, a woman who devoted herself to helping those less fortunate than herself – worked with Mary raising money for the International Students House. In an interview after Mary's death she recalled the events of early 1957:

> Their relationship was like a platonic marriage. Going to church together, always one evening a week together . . . And almost before anyone realised what he was up to he walked out of his flat with John Hayward and got married to his secretary with never a word to Mary until afterwards . . . He did the same to John, his best friend, as he did to Mary. They were both equally hurt at the way he had done it. They couldn't get over it . . . She used to call it 'my jilting' but she was very hurt underneath. And she told me everything . . . She felt Eliot couldn't do without the spiritual side she had shared with him. It was very strong in her. She was a very attractive person – intensely attractive in a non-sexual way. Charisma. She talked to you so personally. So it was killing for her to think of Eliot being with Valerie. She couldn't see it like others saw it. She never did accept it. She could never see he needed this sexual side. Eliot didn't take Mary seriously as a woman. He wanted her friendship.

When Eliot died in 1965, neither John nor Mary attended his funeral: that was how deep what they both felt as his betrayal cut.

Mary was mystified by her friend's devotion to Valerie. 'Naturally I thought Tom had gone out of his mind.' Yet he was, by all accounts, blissfully happy in this late love: 'Eliot came to recognise in his secretary the absolute dedication of an ideal heir,' Lyndall Gordon writes. But it was much more than Valerie's dedication to his work that moved him: at parties they stood arm in arm; in company, he would hold her hand. When they moved to the flat which still houses Eliot's archive, in Kensington Court Gardens, he would write at home in the mornings; later in the day the pair would walk in Kensington Gardens. In some respects, their entertainments – the cinema, the theatre, listening to the gramophone – replicated the evenings he had spent with Mary.

Eliot was happier, more relaxed. His final play, *The Elder Statesman*, did not receive the warmest notices; he was, however, sanguine. 'Love reciprocated is always rejuvenating. Before my marriage I was getting older. Now I feel younger at seventy than I did at sixty . . . An experience like mine makes all the more difference because of its contrast with the past.' Mary had often written of Eliot as an old man; his marriage – and no doubt his sexual relationship with Valerie – had a tonic effect. Interviewing Valerie Eliot thirty years after the poet's death, Blake Morrison alluded to the sexual difficulties Eliot might have encountered with Vivien. Valerie Eliot answered briskly: 'There was nothing wrong with Tom, if that's your implication.'

It is hardly surprising, however, that Mary failed to come to terms with the end of their friendship – with the way Eliot treated her. It is difficult to get away from the sense that once she – and indeed John Hayward – were no longer strictly useful to Eliot, he could dispense with them, despite his offer of continued friendship. He may also have been embarrassed: fearing their judgement of Valerie, fearing their judgement of himself for falling for her. Mary's questions to herself, about whether she ever knew the real person, the real man, have the ring of truth about them. Lyndall Gordon has written perceptively about the way in which the women who were connected to Eliot's creative life were 'kept under wraps'; she has also noted that despite the cleverness of his sisters Ada and Charlotte, and their accomplishments – not to mention the accomplishments of his 'sensible Boston cousins Martha and Abigail Eliot', themselves distinguished professional women – he struggled to perceive women as complete human beings. 'It is puzzling that women kin to Eliot in no way shaped his judgement of their sex, as though that judgement excluded every attribute women share with men beyond sexual instinct,' as Gordon writes. His relationship with Emily Hale came to a final end at this point too, though their intimate connection had long ago ceased; she was devastated at the news of his marriage and retired from Abbot Academy. Their correspondence, given to Princeton University, was only unsealed in the first weeks of 2020.

Stephen Spender's judgement of 'The Waste Land' is interesting in its observation regarding Eliot's interest – or lack of interest – when it came to the question of character: 'The psychology of his people is just as crude,' Spender wrote.

His ladies, his bank clerks, his Sweeneys, his Mrs Porters, his pub conversationalists, are all part of the world of thugs. Psychologically they are far cruder than the Babbitts and other creations of Sinclair Lewis. One of the most astonishing things about Eliot is that a poet with such a strong dramatic style should seem so blinded to the existence of people outside himself.

Eliot was, it seems, genuinely startled that Mary could take his marriage amiss in the way that she did, but it is clear – finally – that throughout their friendship his focus was always on himself, and on his own needs and requirements.

Mary – unsurprisingly, given her strong will, her enthusiasm for the world around her, her strength and energy – picked herself up, dusted herself off, and continued to lead a vigorous life. Her travels continued unabated: in 1962, for instance, she spent the month of April studying the educational systems of the United States, also discussing, while she was there, the teaching being done across the African continent. She had been invited by the National Association of Foreign Student Advisors, and among the institutions she visited were Teachers College at Columbia University in New York City. She looked in at the UN, to examine the United Nations Interns Programmes and Fellowships, and there was the Greater New York Council for Foreign Students at New York University. She went on to Boston, to Harvard, to Brandeis, then over to the University of Minnesota and to Berkeley, in California. She went to Atlanta, Georgia, too, where she was especially concerned with the situation of Black students. 'A luncheon (held, significantly, in a restaurant on the outskirts of the town) was arranged for me to meet Negro educators,' she wrote in her account of the trip.

> Presidents, Deans and Foreign Student Advisers in Negro colleges. Fourteen were present, including Dr Benjamin Mays, President of Morehouse . . . after a very lively and friendly lunch there was a long discussion, in which everybody spoke with freedom. I was impressed (not for the first time) with the patience, restraint and humour of these Negro leaders.

On a day off in New York she made time to visit the Frick Collection on Fifth Avenue: she pasted the postcards she collected into her diary, just as she had pasted postcards into the manuscript of *The Pope of Russell Square*. But it wasn't all high art: she was taken off for a tour of the city by her friends Al and Christine Kibel:

> I don't know where we didn't go. First to lunch in an Automat in the Bronx (a splendid inspiration, as I was determined not to be an expense to them) – the food was trying, the crowd fascinating – poor, old, beatniks. Christine, who is really very nice, said she hated coming there at night, because there were so many old poor men, who couldn't afford proper meals.

They went on to the Cloisters, to Wall Street, to the Village, 'ending with an ice cream soda in a low dive!' What a day!

At the end of 1964 and the beginning of 1965 she travelled to Moscow, where her brother Humphrey was now British Ambassador. She stayed at the ambassadorial residence: 'From my bed I can see the towering Kremlin – with the great towers sporting great RED STARS, electrically lit.' She had to find herself a German hairdresser; the Russian ones took three hours, apparently. As ever, her open-mindedness is on display. She was the first person from the Embassy to visit the Peoples' Friendship University 'Patrice Lumumba' – named for the African nationalist leader who was the first Prime Minister of the Democratic Republic of the Congo; he was assassinated in 1961. The university had been founded in 1960 for students from developing countries and was a beacon of Soviet internationalism. Yet it was only Mary who had the vim to actually go there. She travelled by sleeper train – on the famous 'Red Arrow' – to Leningrad, as St Petersburg was called then. The city, she said simply, 'bears some likeness to Bath'. Somehow, that remark is Mary in a nutshell.

She returned from the Soviet Union on 11 January; Eliot had died just the week before. Her travels did not cease. She went 'round the world in ninety days', from the beginning of October 1967 through to February of the following year, visiting twenty-six different places in twelve countries and travelling by sixteen different airlines: her business to see as many International Student Houses and Centres as possible in the four months at her disposal. She spent a month in the United States and Canada, a month in South-East Asia, a month in Australia and New Zealand and a month in India, Ceylon and Pakistan. The trip was enabled by a Ford Foundation Award in order to make a study of the principal International Houses and Centres for students, and to confer with leaders on the issues students faced, to meet with the Houses' directors and to consider the impact of international and race relations on student communities across the globe. She would travel through the Middle East and North Africa, visiting Tangier, Cairo – from where her brother had been expelled – Cyprus and Jerusalem.

In October 1956 she established her 'Goats Club' (see above, p. 240). By then there were tens of thousands of foreign students in London; it was clear to Mary that there was a real need for an International House. With her customary energy, she was able to form a charitable trust in 1962; this would bring International Students House in Park Crescent, W1, into being at last. When it opened in May 1965, 'she had achieved her cherished dream and the peak of her career', as *The Times* would put it; she was its first Director until her retirement in 1967.

Mary was made a CBE in 1968. She always took special pride in what she had achieved with her 'Goats': 'Goats have spread all over the world in the short space of four years,' she wrote in 1962.

Former members, Old Goats, go to endless trouble after they have returned home to keep in touch by writing and by meeting each other in many different countries. Last year a Japanese 'goat' met a Scottish 'goat' on the streets of Tokyo, by chance, and wrote an enthusiastic letter describing this reunion. A West Indian 'goat' holidaying in Norway met a Norwegian 'goat', also by chance and was promptly invited to his wedding.

When Mary died in January 1983, a letter of condolence letter was sent to her brother, Humphrey Carpenter, from Martin Gilliat, Private Secretary to the Queen Mother:

Queen Elizabeth the Queen Mother has asked me to tell you how much you and the members of your family are in her thoughts at this time. The Queen Mother had such a very high regard for Mary and admired so greatly her wonderful achievements as the Pioneer in the field of international students in the widest sense . . .

The Queen Mother wishes you to know what a privilege she feels it has been to have been associated with Mary in the work of International Students House.

Mary's relationship with T. S. Eliot by no means defined her life. But she carefully preserved her record of their long friendship; even decades later, the pain of its ending rings clear. But as Humphrey Carpenter wrote, she staked a great deal on that friendship:

It is understandable that she interpreted his marriage – whether or not he meant her to – as the final rejection. A more perceptive person might have seen that some such conclusion to their strange relationship was inevitable; but Mary did not think that way, and if she had, Eliot would never have enjoyed her friendship. She was not the sort of person who analysed behaviour. She had offered him jovial, uncomplicated companionship – the same glass of gin, the same sausages in the kitchen, as she gave her nephews and nieces, the same records and piano-playing and cheerful chat, a contact with a certain sort of Englishness that he maybe valued for its roots in his adoptive country's clerical and aristocratic past.

She would have wished for more than those glasses of gin, that cheerful chat. But perhaps now she has – at least – made her true feelings known. 'Although his company was a constant pleasure to me, he was not an easy friend,' she wrote of their years together. But by her lights he was much more than a friend; what she has left is a testament of love.

ABBREVIATIONS AND
BRIEF BIBLIOGRAPHY

ABBREVIATIONS FOR PUBLISHED SOURCES

ENL: Gordon, Lyndall, *Eliot's New Life* (Oxford: Oxford University Press, 1988).

FEE: Trevelyan, Mary, *From the Ends of the Earth* (London: Faber and Faber, 1942).

L1: *The Letters of T. S. Eliot, Volume 1: 1898–1922*, revised edn, ed. Valerie Eliot and Hugh Haughton (London: Faber and Faber, 2009).

L2: *The Letters of T. S. Eliot, Volume 2: 1923–1925*, ed. Valerie Eliot and Hugh Haughton (London: Faber and Faber, 2009).

L5: *The Letters of T. S. Eliot Volume 5: 1930–1931*, ed. Valerie Eliot and John Haffenden (London: Faber and Faber, 2014).

L6: *The Letters of T. S. Eliot, Volume 6: 1932–1933*, ed. Valerie Eliot and John Haffenden (London: Faber and Faber, 2016).

L7: *The Letters of T. S. Eliot, Volume 7: 1934–1935*, ed. Valerie Eliot and John Haffenden (London: Faber and Faber, 2017).

L8: *The Letters of T. S. Eliot, Volume 8: 1936–1938*, ed. Valerie Eliot and John Haffenden (London: Faber and Faber, 2019).

L9: *The Letters of T. S. Eliot, Volume 9: 1939–1941*, ed. Valerie Eliot and John Haffenden (London: Faber and Faber, 2021).

TSEAIL: Gordon, Lyndall, *T. S. Eliot: An Imperfect Life* (London: W. W. Norton, 2000).

UNPUBLISHED SOURCES

These sources were written by Mary Trevelyan and belong to her estate unless otherwise indicated below.

Oxford, Bodleian Libraries, MS. Dep. c. 969, Mary Trevelyan's typescript of *The Pope of Russell Square*

Private diaries, 1951–73.

Letters from Mary Trevelyan to J. D. Hayward, King's College Cambridge archive, HB/L/12/16.

Diary of a journey to Ceylon, India, Burma, Malay, China, Japan, America, December 1936–July 1937.

WD: War Diaries, October 1940–August 1941.

Burma report: Report on Burma recently visited in the course of undertaking educational surveys in war-devastated countries of South East Asia, for UNESCO, 1947–8.

'New Moon on Burma', 1948: a report for the UNESCO Foreign Office of Mary's mission there to make surveys of the damage done to education, science and culture in the war-devastated countries of South-East Asia.

MT/Africa/54: 'Report on a British Council Lecture Tour in West and East Africa', 3 January–12 April 1954.

Report on the National Association of Foreign Student Advisers Study-Tour, 1–29 April 1962.

Notes on a visit to Moscow and Leningrad, 28 December 1964–11 January 1965.

'Round the world in ninety days': notes on a world tour, 1 October 1967–February 1968.

Photo album, Middle East and North Africa tour, 13 April–4 July 1969.

Transcript of Lady Goodman (Anstice Goodman) and Lady Daphne Grierson being interviewed by John Charles, 7 March 1989.

PUBLISHED SOURCES

Ackroyd, Peter, *T. S. Eliot: A Life* (London: Hamish Hamilton, 1984).

Aiken, Conrad, *A Reviewer's ABC: Collected Criticism of Conrad Aiken, from 1916 to the Present* (New York: Greenwich Editions/Meridian Books, 1958).

Behr, Caroline, *T. S. Eliot: A Chronology of His Life and Works* (London: Macmillan, 1983).

Blackmur, R. P., *The Lion and the Honeycomb* (New York: Harcourt Brace, 1955).

Boahen, A. Adu, and John Wolfe, *50 Years of International Students House* (London: International Students House, 2010).

Bourque, Stephen, 'Rouen: La Semaine Rouge', *Journal of Military and Strategic Studies* 14 (2012).

Bradshaw, David, '"Oxford Poets": Yeats, T. S. Eliot and William Force Stead', *Yeats's Mask: Yeats Annual* 19 (2013), pp. 77–102.

Brinnin, John Malcom, *Sextet: T. S. Eliot & Truman Capote & Others* (London: André Deutsch, 1981).

Carpenter, Humphrey, 'Poor Tom: Mary Trevelyan's View of T. S. Eliot', *English* 38 (1989), pp. 37–52.

Clarke, Richard, Elizabeth McKellar and Michael Symes, 'Russell Square: A Lifelong Resource for Teaching and Learning', Faculty of Continuing Education, FCE Occasional Paper No. 5, December 2004.

Cracknell, H. L., and G. Nobis, *Practical Professional Gastronomy* (Basingstoke: Macmillan, 1985).

Crawford, Robert, *Young Eliot: From St Louis to The Waste Land* (London: Vintage, 2016).

Dale, Alzina Stone, *T. S. Eliot, The Philosopher Poet* (Lincoln, NE: Authors Guild, 2004).

Devine Thomas, Kelly, 'T. S. Eliot at the Institute for Advanced Study', 2007, https://www.ias.edu/ideas/2007/ts-eliot-ias (accessed 10 January 2022).

Dickey, Frances, and John D. Morgenstern, *The Edinburgh Companion to T. S. Eliot and the Arts* (Edinburgh: Edinburgh University Press, 2016).

Eliot, T. S., *The Cocktail Party* (New York: Harcourt, Brace and Company, 1950).

———, 'Reunion by Destruction: Reflections on a Scheme for Church Union in South India – Addressed to the Laity', Council for the Defence of Church Principles, pamphlet 7 (London: Pax House, 1943).

———, *Selected Essays, 1917–1932* (New York: Harcourt, Brace and Company, 1932).

———, *To Criticize the Critic*, second edition (London: Faber and Faber, 1978).

———, *The Letters of T. S. Eliot, Volume 1: 1898–1922*, revised edn, ed. Valerie Eliot and Hugh Haughton (London: Faber and Faber, 2009).

———, *The Letters of T. S. Eliot, Volume 2: 1923–1925*, ed. Valerie Eliot and Hugh Haughton (London: Faber and Faber, 2009).

———, *The Letters of T. S. Eliot Volume 5: 1930–1931*, ed. Valerie Eliot and John Haffenden (London: Faber and Faber, 2014).

———, *The Letters of T. S. Eliot, Volume 6: 1932–1933*, ed. Valerie Eliot and John Haffenden (London: Faber and Faber, 2016).

———, *The Letters of T. S. Eliot, Volume 7: 1934–1935*, ed. Valerie Eliot and John Haffenden (London: Faber and Faber, 2017).

———, *The Letters of T. S. Eliot, Volume 8: 1936–1938*, ed. Valerie Eliot and John Haffenden (London: Faber and Faber, 2019).

———, *The Letters of T. S. Eliot, Volume 9: 1939–1941*, ed. Valerie Eliot and John Haffenden (London: Faber and Faber, 2021).

———, *The Poems of T. S. Eliot, Volume I, Collected and Uncollected Poems*, ed. Christopher Ricks and Jim McCue (London, Faber and Faber, 2015).

———, *The Poems of T. S. Eliot, Volume II, Practical Cats and Further Verses*, ed. Christopher Ricks and Jim McCue (London, Faber and Faber, 2015).

Eliot, T. S., et al., *Murder in the Cathedral* film leaflet (London: Westminster Press, 1952).

Evans, T. F. (ed.), *Shaw: The Critical Heritage* (London: Routledge & Kegan Paul, 1976).

Faber, Toby, *Faber and Faber: The Untold Story* (London: Faber and Faber, 2019).

Forster, E. M., 'T. S. Eliot and His Difficulties', *Life and Letters* 2 (1929), pp. 417–25.

Gates, Henry Louis, Jr, and Evelyn Brooks Higginbotham (eds), *Harlem*

Renaissance Lives from the African American National Biography (Oxford: Oxford University Press, 2000).

Geary, M., 'The "Agèd Eagle": Jacob Epstein, T. S. Eliot (1952)', *Midlands Art Papers* 2 (2018/19).

Gordon, Lyndall, *Eliot's New Life* (Oxford: Oxford University Press, 1988).

Gordon, Lyndall, *T. S. Eliot: An Imperfect Life* (London: W. W. Norton, 2000).

Hall, Donald, *Remembering Poets: Reminiscences and Opinions* (New York and London: Harper & Row, 1978).

Harrison, Brian, *Seeking a Role: The United Kingdom 1951–70* (Oxford: Clarendon Press, 2009).

Haughton, Hugh, 'The Possum and the Salamander: T. S. Eliot and Marianne Moore', https://poetrysociety.org.uk/essay-hugh-haughton-on-the-possum -and-the-salamander-t-s-eliot-and-marianne-moore (accessed 11 January 2022).

Ikonne, Chidi, 'Opportunity and Black Literature, 1923–1933', *Phylon* 40 (1979), pp. 86–93.

Isaacs, Jacob, *An Assessment of Twentieth-Century Literature: Six Lectures Delivered in the BBC Third Programme* (London: Secker & Warburg, 1952).

Johnson, Douglas, 'Churchill and France', in Robert Blake and Wm Roger Louis (eds), *Churchill* (Oxford: Clarendon Press, 1996).

Jolly, Emma, 'Cultural Imperialism at Home? Mary Trevelyan and Student Movement House, 1932–1946', unpublished thesis, Sheffield Hallam University, 2014.

Julius, Anthony, *T. S. Eliot, Anti-Semitism, and Literary Form* (Cambridge: Cambridge University Press, 1995).

Kindley, Evan, 'The Insanity Defense: Coming to Terms with Ezra Pound's Politics', *The Nation*, 23 April 2018, https://www.thenation.com/article/ archive/coming-to-terms-with-ezra-pounds-politics (accessed 10 January 2022).

Levy, William Turner, *Affectionately, T. S. Eliot: The Story of a Friendship: 1947– 1965* (London: Dent, 1968).

Manning, Sam, *Cinemas and Cinema-going in the United Kingdom: Decades of Decline, 1945–65* (London: University of London Press, 2020).

Matthews, T. S., *Great Tom: Notes towards the Definition of T. S. Eliot* (London: Weidenfeld and Nicolson, 1974).

Miller, James E., Jr, *T. S. Eliot: The Making of an American Poet, 1888–1922* (University Park, PA: Pennsylvania State University Press, 2005).

Morley, Frank Vigor, and J. S. Hodgson, *Whaling, North and South* (New York: Century, 1926).

Morrell, Ottoline, *Ottoline at Garsington: Memoirs of Lady Ottoline Morrell, 1915– 1918*, ed. Robert Gathorne-Hardy (London: Faber and Faber, 1974).

Murray, Alan, 'I'll walk beside you', words by E. Lockton (London: Chappell & Co., 1936).

Nott, John, *The Cook's and Confectioner's Dictionary, or, the Accomplish'd Housewife's Companion*, fourth edition (London: Charles Rivington, 1733).

Orwell, George, *Seeing Things As They Are: Selected Journalism and Other Writings*, ed. Peter Davison (London: Penguin, 2016).

Oxford Dictionary of National Biography, www.oxforddnb.com.

Pasternak Slater, Ann, *The Fall of a Sparrow: Vivien Eliot's Life and Writings* (London: Faber and Faber, 2020).

Pearson, Graham, 'Mrs Edith Carroll Perkins and Chipping Campden Gardens', *Signpost: The Journal of Chipping Campden History Society* 8 (spring 2018), pp. 12–15.

The Queen's Book of the Red Cross (London: Hodder & Stoughton, 1939).

Ridler, Anne, *Working for T. S. Eliot: A Personal Reminiscence* (London: Enitharmon Press, 2000).

Rochester, John Wilmot, Earl of, *Collected Works*, ed. John Hayward (London: Nonesuch Press, 1926).

Rubin, Martin, *Sarah Gertrude Millin: A South African Life* (Johannesburg: Ad. Donker, 1977).

Schneider, Elisabeth W., *T. S. Eliot: The Pattern in the Carpet* (Berkeley: University of California Press, 1975).

Scholes, Robert, *Paradoxy of Modernism* (New Haven and London: Yale University Press, 2006).

Simpson, Eileen, *Poets in their Youth: A Memoir* (New York: Farrar, Straus and Giroux, 2014).

Smart, John, *Tarantula's Web: John Hayward, T. S. Eliot and Their Circle* (Norwich: Michael Russell, 2013).

Spender, Stephen, *The Destructive Element: A Study of Modern Writers and Beliefs* (London: Jonathan Cape, 1935).

——, *World Within World: The Autobiography of Stephen Spender* (Berkeley: University of California Press, 1966).

Tambimuttu and Richard March (eds), *T. S. Eliot: A Symposium* (London: Frank & Cass, 1965).

Tomlin, E. W. F., *T. S. Eliot: A Friendship* (Abingdon: Routledge, 2016).

Trevelyan, Laura, *A Very British Family: The Trevelyans and their World* (London: I. B. Tauris, 2006).

Trevelyan, Mary, *From the Ends of the Earth* (London: Faber and Faber, 1942).

——, *I'll Walk Beside You: Letters from Belgium, September 1944–May 1945* (London: Longmans, Green & Co., 1946).

Wearing, J. P., *The London Stage 1950–1959: A Calendar of Productions, Performers, and Personnel* (Plymouth: Rowman & Littlefield, 2014).

Williams, Charles, *All Hallows' Eve*, introduction by T. S. Eliot (New York: Pellegrini & Cudahy, 1948).

Wilson, Sondra Kathryn (ed.), *The Opportunity Reader* (New York: Random House, 1999).

Winston Dixon, Wheeler, 'Cinema and Poetry: T. S Eliot's *Murder in the Cathedral*', *Senses of Cinema*, 2016, https://www.sensesofcinema.com/2016/feature-articles/murder-in-the-cathedral *(accessed 21 January 2022)*.

Woolf, Virginia, *The Diary of Virginia Woolf*, volume 2: *1920–24*, ed. Anne Oliver Bell and Andrew McNeillie (London: Penguin, 1981).

——, *A Moment's Liberty: The Shorter Diary*, ed. Anne Olivier Bell (London: Hogarth Press, 1990).

NOTES

Quotations from Eliot's poetry throughout the volume are taken from *The Poems of T. S. Eliot*, volumes 1 and 2, *Collected and Uncollected Poems*, ed. Christopher Ricks and Jim McCue (London: Faber and Faber, 2015).

INTRODUCTION

2   *'He feels very superior'*: Mary Trevelyan, *The Pope of Russell Square*, unpublished MS, 8 September 1955.

2   *'the Saint of the West'*: James E. Miller, Jr, *T. S. Eliot: The Making of an American Poet, 1888–1922* (University Park, PA: Pennsylvania State University Press, 2005), p. 10.

2   *Noah Webster, Herman Melville, Nathaniel Hawthorne*: ENL, pp. 15–16.

2   *'Eliots, non-Eliots and foreigners'*: Trevelyan, *Pope*, 2 April 1951.

3   *'In their speech'*: Humphrey Carpenter, 'Poor Tom: Mary Trevelyan's View of T. S. Eliot', *English* 38 (1989), pp. 37–52, at p. 37.

3   *'the supreme social self-confidence'*: Carpenter, 'Poor Tom', p. 37.

3   *'not tall, but broadly built'*: Carpenter, 'Poor Tom', p. 38.

3   *more than just the daughter of a Victorian vicarage*: Emma Jolly, 'Cultural Imperialism at Home? Mary Trevelyan and Student Movement House, 1932–1946', unpublished thesis, Sheffield Hallam University, 2014, p. 33.

4   *'integrity to the point of eccentricity'*: quoted in Laura Trevelyan, *A Very British Family: The Trevelyans and their World* (London: I. B. Tauris, 2006), p. 1.

4   *'The door would swing open'*: Carpenter, 'Poor Tom', p. 38.

4   *Music was her love*: Carpenter, 'Poor Tom', p. 37.

5   *'In London, I noticed groups of Indians'*: A. du Boahen and John Wolfe, *50 Years of International Students House* (London: International Students House, 2010), p. 1, quoting Mary Trevelyan typescript, 'The World on our Doorstep', p. 4.

6   *'mobile canteen trucks'*: Mary Trevelyan, *I'll Walk Beside You: Letters from Belgium, September 1944–May 1945* (London: Longmans, Green & Co., 1946), p. 11.

6   *'I found it rather tedious'*: Trevelyan, *I'll Walk*, pp. 11–12.

6   *a strong proponent of ecumenism*: Jolly, 'Cultural Imperialism', p. 20.

7   *'It became evident'*: Carpenter, 'Poor Tom', p. 38.

7 *'tied together with string'*: FEE, p. 101.

7 *'glad to give the last twenty years of its life'*: Boahen and Wolfe, *50 Years*, p. 6, from an unpublished typescript by Mary Trevelyan, p. 6.

8 *pay what they could afford*: FEE, p. 39.

8 *no fear of the doors being closed*: FEE, p. 19. The Trinidadian historian C. L. R. James would write that: 'Were it not for a few institutions like the Student Movement House . . . the average West Indian student would have a dreadful time.' C. L. R. James, *Christian Høgsbjerg Toussaint Louverture: The Story of the Only Successful Slave Revolt in History* (Durham, NC: Duke University Press, 2012), 'Appendix', p. 206.

8 *'Just because he has been born under a tropical sun?'*: FEE, p. 50.

8 *'Dear Mr Elliott'*: Correspondence between T. S. Eliot and Mary Trevelyan, T. S. Eliot Estate.

9 *'I decided to write a diary'*: Trevelyan, *Pope*, Preface. She kept a daily journal too; it seems, however, that the notes on her meetings with Eliot were always recorded separately.

10 *'gossip about Church of England matters'*: Carpenter, 'Poor Tom', p. 40.

11 *'felt this to be quite unfair . . . strength of feeling'*: Carpenter, 'Poor Tom', p. 40.

11 *'I went there in rather a bad temper'*: Carpenter, 'Poor Tom', p. 40.

11 *'the fullest record we shall have'*: TSEAIL, p. 439.

11 *'severely bowdlerised . . . full story'*: Carpenter, 'Poor Tom', p. 41.

12 *'the moral spokesman . . . stranger and more intolerant'*: TSEAIL, p. 2.

1938

15 *three aims for this round-the-world trip*: FEE, p. 70.

15 *'as if the whole British Empire was crumbling'*: FEE, pp. 73–4.

16 *'once there it was marvellous'*: FEE, p. 81.

16 *'the behaviour of some English people'*: FEE, p. 79.

16 *'the "stalls" had no seats'*: FEE, p. 90.

16 *'a completely new country to me'*: FEE, p. 90.

16 *'appeared to be tied together with string'*: FEE, p. 101.

16 *'I could not fail to be charmed'*: FEE, p. 104.

16 *to see the International Houses*: FEE, p. 114.

16 *'True international friendship'*: FEE, p. 118.

16 *a 'particular problem'*: FEE, p. 121.

17 *a significant figure in the civil rights movement*: Henry Louis Gates, Jr, and Evelyn Brooks Higginbotham (eds), *Harlem Renaissance Lives from the African American National Biography* (Oxford: Oxford University Press, 2000), p. 103.

17 'a man of great wisdom and balance': FEE, p. 122.

17 'I thought of the many coloured students': FEE, pp. 122–3.

17 'a very tall, thin house': FEE, p. 128.

17 'now, if ever, was the time': FEE, p. 135.

18 'the most difficult period': FEE, p. 134.

18 'Mr Eliot's work . . . most important author of their day': E. M. Forster,
    'T. S. Eliot and His Difficulties', in Life and Letters 2 (June 1929), pp. 417–25.

18 He spent eight years working there: https://tseliot.com/foundation/t-s-eliot
    -at-lloyds-bank-2 (accessed 4 August 2021); Robert Crawford, Young Eliot:
    From St Louis to The Waste Land (London: Vintage, 2016), p. 270.

19 firmly established in the literary firmament: Caroline Behr, T. S. Eliot: A
    Chronology of His Life and Works (London: Macmillan, 1983), p. 24.

19 Eliot had been invited by George Bell: Behr, Chronology, p. 46.

19 'here at last was the English language literally being used': Conrad Aiken,
    A Reviewer's ABC: Collected Criticism of Conrad Aiken, from 1916 to the
    Present (New York: Greenwich Editions/Meridian Books, 1958), p. 192.

19 The play opened in London . . . before crossing the Atlantic: Behr, Chronology,
    pp. 47–50.

20 'I well remember that first visit': And yet in the manuscript she mis-dates this
    first encounter, placing it in 1938, not 1936 when it in fact occurred (L8,
    p. 298). It seems likely too that Emily Hale did not accompany him to this
    first encounter, but to another reading in London; Mary's insertion of Hale
    here may – perhaps – indicate a romantic perception from Eliot from their
    earliest meeting.

20 'Here is Lady Proctor': L8, p. 299.

21 'Pale, marmoreal Eliot': Wednesday 16 February 1921, Virginia Woolf,
    A Moment's Liberty: The Shorter Diary, ed. Anne Olivier Bell (London:
    Hogarth Press, 1990), p. 121.

21 'a very confused and unintelligible manner': Ann Pasternak Slater, The Fall of a
    Sparrow: Vivien Eliot's Life and Writings (London: Faber and Faber, 2020),
    p. 369.

21 'she had been committed to Northumberland House': TSEAIL, p. 301 ff.

21 Her father was a Unitarian minister . . . : Crawford, Young Eliot, p. 189.

21 She attended Miss Porter's School in Connecticut: TSEAIL, pp. 76, 80–1.

22 Emily's 'attachment to Eliot': TSEAIL, p. 83.

1940

23 Student Movement House departed Russell Square: FEE, p. 141.

23 'We all crowd in': FEE, p. 146.

23   *the last edition of the Criterion appeared*: Behr, *Chronology*, p. 52.

23   *its cover drawn by Eliot himself*: Behr, *Chronology*, p. 53.

23   *In February came 'The Waste Land' and Other Poems*: Behr, *Chronology*, p. 54.

24   *'interminable night'*: Ricks/McCue, vol. 1, p. 203; Behr, *Chronology*, p. 57.

24   *'For the first time in its history'*: *FEE*, p. 153.

24   *'We were windowless'*: *FEE*, p. 154.

24   *'A perfectly hellish night'*: WD.

24   a recital by Peter Stadlen: https://www.rcm.ac.uk/singingasong/ featuredmusicians/peterstalden (accessed 10 January 2022); *FEE*, p. 151.

24   *Pre-Internment Dance*: *FEE*, p. 152.

25   *'All over the world, in Germany, Japan'*: *FEE*, pp. 156–7.

1941

26   *'new Christian activism'*: Peter Ackroyd, *T. S. Eliot: A Life* (London: Hamish Hamilton, 1984), p. 242.

27   *participation in traditional Christian life was beginning to decline*: Clive D. Field, 'Puzzled People Revisited: Religious Believing and Belonging in Wartime Britain, 1939–45', *Twentieth Century British History* 19 (2008), pp. 446–79; Thomas William Heyck, 'The Decline of Christianity in Twentieth-Century Britain', *Albion* 28 (1996), pp. 437–53.

27   *It wasn't only his decision . . . His doubts were overruled*: T. S. Eliot, Report to the Faber Book committee on Mary Trevelyan's *Strangers and Sojourners*, 1941, Faber Archive.

27   *'Christians meet to answer listeners' questions'*: *Radio Times*, 6 May 1943, https://genome.ch.bbc.co.uk/schedules/bbchomeservice/basic/1943-05-06 (accessed 10 January 2022).

28   *He wrote to Martin Browne*: *TSEAIL*, p. 385, from E. Martin Browne, *The Making of T. S. Eliot's Plays* (Cambridge: Cambridge University Press, 1969; revised edn, 1970), p. 158, letter 20 October 1942.

28   *'bleak resignation'*: Behr, *Chronology*, p. 55.

28   *a limerick on the title page*: *The Poems of T. S. Eliot*, ed. Christopher Ricks and Jim McCue, vol. 2 (London: Faber and Faber, 2015), p. 187.

1942

31   Meary James Thurairajah Tambimuttu: http://www.open.ac.uk/ researchprojects/makingbritain/content/meary-james-tambimuttu (accessed 10 January 2022).

31   *the marriage was difficult*: information provided by John Haffenden.

31   *Mary and Eliot together tried to persuade*: unpublished letter, 1107/72/42, T. S. Eliot to Philip Cox, 16 February 1942, and footnotes; courtesy John Haffenden.

31   *He often wrote to her from Shamley Green*: *L8*, note to letter dated 17 August 1936.

31   *The household was a large one*: *TSEAIL*, p. 367.

32   *The first complete typescript*: *TSEAIL*, p. 379.

32   *Eliot often read the Remus stories aloud*: *TSEAIL*, p. 367.

33   'singularly moving, singularly beautiful': Desmond MacCarthy, 'A Religious Poem', *Times Literary Supplement*, 19 December 1942, p. 622.

33   'They talk a lot of nonsense': *FEE*, p. 12.

35   'The dislocating effects of war': *Irish Independent*, 18 May 1942, p. 2.

35   *According to Tatler*: *Tatler*, 8 July 1942, p. 56.

35   'a fascinating account': *Manchester Evening News*, quote reproduced on front flap of *FEE*.

35   *a lively woman and a fine dancer*: Crawford, *Young Eliot*, p. 226; *L2*, p. 740.

35   *They married at the end of June*: *TSEAIL*, pp. 114–15.

36   *all I wanted of Vivien was a flirtation*: *L1*, p. xix.

36   *The qualities that had attracted him*: *TSEAIL*, pp. 114–15, 120.

36   'black silent moods': V. to Charlotte Eliot, 8 April 1917, *L1*, p. 173.

36   'Tom is IMpossible': V. to Mary Hutchinson, 16 July 1919, *L1*, p. 320.

36   'Was there ever such a torture': Woolf, *A Moment's Liberty*, p. 289.

36   *Eliot had left her in 1933*: Pasternak Slater, *The Fall of a Sparrow*, p. 369.

36   '"irrevocably"; and she sits meanwhile': Woolf, *A Moment's Liberty*, p. 339.

36   'wandering in the streets': *TSEAIL*, pp. 306–8; letters printed as part of Blake Morrison's interview with Valerie Eliot, 'The Two Mrs Eliots', *Independent on Sunday*, 24 April 1994; *L8*, p. 928.

37   *he anticipated spending the rest of his life in solitude*: *L6*, p. 552.

37   *he removed that dedication*: *TSEAIL*, p. 310.

38   *Eliot had participated in the discussion groups*: *L6*, p. 195.

1943

40   *British students 'who make friends'*: Jolly, 'Cultural Imperialism', p. 2, quoting A. Herbert Gray, 'The Student Christian Movement', *Expository Times* 43 (1932), p. 559.

41   *Salvation came from human effort*: *ENL*, p. 18.

41   'intellectual and puritanical rationalism': *ENL*, p. 20, quoting 'A Sermon Preached in Magdalene Chapel', Cambridge, 1948, p. 5.

41   *he admired too the Church*: *TSEAIL*, p. 213.

41 *first visited the Anglican chapel*: Behr, *Chronology*, p. 7; *TSEAIL*, p. 212.
41 'between Papacy and Presbytery': *For Lancelot Andrewes: Essays on Style and Order* (1928), reprinted in T. S. Eliot, *Selected Essays, 1917–1932* (New York: Harcourt, Brace and Company, 1932), p. 290.
41 *he was Vicar's Warden*: *L7*, p. 37.
41 *Lang's Anglo-Catholic views*: Alan Wilkinson, 'Lang, (William) Cosmo Gordon, Baron Lang of Lambeth (1864–1945), archbishop of Canterbury', *Oxford Dictionary of National Biography*.
42 *Miss Swan*: E. W. F. Tomlin, *T. S. Eliot: A Friendship* (Abingdon: Routledge, 2016), pp. 16–17.
42 Miss Melton: https://hollisarchives.lib.harvard.edu/repositories/24/resources/3309 (accessed 10 January 2022).
42 *Dai Jones*: *L8*, p. 604.
43 *Wall, a Catholic intellectual*: *L8*, p. 203.
43 *health benefits of cigarettes*: https://www.history.com/news/cigarette-ads-doctors-smoking-endorsement (accessed 10 January 2022).

1944

45 *more than 1.5 million*: https://historicengland.org.uk/whats-new/features/blitz-stories/london-the-baby-blitz-and-v-weapons-1941-1945 (accessed 10 January 2022).
45 *The V-1 . . .*: https://www.iwm.org.uk/history/the-terrifying-german-revenge-weapons-of-the-second-world-war (accessed 10 January 2022).
46 *The thing fell bang*: Toby Faber, *Faber and Faber: The Untold Story* (London: Faber and Faber, 2019), pp. 174–5. For the date of the bombing see also: Richard Clarke et al., 'Russell Square: A Lifelong Resource for Teaching and Learning', Faculty of Continuing Education, FCE Occasional Paper No. 5, December 2004, p. 46.
48 *The first British edition*: Behr, *Chronology*, p. 61.
48 'one of the few good results': Trevelyan, *I'll Walk*, p. 8.
49 *the notion is revealing*: Jolly, 'Cultural Imperialism', p. 36.
50 *'I'll walk beside you'*: Alan Murray, 'I'll walk beside you', words by E. Lockton (London: Chappell & Co., 1936).
50 *'I have often wondered'*: Trevelyan, *I'll Walk*, pp. 8, 9.
50 *international alliance of YMCA organisations*: https://www.ymca.org.uk/about/history-heritage/ymca-and-ww2 (accessed 10 January 2022).
50 *'they were all so young'*: Trevelyan, *I'll Walk*, p. 20.
51 *devastation of the city of Rouen*: Stephen Bourque, 'Rouen: La Semaine Rouge', *Journal of Military and Strategic Studies* 14 (2012).

NOTES

51 'how long it would take for France': Trevelyan, I'll Walk, pp. 25–6.
51 'the occupants had just gone out': Trevelyan, I'll Walk, p. 32.
51 'Almost every family': Trevelyan, I'll Walk, p. 33.
51 'The war is certainly not over': Trevelyan, I'll Walk, p. 34.
51 He promised to send her Four Quartets: Behr, Chronology, p. 60; Pope, Eliot to Mary, 13 October.
51 'King Uzziah died': Eliot to Mary, Pope, 12 November, 18 November.
52 'living like civilians': Trevelyan, I'll Walk, p. 37.
52 'much our best opportunity': Trevelyan, I'll Walk, p. 38.
52 'I asked one man': Trevelyan, I'll Walk, p. 39.
52 'Hands are as interesting as faces': Trevelyan, I'll Walk, p. 57.
52 'the work is a considerable strain': Trevelyan, I'll Walk, p. 40.
52 'I ask every man': Trevelyan, I'll Walk, p. 41.
53 'the Light shining in darkness': Trevelyan, I'll Walk, p. 43.
54 'I think quite differently about euthanasia now': Correspondence between T. S. Eliot and Mary Trevelyan, T. S. Eliot Estate.
54 'The only trouble we have': Correspondence between T. S. Eliot and Mary Trevelyan, T. S. Eliot Estate.
54 'I share your opinion of the Americans': Pope, 12 November 1944.
54 'keep out of harm's way': Pope, Eliot to Mary, 28 November 1944.
54 Winston Churchill had come to make a speech: Douglas Johnson, 'Churchill and France', in Robert Blake and Wm Roger Louis (eds), Churchill (Oxford: Clarendon Press, 1996).
54 'I bought a Guide Bleu of Brussels': Trevelyan, I'll Walk, p. 50.
55 'an engagement book in French': Correspondence between T. S. Eliot and Mary Trevelyan, T. S. Eliot Estate.
55 'an excellent writer of detective fiction': Correspondence between T. S. Eliot and Mary Trevelyan, T. S. Eliot Estate.
55 'I now prefer Burgundy': Robert Scholes, Paradoxy of Modernism (New Haven and London: Yale University Press, 2006), p. 196.
55 'Did I first introduce you?': Pope, 12 May 1954.
55 'been reading Simenon for many years': L5, p. 751.
55 'consumed with admiration': Pope, Eliot to Mary, 30 October 1944.
55 'safety valve': Correspondence between T. S. Eliot and Mary Trevelyan, T. S. Eliot Estate.
55 'a small remark as to their toughness': Trevelyan, I'll Walk, p. 54.
56 'Yesterday I had a friend to tea': Correspondence between T. S. Eliot and Mary Trevelyan, T. S. Eliot Estate.
56 'The Angel Gabriel': Trevelyan, I'll Walk, p. 72.
56 'At 6 a.m. on Christmas morning': Trevelyan, I'll Walk, p. 73.
56 'no state to face a strain': Trevelyan, I'll Walk, p. 74.

1945

57   'Have you ever read': Pope, Eliot to Mary, 19 December 1944.

57   'A huge Scot': Trevelyan, *I'll Walk*, p. 77.

57   'What you say of the troops': Pope, Eliot to Mary, 2 January 1945.

58   'I shan't send it': Pope, Eliot to Mary, 21 January 1945.

58   small-town Shamley affairs: Pope, Eliot to Mary, 29 January 1945.

58   delivered at the Virgil Society: Behr, *Chronology*, p. 60.

58   'a swindling price': Pope, Eliot to Mary, 21 January 1945.

58   'chasing' a flying bomb: Trevelyan, *I'll Walk*, p. 86.

58   'the more one can share': Trevelyan, *I'll Walk*, p. 86.

59   'a town continually in the front line': Trevelyan, *I'll Walk*, p. 87.

59   Mary noted a sign: Trevelyan, *I'll Walk*, p. 91.

59   'At first it seemed': Trevelyan, *I'll Walk*, p. 91.

59   'all the world was wrecked': Trevelyan, *I'll Walk*, p. 94.

59   'What a field-day for thugs': Pope, Eliot to Mary, 13 March 1945.

59   'must have cost you a pretty penny': Pope, Eliot to Mary, 9 April 1945.

60   'Many of the men are skeletons': Trevelyan, *I'll Walk*, p. 96.

60   'a long and costly process': Trevelyan, *I'll Walk*, p. 97.

60   'The fighting man': Trevelyan, *I'll Walk*, p. 107.

61   'their eyes were full of horror': Trevelyan, *I'll Walk*, p. 105.

61   'sober mood': Trevelyan, *I'll Walk*, p. 105.

61   'gifts of small luxuries': Ackroyd, *T. S. Eliot: A Life*, p. 272.

61   She told . . . Ann Stokes: *TSEAIL*, p. 434.

61   'They won't get anybody else': Houghton Library, Harvard University, MS Am 1691.2, T. S. Eliot's Letters to Mary Trevelyan (1940–1956), 3 April 1945. Jolly, 'Cultural Imperialism', pp. 36–7.

62   'The elderly dachshund': Pope, Eliot to Mary, 1 September 1945.

1946

63   Eliot and Hayward had met: John Smart, *Tarantula's Web: John Hayward, T. S. Eliot and Their Circle* (Norwich: Michael Russell, 2013), p. 45.

63   The breakfast began awkwardly: Smart, *Tarantula's Web*, p. 55.

63   As a schoolboy: Smart, *Tarantula's Web*, p. 11.

63   muscular dystrophy: Smart, *Tarantula's Web*, p. 13; https://www.mda.org/ disease/facioscapulohumeral-muscular-dystrophy/signs-and-symptoms (accessed 10 January 2022).

63   'the only competent editor': Smart, *Tarantula's Web*, p. 51.

64   He was relentlessly social: *TSEAIL*, pp. 257–8.

64   'a court circle': TSEAIL, p. 25.

64   'Faber and Morley': Faber, Faber and Faber, p. 66.

64   each had an animal nickname: Smart, Tarantula's Web, p. 124.

64   'a world of men': TSEAIL, p. 259.

64   'One's easy and dominant memory': Vera Meynell in Smart, Tarantula's Web,
      p. 43.

64   'Everyone wanted to know', 'I know of no one more vitalising': Smart,
      Tarantula's Web, p. 220; Sitwell to John Hayward, 30 September 1947,
      Modern Archives Centre, King's College, Cambridge.

64   a regular reviewer: Smart, Tarantula's Web, p. 73.

64   arbiter of English correctness: Smart, Tarantula's Web, p. 162.

64   Eliot and Hayward would live together: Smart, Tarantula's Web, p. 192.

64   two small dark rooms: Ackroyd, T. S. Eliot: A Life, p. 274.

65   In the mornings after mass: Ackroyd, T. S. Eliot: A Life, p. 249.

65   She would continue to dream: FEE, p. 115.

65   Her dream would become reality: Jolly, 'Cultural Imperialism', p. 37.

66   'confidently recommended': Western Mail, Thursday 20 June 1946, p. 2.

67   'a curiously strangled sound': Anne Ridler, Working for T. S. Eliot: A Personal
      Reminiscence (London: Enitharmon Press, 2000), p. 10.

68   'You let in the Jew': Evan Kindley, 'The Insanity Defense: Coming to Terms
      with Ezra Pound's Politics', The Nation, 23 April 2018, https://www.
      thenation.com/article/archive/coming-to-terms-with-ezra-pounds-politics
      (accessed 10 January 2022).

68   Eliot sought the support of other poets: Ackroyd, T. S. Eliot: A Life, p. 281.

68   Eliot visited him: Ackroyd, T. S. Eliot: A Life, p. 282.

68   seeing friends and relatives: Pope, Eliot to Mary, 'Trinity VI', 28 July 1946.

68   Marion Dorn: https://www.ltmuseum.co.uk/collections/collections-online/
      people/item/1998-111001 (accessed 10 January 2022).

69   'So now we live quiet': Pope, Eliot to Mary; 'Two Christmas Presents', 1946,
      The Poems of T. S. Eliot, ed. Ricks and McCue, vol. 1, p. 288.

1947

70   he had resolved to leave her: Pasternak Slater, The Fall of a Sparrow, p. 490.

70   '"O God! O God!"': TSEAIL, p. 386.

70   'She had worn herself to death': Ackroyd, T. S. Eliot: A Life, p. 283.

71   'nearly the death of me': 'Statement by T. S. Eliot on the opening of the
      Emily Hale Letters at Princeton', written 25 November 1960, released
      to the public 2 January 2020, in Pasternak Slater, The Fall of a Sparrow,
      pp. 492–3.

71   'I go on coughing and spitting': Pope, Eliot to Mary, 17 February 1947.

71   'irritates me exceedingly': Pope, Eliot to Mary, 3 February 1947.

72   'This new work': Boahen and Wolfe, 50 Years, pp. 7–8.

72   In April Eliot flew to America: Ackroyd, T. S. Eliot: A Life, p. 285.

72   'I am going to tell you': EH to Lorraine Havens, 7 August 1947, in TSEAIL, pp. 411–12.

73   'You have made me perfectly happy': quoted by Edward Helmore, 'T. S. Eliot's Hidden Love Letters Reveal Intense, Heartbreaking Affair', Guardian, 2 January 2020, https://www.theguardian.com/books/2020/jan/02/ts-eliot-hidden-love-letters-reveal-intense-heartbreaking-affair-emily-hale (accessed 10 January 2022).

73   operation for a hernia: TSEAIL, p. 391.

74   'His appearance was grave': Stephen Spender, World Within World: The Autobiography of Stephen Spender (Berkeley: University of California Press, 1966), pp. 145–6.

74   'a complete false upper set': Pope, Eliot to Mary, 22 October 1947.

75   'exports first': Peter Clarke and Richard Toye, 'Cripps, Sir (Richard) Stafford (1889–1952), politician and lawyer', Oxford Dictionary of National Biography.

75   the Inland Revenue: Tomlin, T. S. Eliot: A Friendship, p. 174.

75   'After the Holocaust': TSEAIL, p. 109.

75   he had had a cold: Pope, Eliot to Mary, 22 October 1947.

75   some correspondence about her poetry: https://archiveshub.jisc.ac.uk/data/gb532-haw (accessed 10 January 2022).

76   he would head to Amsterdam and Rome: Ackroyd, T. S. Eliot: A Life, p. 286.

76   'the worries of the Burmese': Pope, Eliot to Mary, 1 Advent/30 November 1947.

1948

77   her work with UNESCO: Boahen and Wolfe, 50 Years, pp. 7–8.

77   'A week before Independence': Burma report, p. 3.

77   'We need our British friends': Burma report, p. 8.

78   'Nationalisation of everything': Burma report, p. 10.

78   'And at nightfall': 'New Moon on Burma', p. 21.

79   Eliot had been informed of the decision: Ackroyd, T. S. Eliot: A Life, p. 289.

79   George Orwell's review: Observer, 28 November 1948, p. 4.

80   'apathy and delight': Pope, Eliot to Mary, 5 January 1948.

80   'looked in on the Pope': Pope, Eliot to Mary, 11 January 1948.

80   his cousin Martha: 'Child health pioneer Martha May Eliot: A woman ahead

of her time', https://www.hsph.harvard.edu/news/centennial-martha-may
-eliot (accessed 10 January 2022).

81 'Does U mean Mister': Pope, Eliot to Mary, 26 January 1948.

81 preached a sermon on Easter Day 1765: TSEAIL, p. 240.

81 he told her in February: Pope, Eliot to Mary, 23 February 1948.

82 Edith Carroll Perkins: Graham Pearson, 'Mrs Edith Carroll Perkins and
Chipping Campden Gardens', Signpost: The Journal of Chipping Campden
History Society 8 (2018), pp. 12–15.

82 he was 'distressed': Pope, Eliot to Mary, 2 July 1948.

83 Martin Browne noted: Behr, Chronology, p. 64.

83 'a cocktail party at the Perths'': Pope, Eliot to Mary, 6 August 1948.

83 'come to the Institute for Advanced Study': Kelly Devine Thomas, 'T. S. Eliot at
the Institute for Advanced Study', 2007, https://www.ias.edu/ideas/2007/
ts-eliot-ias (accessed 10 January 2022).

83 He sailed at the end of September: Ackroyd, T. S. Eliot: A Life, p. 288.

84 'aren't they the jolly boys': Pope, Eliot to Mary, St Wenceslas, 28 September 1948.

84 He settled into a house: Thomas, 'T. S. Eliot at the Institute for Advanced
Study'.

84 he was even provided with a servant: Ackroyd, T. S. Eliot: A Life, p. 288.

84 'atom bombers or Einstein or Dirac': Pope, Eliot to Mary, St Wenceslas, 15
October 1948.

84 the American poet Robert Lowell: Faber, Faber and Faber, p. 189.

84 'the chief formative influence': The Times, 5 November 1948, p. 5.

84 Eileen Simpson: Eileen Simpson, Poets in their Youth: A Memoir (New York:
Farrar, Straus and Giroux, 2014), pp. 172–3.

86 'One-Eyed Riley': Pope, Eliot to Mary, 15 September 1948.

1949

88 'a collaborator': TSEAIL, p. 332, letter 27 September 1959, EH papers,
Sophia Smith Collection, Smith College.

88 'hidden meaning': TSEAIL, p. 400, EH to Willard Thorpe, 5 January 1964,
Princeton.

88 'my East Indian Island': Pope, Eliot to Mary, 13 March 1949.

89 Poe's 'negligible' influence: Behr, Chronology, p. 65.

90 Lady Fidget: Anthony Cuda, 'Evenings at the Phoenix Society: Eliot
and the Independent London Theatre', in Frances Dickey and John D.
Morgenstern (eds), The Edinburgh Companion to T. S. Eliot and the Arts
(Edinburgh: Edinburgh University Press, 2016), p. 217.

91 *Kees van Baaren*: http://www.musicweb-international.com/classrev/2004/
octo4/Baaren.htm (accessed 10 January 2022).

91 *'the seven characters are a nuisance'*: Pope, Eliot to Mary, 21 March 1949.

91 *He was very busy*: Ackroyd, *T. S. Eliot: A Life*, pp. 292–3.

92 *'a lot of fun in him'*: Tatler, 17 May 1950, p. 18.

94 *break with Emily Hale*: TSEAIL, p. 412.

97 *'arguably the most important years'*: Ackroyd, *T. S. Eliot: A Life*, pp. 78–9.

98 *'highbrows' and 'experts'*: Brian Harrison, *Seeking a Role: The United Kingdom
1951–70* (Oxford: Clarendon Press, 2009), p. 382.

99 *its first outing*: Ackroyd, *T. S. Eliot: A Life*, pp. 292–3.

100 *'I will now read the play to you'*: Ackroyd, *T. S. Eliot: A Life*, p. 294, from
Henry Sherek, *Not In Front of the Children* (London: Heinemann, 1959).

100 *'industrious, honest'*: Houghton Library, Harvard University, MS Am
1691.2, T. S. Eliot's Letters to Mary Trevelyan (1940–1956), 28 September
1946.

100 *Sir Owen Morshead*: Oliver Everett, 'Morshead, Sir Owen Frederick (1893–
1977), librarian', *Oxford Dictionary of National Biography*.

101 *'brilliantly entertaining analysis'*: The Times, 24 August 1949, p. 8.

103 *'The Eliotians were saying'*: Observer, 28 August 1949.

103 *'I understand indirectly'*: Faber, *Faber and Faber*, p. 192.

103 *'a revelation'*: Valerie Eliot to Blake Morrison, 'The two Mrs Eliots',
Independent on Sunday, 24 April 1994.

103 *'In my excitement I'd cut my hand'*: Morrison, 'The two Mrs Eliots'.

103 *she was offered the post*: Faber, *Faber and Faber*, p. 192.

104 *Eliot prepared for a lecture tour*: Ackroyd, *T. S. Eliot: A Life*, p. 297.

104 *The Beethoven had inspired Four Quartets*: L5, pp. 528–9.

106 *murderer of Christopher Marlowe*: https://www.independent.co.uk/news/
people/obituary-leslie-hotson-1561273.html (accessed 3 November
2020).

107 *six weeks in South Africa*: Ackroyd, *T. S. Eliot: A Life*, p. 298.

1950

109 *the Duke and Duchess of Windsor*: Behr, *Chronology*, p. 67.

109 *'Whatever its merits'*: New York Times, 29 January 1950, p. 73.

109 *'a very big success'*: Behr, *Chronology*, p. 67.

110 *'Why are we haunted'*: https://www.poetryfoundation.org/poems/50283/
friendship-after-love (accessed 10 January 2022).

110 *'"Family Reunion" was being televised'*: British Universities Film and Video
Council, broadcast 19 February, live from the studio, and then according to

BUFVC, again at 8.30 p.m. on Friday 24 February 1950 (small discrepancy of date).

112 *'strenuous bonhomie'*: Lee Siegel, 'The Fraught Friendship of T. S. Eliot and Groucho Marx', *New Yorker*, 25 June 2014.

114 *The play would run:* Behr, *Chronology*, p. 68.

118 *Julia is variously described*: T. S. Eliot, *The Cocktail Party* (New York: Harcourt, Brace and Company, 1950), pp. 15, 17, 20, 23, 24.

119 *Abigail Adams Eliot was a pioneer*: Betty Liebovitch, 'Our Proud Heritage', https://www.naeyc.org/resources/pubs/yc/may2016/our-proud-heritage (accessed 10 January 2022).

120 *'Garsington was a theatre'*: Ottoline Morrell, *Ottoline at Garsington: Memoirs of Lady Ottoline Morrell, 1915–18*, ed. Robert Gathorne-Hardy (London: Faber and Faber, 1974), p. 255.

121 *a trip in the autumn*: Ackroyd, *T. S. Eliot: A Life*, p. 302, Behr, *Chronology*, p. 68.

123 *attacks of bronchitis*: Ackroyd, *T. S. Eliot: A Life*, p. 303.

123 *Lyndall Gordon quotes 'Little Gidding'*: TSEAIL, p. 208; Ricks/McCue, vol. 1, p. 204.

1951

124 *'The rats are underneath the piles'*: Ricks/McCue, vol. 1, p. 35.

124 *'radical challenge to the Jewish reader'*: Anthony Julius, *T. S. Eliot, Anti-Semitism, and Literary Form* (Cambridge: Cambridge University Press, 1995), p. 2.

125 *'charged with malevolent meaning'*: Julius, *T. S. Eliot, Anti-Semitism*, p. 2.

125 *'hurts of intimacy'*: Julius, *T. S. Eliot, Anti-Semitism*, p. 179.

125 *'her sensitivity . . . was legendary'*: Martin Rubin, *Sarah Gertrude Millin: A South African Life* (Johannesburg: Ad. Donker, 1977), p. 242.

125 *Speaight was the actor*: TSEAIL, p. 278.

126 *The Confidential Clerk*: Behr, *Chronology*, p. 72.

127 *N. M. Iovets-Tereshchenko*: http://archives.balliol.ox.ac.uk/Modern%20 Papers/eliot.asp (accessed 10 January 2022); *L8*, p. 1044.

129 *'No one can grasp more firmly'*: T. F. Evans (ed.), *Shaw: The Critical Heritage* (London: Routledge & Kegan Paul, 1976), pp. 293–4.

129 *In the late spring*: Ackroyd, *T. S. Eliot: A Life*, p. 304.

130 *His talk to the Friends*: Behr, *Chronology*, p. 69

131 *the Ballet Rambert*: https://www.rambert.org.uk/about-us/our-history (accessed 10 January 2022).

132 *Eliot continued working for Lloyd's Bank*: Ackroyd, *T. S. Eliot: A Life*, p. 101.

132 *he did receive some funds*: TSEAIL, p. 192.
133 *'Eliot was only sixty-three'*: Behr, *Chronology*, p. 69; Donald Hall,
Remembering Poets: Reminiscences and Opinions (New York and London:
Harper & Row, 1978).
135 *it wasn't a city he enjoyed any more*: Ackroyd, *T. S. Eliot: A Life*, p. 307.
135 *The appeal that raised his ire*: *The Times*, 29 November 1951, p. 1.
135 *'a bitter and insensitive polemic'*: Irving Howe, review of *The T. S. Eliot Myth*
by Rossell Hope Robbins, *American Literature* 24 (1952), pp. 400–1.

1952

139 *'A deep sorrow has fallen'*: *The Times*, 7 February 1952, p. 7.
141 *very enthusiastic about the film*: Wheeler Winston Dixon, 'Cinema and
Poetry: T. S. Eliot's *Murder in the Cathedral*', *Senses of Cinema*, 2016, https://
www.sensesofcinema.com/2016/feature-articles/murder-in-the-cathedral
(accessed 21 January 2022).
141 *'Whatever literary merits'*: Bosley Crowther in the *New York Times*, 26 March
1952.
143 *he gave a talk to the girls*: TSEAIL, p. 416.
145 *'small, comfortable, well-appointed'*: *Tatler*, 22 February 1961, p. 12.
147 *Emlyn Williams*: 'Emlyn Williams as Dickens', *New York Times*, 15 January
1981; Paul Tanqueray, 'Williams, (George) Emlyn (1905–1987)', *Oxford
Dictionary of National Biography*.
148 *'a young man of extreme friendliness'*: Claudio Perinot, 'Jean Verdenal, an
Extraordinary Young Man: T. S. Eliot's Mort Aux Dardanelles', *South
Atlantic Review* 76 (2011), pp. 33–50, at p. 38.
148 *Verdenal was killed*: Perinot, 'Jean Verdenal', p. 44.
149 *'His own horror of self-revelation'*: Ackroyd, *T. S. Eliot: A Life*, p. 310.
151 *Martin Browne received a draft*: Behr, *Chronology*, p. 71.
151 *there is a photograph*: Eliot estate photo in Robert McCrum, 'T. S. Eliot's
Restless Ghost Finds Home in Seaside Idyll', *Observer*, 15 February 2015.
152 *'benevolent bird of prey'*: M. Geary, 'The "Agèd Eagle": Jacob Epstein,
T. S. Eliot (1952)', *Midlands Art Papers* 2 (2018/19), p. 2.

1953

153 *'The narrative pattern is staggeringly intricate'*: Kenneth Tynan, *Curtains*
(New York: Atheneum, 1961), p. 102.
153 *'We are never quite sure'*: T. C. Worsley, review of *The Confidential Clerk*, *New
Statesman*, 5 September 1953.

155 *The English Speaking Union*: https://www.esu.org/our-history (accessed 10 January 2022).

155 *Vivien's long-ago affair:* Pasternak Slater, *The Fall of a Sparrow*, p. 98.

159 *Eva Le Gallienne: Discography of American Historical Recordings*, s.v. 'Le Gallienne, Eva', https://adp.library.ucsb.edu/names/326795 (accessed 10 January 2022).

162 *The trip took him*: Behr, *Chronology*, p. 72.

162 *'Some of my strongest impulse'*: T. S. Eliot, *To Criticize the Critic*, second edition (London: Faber and Faber, 1978), p. 56.

163 *'brilliantly entertaining'*: *The Times*, 26 August 1953, p. 4.

163 *It would open in September*: Behr, *Chronology*, p. 72.

167 *'Hosea' by Norman Nicholson*: Alan Beattie, 'A Match for the Devil: Was Norman Nicholson a Feminist?', *Comet: The Newsletter of the Norman Nicholson Society* 6 (winter 2011), pp. 1–6.

168 *one of a sequence created by Boris Anrep*: 'One of a Kind', *New York Times*, 14 September 2003, https://www.nytimes.com/2003/09/14/magazine/one -of-a-kind-london-national-gallery-watch-your-step.html (accessed 10 January 2022).

170 *Cicely Courtneidge*: J. P. Wearing, *The London Stage 1950–1959: A Calendar of Productions, Performers, and Personnel* (Plymouth: Rowman & Littlefield, 2014), p. 227.

171 *a plot in Brookwood Cemetery*: https://brookwoodcemetery.com/plots-and -section (accessed 10 January 2022).

171 *Eliot was not, however, buried there*: Ackroyd, *T. S. Eliot: A Life*, p. 335.

1954

174 *In February 1954*: Behr, *Chronology*, p. 74.

174 *The Confidential Clerk is the logical result*: Brooks Atkinson, *New York Times*, 21 February, 1954, p. 29.

174 *'It was, probably, unwise'*: MT/Africa/54, p. 3.

175 *'the Old Testament come to life'*: MT/Africa/54, p. 6.

175 *She gave lectures*: MT/Africa/54, p. 7

175 *'removed, dramatically'*: MT/Africa/54, p. 14.

175 *'the "suicide road"'*: MT/Africa/54, p. 14.

175 *he suffered heart palpitations*: Ackroyd, *T. S. Eliot: A Life*, p. 314.

177 *Leslie Hotson*: L6, p. 505.

177 *Elizabeth Gaskell met . . . Charles Eliot Norton*: Hannah Rosefield, 'The Unjustly Overlooked Victorian Novelist Elizabeth Gaskell', *New Yorker*, 5 September 2018, https://www.newyorker.com/books/page-turner/the

-unjustly-overlooked-victorian-novelist-elizabeth-gaskell (accessed 10 January 2020).

177 *Eliot was near Littlehampton*: Ackroyd, *T. S. Eliot: A Life*, p. 314.

179 *the Farringford Hotel*: https://farringford.co.uk/farringford-hotel (accessed 10 January 2022).

180 *ordered to give up cigarettes*: Ackroyd, *T. S. Eliot: A Life*, p. 314.

183 *William Force Stead*: William Force Stead papers, Beinecke Rare Book and Manuscript Library, Yale University, https://archives.yale.edu/repositories/11/resources/1039 (accessed 10 January 2022).

184 *'Eliot came down from London'*: *Alumnae Journal of Trinity College Washington* 38 (winter 1965), pp. 59–66, at 64–5, quoted in David Bradshaw, '"Oxford Poets": Yeats, T. S. Eliot and William Force Stead', *Yeats's Mask: Yeats Annual* 19 (2013), pp. 77–102; also *TSEAIL*, p. 223.

191 *A reader for the publishing house looked it over*: Faber, *Faber and Faber*, pp. 224–5.

192 *'The Cultivation of Christmas Trees'*: Ackroyd, *T. S. Eliot: A Life*, p. 315.

1955

195 *The Authors' World Peace Appeal*: University of Leeds Library, Special Collections, https://explore.library.leeds.ac.uk/special-collections -explore/7287/authors_world_peace_appeal_papers_and_correspond (accessed 10 January 2022).

195 *'foreigners cannot be admitted'*: Authors' World Peace Appeal, *Hansard*, 27 January 1955, vol. 536 cc47-8W, https://api.parliament.uk/ historic-hansard/written-answers/1955/jan/27/authors-world-peace -appeal#S5CV0536P0_19550127_CWA_40 (accessed 10 January 2022).

196 *Wilfred Watson's first book*: https://discoverarchives.library.ualberta.ca/index. php/wilfred-watson-fonds (accessed 10 January 2022).

197 *Billy Graham had first come to Britain*: https://billygrahamlibrary.org/ crusade-city-spotlight-london (accessed 10 January 2022).

197 *preached for a week*: *The Times*, 26 April 1955, p. 8.

202 *The mass of the pre-sanctified*: https://www.catholiceducation.org/en/culture/ catholic-contributions/mass-of-the-pre-sanctified.html (accessed 10 January 2022).

203 *I've been meditating on your comment*: MT to John Hayward, 21 April 1955, King's College Archive.

204 *Eliot had written a tribute*: Behr, *Chronology*, p. 75.

205 *Hanseatic Goethe Prize*: Behr, *Chronology*, p. 75.

207 *'My new car'*: Mary Trevelyan, unpublished diary, 1955–6.

209 *À l'Ecu de France:* H. L. Cracknell and G. Nobis, *Practical Professional Gastronomy* (Basingstoke: Macmillan, 1985), p. 328.

211 *Priscilla Stearns Talcott:* Rebecca Rego Barry, 'Found in the Attic: T. S. Eliot's Family Photo Album', *Fine Books Magazine,* 2017, https://web.archive.org/save/https://www.finebooksmagazine.com/fine_books_blog/2017/08/found-in-the-attic-ts-eliots-family-photo-album.phtml (accessed 10 January 2022).

211 *George Lawrence Smith:* obituary for George L. Smith, *New York Times,* 8 September 1962, p. 19.

213 *'A Song for Simeon':* Behr, *Chronology,* p. 35; Ricks/McCue, vol. 1, p. 103.

215 *Eliot's final play:* Behr, *Chronology,* p. 79.

217 *Hogarth Press had published:* https://www.bl.uk/collection-items/poems-by-t-s-eliot-published-by-the-hogarth-press (accessed 10 January 2022).

1956–1957

219 *Robert Ford:* obituary for Robert Ford, https://www.independent.co.uk/news/obituaries/robert-ford-radio-operator-in-tibet-who-was-jailed-by-china-for-being-an-imperialist-spy-8890248.html (accessed 10 January 2022).

220 *back in the London Clinic:* Ackroyd, *T. S. Eliot: A Life,* p. 317.

220 *delivered over loudspeakers: Star Tribune,* 30 April 1956, p. 1.

220 *continued . . . to work on The Elder Statesman: TSEAIL,* p. 500.

221 *awarded an OBE: London Gazette,* 30 December 1955, Supplement: 40669, p. 15.

224 *Starkie was an Irish-born literary critic:* Oliver O'Hanlon, '"A Bit of a Character": An Irishman's Diary on Enid Starkie, Irish-Born Oxford Academic and Literary Critic', *Irish Times,* 19 August 2020.

224 *Mr Little had been at Harvard: L9,* pp. 72–3.

225 *'He had become a kind of totem':* Ackroyd, *T. S. Eliot: A Life,* p. 317.

225 *another attack of tachycardia:* Behr, *Chronology,* p. 76.

225 *'Mr T. S. Eliot, the poet and playwright': Coventry Evening Telegraph,* 13 June 1956, p. 13.

226 *'swarming around him': Shenandoah* (spring 1961), quoted by Ackroyd, *T. S. Eliot: A Life,* p. 299.

229 *'a centre of Evangelical Catholicism':* T. S. Eliot, 'Father Cheetham Retires from Gloucester Road', *Church Times,* 9 March; Behr, *Chronology,* p. 76.

232 *'Tell him to cheer up!':* Michael T. Thornhill, 'Trevelyan, Humphrey, Baron Trevelyan (1905–1985), civil servant in India and diplomatist', *Oxford Dictionary of National Biography.*

233 *a month's holiday in Switzerland*: Behr, *Chronology*, p. 77.

234 *Bateson was the editor*: Elisabeth W. Schneider, *T. S. Eliot: The Pattern in the Carpet* (Berkeley: University of California Press, 1975), p. 32; Timothy Materer, 'T. S. Eliot and his Biographical Critics', *Essays in Criticism* 62 (2012), pp. 41–57.

239 *Anne Ridler had been Eliot's secretary*: Ridler, *Working for T. S. Eliot*, p. 5.

240 *Miss Fletcher . . . had begun looking after*: TSEAIL, p. 501.

240 *'an attempt to bring a few more students together'*: Mary Trevelyan, 'The Welfare of Overseas Commonwealth Students in the United Kingdom', *Journal of the Royal Society of Arts* 110 (April 1962), pp. 333–44, at p. 338.

241 *'Without people like you'*: Boahen and Wolfe, *50 Years*, p. 15; unpublished typescript by Mary Trevelyan, p. 109.

242 *My most vivid memory*: Boahen and Wolfe, *50 Years*, pp. 20–1.

242 *'Nanny Goat – the one and only M. T.'*: Boahen and Wolfe, *50 Years*, p. 17.

242 *'She was always available'*: Boahen and Wolfe, *50 Years*, p. 18.

244 *'noticeably radiant'*: TSEAIL, p. 501.

244 *'it is a very different play'*: letter to William Turner Levy, quoted in William Turner Levy, *Affectionately, T. S. Eliot: The Story of a Friendship: 1947–1965* (London: Dent, 1968), p. 101; TSEAIL, p. 503.

POSTSCRIPT

The correspondence quoted in this section is courtesy of the T. S. Eliot Estate.

247 *The priest who married them*: Ackroyd, *T. S. Eliot: A Life*, p. 319; TSEAIL, p. 488.

247 *the swift recklessness of his first marriage*: TSEAIL, p. 505.

247 *'The Bard's elopement'*: Smart, *Tarantula's Web*, p. 264; John Hayward to Helen Gardner, 5 February 1957, Modern Archives Centre, King's College, Cambridge.

247 *'puzzled in the extreme'*: Smart, *Tarantula's Web*, p. 269, John Hayward to Anne Ridler, 3 February 1957, Modern Archives Centre, King's College, Cambridge.

247 *began to thin and falter*: TSEAIL, p. 505.

248 *'I have an informed suspicion'*: Smart, *Tarantula's Web*, p. 263, quoting John Malcolm Brinnin, *Sextet: T. S. Eliot & Truman Capote & Others* (London: André Deutsch, 1981), p. 274.

248 *'I am sorry to have had to leave you'*: T. S. Eliot to Geoffrey Faber, 9 January 1957, quoted in Faber, *Faber and Faber*, p. 242.

248 *'I tried to find out everything I could'*: TSEAIL, p. 498; 'The Poet's Wife and Letters', *The Times*, 17 September 1988.

248 *'This last part of my life'*: TSEAIL, p. 520; Levy, *Affectionately, T. S. Eliot*, p. 110.

AFTERWORD

259 *Anstice Goodman*: https://www.voluntarywork.org.uk/about-us/ history/#ladyanstice (accessed 10 January 2022).

259 *'like a platonic marriage'*: transcript of Lady Goodman Anstice Goodman and Lady Daphne Grierson being interviewed by John Charles, 7 March 1989.

259 *neither John nor Mary attended his funeral*: Smart, *Tarantula's Web*, p. 287.

260 *'the absolute dedication'*: TSEAIL, p. 497.

260 *he would write at home in the mornings*: Ackroyd, *T. S. Eliot: A Life*, pp. 321–2.

260 *their entertainments*: Ackroyd, *T. S. Eliot: A Life*, p. 322.

260 *did not receive the warmest notices*: Behr, *Chronology*, p. 79.

260 *'Love reciprocated is always rejuvenating'*: TSEAIL, p. 514; interview with Henry Hewes, *Saturday Review*, 13 September 1958, p. 32.

260 *'There was nothing wrong with Tom'*: VE to Blake Morrison, *Independent on Sunday*, 24 April 1994.

260 *'kept under wraps'*: ENL, p. viii.

261 *'It is puzzling'*: TSEAIL, p. 37.

261 *Their correspondence . . . was only unsealed*: TSEAIL, pp. 421–4.

261 *'The psychology of his people is just as crude'*: Stephen Spender, *The Destructive Element: A Study of Modern Writers and Beliefs* (London: Jonathan Cape, 1935), p. 145.

262 *'A luncheon . . . leaders'*: Mary Trevelyan, private diaries, 1962.

262 *'I don't know . . . proper meals'*: Mary Trevelyan, private diaries, 1962.

263 *The university had been founded in 1960*: Constantin Katsakioris, 'The Lumumba University in Moscow: Higher Education for a Soviet–Third World Alliance, 1960–91', *Journal of Global History* 14 (2019), pp. 281–300.

264 *'her cherished dream'*: 'Miss Mary Trevelyan: Pioneer Work for Overseas Students', *The Times*, 12 January 1983, p. 12.

264 *'Former members, Old Goats'*: Trevelyan, 'The Welfare of Overseas Commonwealth Students', p. 339.

264 *'Queen Elizabeth . . . has asked me'*: Private papers.

265 *'It is understandable'*: Carpenter, 'Poor Tom', p. 52.

265 *'Although his company was a constant pleasure'*: Pope, Preface.

ACKNOWLEDGEMENTS

My thanks go first to Gill Coleridge, who, along with Parisa Ebrahimi and Clara Farmer, first reached out to me in regard to this wonderful project. At Rogers, Coleridge and White, Cara Jones picked up the baton, and my dear friend Zoë Waldie was also of enormous help. Thanks are also due to my own agents, first Antony Harwood and then Eleanor Birne of PEW.

It was in Gill's offices that I first met Kate Trevelyan, who entrusted this project to me. Her thoughtfulness and care have been invaluable, and I can only hope I've done the Trevelyan family justice.

This book could not have been completed without the help of Clare Reihill, literary executor of the T. S. Eliot estate, who welcomed me so warmly to the thrilling Eliot archives at Kensington Court Gardens. My thanks to Nancy Fulford there too, and of course to John Haffenden, indefatigable and charming editor of Eliot's correspondence: my thanks for his wisdom, knowledge and good humour.

At Faber and Faber, Mitzi Angel acquired this work and I was so lucky to have her enthusiasm. Laura Hassan later became my terrific editor; working with her and Ella Griffiths has been a joy. I am of course indebted to the whole Faber and Faber team, not least Stephen Page and Rachel Alexander and archivist Robert Brown; also to Robert Davies, Anne Owen and Sarah Barlow. Huge thanks to my American editor, the wonderful Jonathan Galassi at Farrar, Straus and Giroux.

I have loved working at the Bodleian, where the manuscript of *The Pope of Russell Square* resides. Thanks ever to my friend Richard Ovenden OBE, Bodley's Librarian. Assisting me at the library were Dr Judith Priestman, then Curator, Literary Manuscripts; Oliver

ACKNOWLEDGEMENTS

House, Superintendent, Special Collections Reading Rooms; Nicola O'Toole, Special Collections Library Assistant; also Lucy McCann and Rachael Marsay. Elizabeth Garner was my dear friend and companion in Oxford. At King's College, Cambridge, I owe thanks to Dr Patricia McGuire.

I am as ever very grateful to the London Library, where T. S. Eliot was first member and later President: in particular I thank Julian Lloyd, Head of Communications, and Rosalie Davidson too. I am always grateful to the British Library.

The Right Reverend Dr Andrew Rumsey, Bishop of Ramsbury, read a draft and kept me clear of religious error; Lyndall Gordon offered her keen eye and her support, both so meaningful to me. Robert McCrum gave early encouragement; Blake Morrison's thoughts were very helpful. Liz Dexter transcribed the manuscript, a great blessing. My dear friend Jill Waters gave me an important new way to think about the book as I wrote it; Ruth Scurr, as ever, was always there for me. Paddy Crewe listened. My husband, Francis Gilbert, was – as always – tirelessly loving, supportive and encouraging, as was our son Theo.

Robin Weigert: she truly helped me over the finish line, though I know she finds that hard to believe.

INDEX

Page references in *italics* refer to illustrations.

Ackroyd, Peter, 26, 70, 97, 149, 225
Aiken, Conrad, 19, 79
Aldington, Richard, 237
Allen, Percy, 66
Alliance Française, 43, 91, 129, 144, 153
'American Literature and the American Language' lecture (Eliot), 162–3
Anrep, Boris, 168, 169
'The Anvil' (BBC radio programme), 27, 30, 32
Archer, William, 66–7
'Ash Wednesday' (Eliot), 19, 37
Ashton, Frederick, 131
Athlone, Lord, 106
Atkinson, Brooks, 109, 174
Attlee, Clement, 110
Auden, W. H., 196, 223–4, 239
Aung San, 77, 78
Auriol, Vincent, 111, 112
Authors' World Peace Appeal, 195, 236
Aydelotte, Frank, 83

Balcon, Jill, 239
Bartlett, Vernon, 136
Bartok Quartet, 216
Bateson, F. W., 234–5
Beethoven: Allegretto from 7th Symphony, 107; Coriolan Overture, 99, 103–4, 107, 137; Op. 59, No. 1, 136; Quartet Op. 132, 104
Behrens, Margaret, 240, 245
Bell, Clive, 120, 168
Bell, George, Bishop of Chichester, 19
Bell, Vanessa, 120
Berryman, John, 84

Betjeman, John, 192
'Billy M'Caw: The Remarkable Parrot' (Eliot), 68–9
Blake, William, 191
Bland, Mary, 93
Blonay, André de, 54
Bloomsbury Set, 216–17, 234
Boahen, Adu, 241–2
Bonham Carter, Lady Violet, 64
Bosanquet, Theodora, 126–7, 241
Boult, Sir Adrian, 4
Bradley, Omar N., 73
Brinnin, John Malcolm, 248
British Council: Eliot's involvement, 75; Eliot's tours, 32, 42, 76, 80; letter of protest sent to, 234; Mary's African tour, 174–5
Brook, Peter, 229, *230*
Brown, Ivor, 103
Browne, Martin: *The Cocktail Party* direction, 83, 91, 109, 114; *The Confidential Clerk* direction, 126, 151; correspondence with Eliot, 28, 109; *Murder in the Cathedral* direction, 28; party (1950), 109
Browning, Elizabeth Barrett, 98
Browning, Robert, 106
Buckle, Richard, 152
Bunyan, John, 191
Butler, R. A. ('Rab'), 108

Carlyle, Thomas, 232, 252
Carpenter, Humphrey, 3, 4, 7, 10–11, 21, 264–5
Carrington, Dora, 120
Carroll Perkins, John and Edith, 82
Carter, Elmer, 17
Casey, William Francis, 236
Cecil, Lord David, 147, 172

Chamberlain, Neville, 17
Cheetham, Rev. Eric, 107, 229
Christie, Agatha, 67
Clair, René, 67
Claudel, Paul, 204
The Cocktail Party (Eliot): Broadway opening, 109; character of Julia, 92, 101, 118, 218, 254; *The Confidential Clerk* compared with, 188; Edinburgh production, 99, 101–3, *102*; financial success, 118–19, 152; first night party (3rd May 1950), *114*, 122; London (New Theatre) opening, *114*, 122; Mary's contribution to, 87–8, 112; 'One-Eyed Riley' song, 86, 88, 101, 112; performances, 107, 114; prayer, 207; programme, *102*; reception, 92, 101–3, 109, 118, 126, 163; records, 143; rehearsals, 98, 101; 'seven imaginary characters', 88, 92, 94, 101; text published, 109, 112; title, 83, 92; translations, 134, 214; working on, 83, 91
Colville, Lady Cynthia, 241
Comfort, Alex, 195
The Confidential Clerk (Eliot): cast, 163, *166*; characters, 124, 126, 131, 139–40, 152, 153; copies of, 187, 214; Mary's reaction to, 187–8; origins, 182; performances, 163, 165–7, *166*, 174, 188; reception, 163, 168–9, 170–1, 174; Simenon references, 156; working on, 126, 133, 141, 147, 151, 154–5, 160
Conservative Association, 214
Cooper, Duff, Viscount Norwich, 147
Cooper, Lady Diana, 147
Courtneidge, Cicely, 170
The Criterion: contributors, 167, 236; Eliot's role, 19, 43, 129, 236; Hayward's reviews, 64; last edition, 23; launch, 19
'The Cultivation of Christmas Trees' (Eliot), 192, *193*
Cummings, Constance, 101

D'Arányi, Jelly, 106
Day-Lewis, Cecil, 195, 223, 239
Day-Lewis, Mary, 239
de la Mare, Richard, 239
de la Mare, Walter, 227, 228, 229
Donat, Robert, 158, 161–2, 218
Doolittle, Hilda (H. D.), 132, 237
Dorn, Marion, 68
Dukes, Ashley, 131
Durrell, Lawrence, 79

Eden, Anthony, 232–3
Edinburgh, Philip, Duke of (later Prince Philip), 155
Edward VIII, King (later Duke of Windsor), 15, 109
Einstein, Albert, 84, 91
The Elder Statesman (Eliot), 215, 217, 219, 220–1, 244, 260
Eliot, Abigail Adams (cousin), 119, 261
Eliot, Ada (sister), 261
Eliot, Andrew, Reverend, 81
Eliot, Charlotte Champe Stearns (mother), 3, 106, 151, 182, 224
Eliot, Charlotte (sister), *see* Smith
Eliot, Christopher (uncle), 214–15
Eliot, Henry Ware (brother), 72, 85, 113, 186, 192
Eliot, Henry Ware (father), 3, 137, 182, 199
Eliot, Margaret Dawes (sister), 226–7, 238
Eliot, Marian Cushing (sister): account of hurricane, 188; appearance, 100, 178, *184*; childhood, 151; Eliot's relationship with, 121, 171, 183, 222; Eliot's visits, 121; health, 178, 181; Isle of Wight trip, 178–83, *184*; Prospect of Whitby trip, 185; relationship with Mary, 113, 168, 176, 180, 186, 207, 258; sister Margaret's death, 226–7; visiting England, 98–101, 171, 178–86, 189, 240; Windsor trip, 100–1
Eliot, Martha May (cousin), 80–1, 261
Eliot, Theodora (niece, daughter of Marian): appearance, 101; Edinburgh visit, 165, 167; opinion

of Wodehouse, 186; Prospect of
Whitby trip, 185; relationship
with Mary, 120, 133, 168, 208, 258;
visiting England, 98–101, 120, 231–3;
Windsor trip, 100–1
Eliot, T. S.: anti-Semitism issues,
75, 124–5; appearance, 19, 20–1,
74, 85, 97, 133, 137, 154, 160, 177, *182*,
184, 224, *226*; attending students'
nativity play, 25, 26, 38–9; attitude
to foreigners, 2, 32, 96, 100, 129;
attitude to race and colour, 75, 80,
81, 198; attitude to women, 150, 158,
222, 234, 260–1; British Council
involvement, 32, 42, 75, 76, 80, 234;
British naturalisation, 41, 152; burial
plans, 171, 228; career, 18–19, 131, 132,
144, 199–200; childhood, 57, 106, 113,
151, 158–9, 181–2, 224; churchwarden,
40, 41, 49, 104, 113, 251; conversations
on hurting people, 146, 148, 150;
conversion to Church of England,
41, 172, 183–4, 243, 247; crossword
puzzles, 74, 124, 128, 145, 183, 223;
death, 259, 263; deceptions, 122, 146,
200–1, 244, 249, 251, 252; describing
Mary, 27, 100; dress, 19, 40, 85, 105,
112, 128, 137, 139, 154, 155, 160, 177,
179, 192, 212–13, 216; engagement
to Valerie, 244; family background,
2–3, 32, 64, 75, 106, 158, 188, 211;
fear of death, 101, 228, 251; final
correspondence with Mary, 255–8;
finances, 75, 118–19, 127, 151–2, 202–3,
206; flat sharing with Hayward (19
Carlyle Mansions), 63, 64–5, 67, 89,
247, 250; friendship with Mary, 1–2,
13, 26, 82–3, 140, 197, 265; funeral,
259; gifts to Mary, 28–9, 48, 68–9,
72, 86, 87, 89, 91, 98, 127, 135, 136,
137, 143, 158, 160, 163, 170, 176, 189,
192, 197, 207, 208, 210, 216, 221; gin
drinking, 66, 93, 101, 105, 113, 119, 122,
132, 143, 148, 153, 156, 187; Hanseatic
Goethe Prize, 205; Harvard
honorary degree, 72; health, 10, 20,

36, 43, 51, 70–1, 73–4, 75, 123, 124,
126, 127–8, 137, 175–6, 196, 200, 202,
211–12, 220, 221, 222, 225, *226*, 227–8,
231, 234, 236–7, 238, 244; hearing
voices, 140, 147, 156; holidays, 107,
109, 111, 115, 128, 129, 143, 173, 233–4;
homosexuality 'accusations', 148–9,
234–5; homosexuality opinions,
154; house in Chester Terrace, 128;
humour, 20, 40, 112, 165, 172, 212;
ideas of friendship, 112–13; influence
on young people, 15, 18; laughter,
153, 161, 205, 235, 237; legacy, 12–13;
letters to Mary, 8–9, 10–11, 31, 43;
literary advice to Mary, 27, 49, 65–6;
marriage to Valerie, 2, 64, 246–8,
251, 257; marriage to Vivien, 21, 35–7,
70–1, 113, 115, 120–1, 190, 215–16, 234,
251, 253; memory, 129, 132; money-
raising plan on his behalf, 132,
199–200; moods, 36, 112, 118, 130–1,
133, 134, 144, 158, 167, 179, 205, 208–9,
212, 218, 223, 238; nickname, 64;
Nobel Prize in Literature, 1, 78–9,
84–5, 89–90, 101, 128; office at Faber,
6, 48, 61, 127, 155, 176, 200, 214, 244,
247; opinion of Mary's writing, 27,
49, 65–6; opinion of other poets, 132,
147, 168, 195, 196, 223, 236, 239–40;
opinion of other writers, 129, 135,
137, 144, 195, 237–8; Order of Merit
(OM), 78–9, 82, 90, 99, 128; Paris
visits, 61, 128, 133, 134–5, 148, 245;
'people in his plays', 111, 187–8, 219;
playing patience, 110, 126, 181, 192,
202; political views, 28, 69, 135, 137,
198; Possum nickname, 32, 38, 44;
pronunciations, 91; readings for
students, 15, 18, 19–20, 23, 35, 45,
241–2; 'the real man', 12, 31, 123, 252,
260; relationship with Emily Hale,
2, 21–2, 72–3, 87, 88, 94, 116, 120, 143,
167, 169; relationship with Ezra
Pound, 32, 68, 131–2, 162, 199–200,
207, 208; relationship with Janes
(handyman), 128; relationship with

Jean Verdenal, 148, 235; relationship
with John Hayward, 63, 64–5, 67,
89, 143, 146, 148, 150, 197, 202–3, 247,
250–1, 252, 259, 260; relationship
with Mary, 30–1, 47–8, 55, 66, 87–9,
92–3, 94–8, 113–18, 121, 122, 123, 140,
145–6, 150–1, 158, 163–4, 170–1, 188–9,
203, 220, 222, 224; relationship with
parents, 106, 182; religion, 26–7, 32,
40–2, 72, 86, 93, 105, 110, 113, 134, 145,
156, 159–60, 172, 183, 201–2, 206–7,
251–2; rules on meeting friends, 112,
140–1, 145–6, 208–9; 'runner-away',
90, 146, 231–2, 252; secrecy, 21–2, 122,
149, 200–1, 228, 231–2, 244, 247, 248–
9; sense of duty, 41, 112, 223, 233, 240;
separation between spheres of his
life, 22, 87, 236; sherry drinking, 148,
188, 189, 201, 210, 223, 228, 232, 250,
258; singing, 86, 106, 126, 130–1, 152,
153, 172, 201, 218; sister Margaret's
death, 226–7, 238; sixtieth birthday,
78; smoking, 2, 44, 133, 180, 181, 190,
210, 228; snobbery, 129, 131, 195, 211,
224; teeth, 74, 137, 238; telephoning,
42, 67, 89, 164, 172, 173, 200, 214,
236, 238; temper, 36, 130, 134, 143,
185, 237; travels, 76, 80, 109; trips to
America, 67–8, 72, 83–5, 121, 122–3,
143, 162, 205–8, 224–5, 249; verses for
Mary, 28–9, 33, 35, 51, 68–9; voice,
20, 67, 74, 106, 133, 152, 153, 173, 207,
228; wartime fire-watching, 23–4,
25, 31, 46; worrying, 47, 109, 121, 162,
178, 183, 205–6, 222, 228, 240; writing
poetry, 191; writing prose, 231
Eliot, Valerie (Fletcher, second wife):
copyright issues, 10–11; Eliot's
accounts of, 104, 156, 200–1, 244, 249;
Eliot's illnesses, 176, 196, 248; Eliot's
secretary at Faber, 2, 103, 104, 247;
management of Eliot's affairs, 156,
169, 170, 176, 240, 247; marriage, 2, 64,
246–8, 257; new flat, 250; relationship
with Eliot, 2, 248, 251, 259–60; secret
engagement, 244

Eliot, Vivien (Haigh-Wood, first
wife): appearance, 35; breakdown,
253; committed to asylum
(Northumberland House), 21, 36–7,
46, 245; death, 70–1, 137, 139; Enid
Faber's visits, 106; marriage, 2, 35–7,
120–1, 190, 215–16, 234, 260; Miss
Swan's kindness, 244; relationship
with Bertrand Russell, 155
Eliot, William Greenleaf
(grandfather), 2, 158
Elizabeth, Queen (later Queen
Mother), 39, 147, 264–5
Elizabeth II, Queen (earlier Princess
Elizabeth), 39, 158
Emerson, Ralph Waldo, 2
Empson, William, 196
Epstein, Jacob, 152
Evans, Ifor, 158, 159

Faber, Enid: Eliot's weekend visit,
218; lunching with Eliot, 178; South
African holidays, 107, 109, 173;
Spanish holidays, 128, 129; theatre-
going, 147–8; visiting Vivien in
asylum, 106
Faber, Geoffrey: account of bomb
damage, 46; Eliot's marriage, 247,
248, 250; Eliot's weekend visit, 218;
lunching with Eliot, 178; nickname,
64; relationship with Eliot, 64, 247,
250; South African holidays, 107,
109, 173; Spanish holidays, 128, 129;
theatre-going, 147–8
Faber and Faber: bomb damage to
office building, 46; caretaker, 46;
Eliot's career, 1, 2, 65, 131; Eliot's
secretaries, 2, 43, 93, 103, 239; name,
64, 131; office building, 6, 7, 46, 65,
89, 244; publication of Eliot's works,
23, 28, 48, 109, 112, 192; publication
of Mary's work, 27; publications,
84, 93, 127, 132, 149, 167, 190–1, 196;
receptionist, 43
The Family Reunion (Eliot): BBC
TV production, 110–11; Brook's

production, 229, *230*; characters, 106; Emily Hale's involvement, 88; opening, 23, 164; reception, 164, 231; Swedish production, 85; theme of 'expiation', 251

Farringford House, Isle of Wight, 179, *180*

Fisher, Geoffrey, Archbishop, 81

Ford, Robert, 219

Forster, E. M., 18

Four Quartets (Eliot): 'Burnt Norton', 28; copy sent to Mary, 51; dedication to Hayward, 247; 'The Dry Salvages', 28; 'East Coker', 23, 97, 117; first British edition, 48; impact of, 135; inspired by Beethoven, 104; 'Little Gidding', 23, 24, 26, 30, 32, 33, 123; recording of Eliot's reading, 91

From the Ends of the Earth (Trevelyan), 7, 27, 33–5, *34*

'The Frontiers of Criticism' lecture (Eliot), 220, 221

Frost, Robert, 250

Fry, Roger, 216, 217

Gallico, Paul, 207

Gardner, Helen, 104, 149, 247

Garrick Club: dining at, 104, 106, 111, 125, 130, 136, 140, 144, 146, 162, 172, 224, 236–7; Eliot's membership, 99; Ladies' Night, 99; portraits, 236; renovation, 198; table, 236

Gaskell, Elizabeth, 177

George VI, King, 82, 99, 139, 140

Gide, André, 204

Gielgud, John, 35, 63, 103, 248

Gilliat, Martin, 264

Giroux, Robert, 207

Goats' Club, 240–2, 264

Goethe, Johann Wolfgang von, 177

Golding, William, 190–1

Goodman, Anstice, 259

Gordon, Lyndall: on Eliot's attitude to women, 260–1; on Eliot's divided nature, 123; on Eliot's engagement to Valerie, 244, 260; on Eliot's legacy,

12, 75; on Emily Hale's relationship with Eliot, 21–2; on *The Pope of Russell Square*, 11

Gosse, Edmund, 63

Graham, Billy, 197–8

Groser, John, 107, 122, 142, 161

Guinness, Alec, 100, 101, 233

Haigh-Wood, Maurice, 21, 36–7, 46, 70–1

Hale, Emily: Eliot's visits, 68, 72, 143; family background, 21, 82; Mary's awareness of, 22, 87, 116, 120, 164, 167, 169; relationship with Eliot, 2, 21–2, 72–3, 87, 88, 94, 116, 167, 248; response to death of Vivien, 72–3; response to Eliot's marriage to Valerie, 261; visiting Eliot in England, 120, 163, 164, 167, 169

Hall, Donald, 133

Hamilton, Lord David, 147

Harris, Joel Chandler, 32

Harrison, Rex, 114

Hawkes, Jacquetta, 75–6, 177

Hawkins, Desmond, 79

Hawthorne, Nathaniel, 2

Hayward, John: Alliance Française, 153; appearance and character, 64; background, 63; career, 63–4; editing Eliot's work, 158; Eliot's burial plans, 228; Eliot's health concerns, 176, 202, 220; Eliot's marriage to Valerie, 246, 247–8, 250, 259; end of relationship with Eliot, 250–1, 259, 260; first meeting with Eliot, 63; flat-sharing with Eliot (19 Carlyle Mansions), 63, 64–5, 67, 89, 247, 250; health, 63; homosexuality 'accusations', 148; news of Vivien's death, 70; nickname, 64; 'One-Eyed Riley' recording discovery, 93; relationship with Eliot, 64–5, 67, 89, 143, 146, 148, 150, 197, 202–3, 247, 250–1, 252, 259, 260; relationship with Mary, 114, 143, 146, 150, 197, 203; social life, 64, 110, 147–8;

usefulness to Eliot, 64, 260; view of Hope Mirrlees, 235; wheelchair, 63, 64, 67

Helpmann, Robert, 158, 161

Herbert, George, 103

Higginson, Mr (solicitor), 148, 149, 228, 234, 247, 248, 250

Higham, David, 147

Hinkley, Eleanor, 21

Hitler, Adolf, 17, 45, 51, 56, 137

Hoellering, George, 65, 107, 141–2

'The Hollow Men' (Eliot), 19, 20–1, 91

Holman, Anna, 119

Hope, Lord John, 219

Hotson, Leslie, 106–7, 177, 209

Hotson, Mary May (Peabody), 106–7, 177, 209

Howe, Irving, 135

Huxley, Aldous, 106, 119, 120, 172, 198–9

Huxley, Julian, 106, 119, 130, 172, 205

Huxley, Juliette, 106, 119, 130, 205

I'll Walk Beside You (Trevelyan), 5, 49–50, 53, 55, 60, 65–6

International Students House, 65, 259, 264–5

Iovetz-Tereshchenko, N. M., 127, 163; widow, 178, 179

Irwin, Robert, 93

Isaacs, Jacob, 89

Jameson, Storm, 33

Janes (handyman and ex-police detective), 128

John, Augustus, 168

Johnson, Hewlett, Dean of Canterbury, 71

Jones, Dai, 42, 43

Jones, Duncan, Dean of Chichester, 130

Julius, Anthony, 124–5

Keynes, John Maynard, 216–17

Keynes, Lydia (Lopokova), 216–17

Kibel, Al and Christine, 262–3

Lanchester, Elsa, 214

Lang, Cosmo, Archbishop, 41–2

Lawrence, D. H., 179, 237–8

Lawrence, Frieda, 237

Le Gallienne, Eva, 158, 159

Leblanc, Maurice, 55

Lehmann, Rosamond, 239, 250

Leighton, Margaret, 163

Lister, Mrs (Faber caretaker), 46

'The Literature of Politics' lecture (Eliot), 201

Little, Mr and Mrs Leon M., 224

Lloyd, Marie, 66–7, 90

Lloyd Webber, Andrew, 214

Lloyd's Bank: Eliot's career, 18–19, 97, 132, 144, 152; Eliot's creative work while working at, 97; Pound's fundraising to release Eliot from, 131, 132, 199–200

London Clinic, Eliot's visits, 127, 175–6, 196–7, 211–12, 220, 234, 245

London Library, 232

Longman's, 49, 65

'The Love Song of J. Alfred Prufrock' (Eliot), 19, 97, 132, 148

Lowell, Amy, 131, 132

Lowell, Percival, 132

Lowell, Robert, 84

Lyceum Club, 198–9

MacCarthy, Desmond, 33, 144

MacDiarmid, Hugh, 168

Mackenzie, Compton, 189, 195

MacLeish, Archibald, 68

Macmillan, Margaret, 119

Macmillan, Rachel, 119

Magnani, Anna, 91

March, Richard, 79

Marciano, Rocky, 162

Margaret, Princess, 39, 213

Marshall, George C., 73

Marx, Groucho, 111–12

Masefield, John, 98

Maung Ohn, 122

Mauriac, François, 204

May, Clarence, 109–10

Mays, Dr Benjamin, 262
Melton, Miss (Eliot's secretary at Faber), 42–3
Melville, Herman, 2
Merton College, Oxford, 41, 128
Millin, Sarah Gertrude, 121–2, 124–5
Mirrlees, Emily Lina, 31
Mirrlees, Hope, 31, 208, 235–6, 244
'Mr. Pugstyles: The Elegant Pig' (Eliot), 69
Mitchison, Naomi, 195
Monro, Alida, 37
Monroe, Harriet, 131, 132
Monteith, Charles, 191
Montgomery, Field Marshal, 58
Moore, Henry, 106
Moore, Irina (Radetsky), 106
Moore, Marianne, 88, 132, 239–40
Morgan, Charles, 103
Morley, Frank, 64
Morrell, Lady Ottoline, 119–20, 172, 237
Morrison, Blake, 260
Morshead, Paquita (Hagemeyer), Lady, 100–1, 130, 164, 168, 258
Morshead, Sir Owen, 100–1, 129–30, 164, 168, 258
Mortimer, Raymond, 79, 252
Mozart: clarinet quintet, 98, 137; Haffner Symphony, 153; Oboe Quartet, 99, 153
Muggeridge, Malcolm, 236
Muir, Edwin, 168, 239
Munich Agreement (1938), 17–18
Munnings, Sir Alfred, 97, 98
Murder in the Cathedral (Eliot): Becket casting, 19, 107, 122, 125, 157, 158, 161–2, 210; direction, 28, 158; Eliot's view of, 70, 130, 142; film, 65, 107, 122, 130, 138, 139, 141–2; first performance, 1, 19; London opening (1935), 19; Old Vic production (1953), 157, 158, 160–2; origins, 19; post-war performances, 71; reviews of film, 141–2; success, 15, 19, 135, 163; televised, 19; translation, 214
Mussolini, Benito, 68, 137

Nasser, Gamal Abdel, 232
'New Moon on Burma' (Trevelyan), 78
Nicholson, Norman, 167–8
Norton, Charles Eliot, 177
Notes Towards the Definition of Culture (Eliot), 9, 78, 79

Old Possum's Book of Practical Cats (Eliot), 23, 28, 161, 214–15, 218
'One-Eyed Riley' (song), 86, 88, 93, 101, 112; see also The Cocktail Party
Oppenheimer, J. Robert, 72, 83
Orwell, George, 79
Osborne House, 181

Peter, John, 148, 235
Pius XII, Pope, 80, 81, 113
'Poe to Valéry' lecture (Eliot), 89, 92, 93, 137
Poetry Book Society, 223
The Pope of Russell Square (Trevelyan), 1, 8–12, 79, 94, 262
Porter, Katherine Anne, 226
Porter, Sarah, 21
Pound, Dorothy (Shakespear), 200
Pound, Ezra: arrest and trial, 67–8; character, 131–2, 199; Eliot's visits to him in hospital, 68, 207, 208; family background, 200; fundraising plan to release Eliot from Lloyd's Bank, 131, 132, 199–200; insanity, 68, 131–2, 199, 200, 208; marriage, 200; political views, 68, 162; published letters, 131, 199; relationship with Eliot, 32, 42, 162
Princeton, Institute of Advanced Study, 83–4
Princeton University, 73, 84, 261

Queen Elizabeth, RMS, 207
Queen Mary, RMS, 225, 226
Quennell, Peter, 147

Raine, Kathleen, 239
Rambert, Marie, 131
Rattigan, Terence, 209

Rawsthorne, Alan, 218
Read, Herbert, 195, 236, 237, 239
Reckitt, Maurice, 38
Rhondda, Margaret Haig Thomas,
Viscountess, 126–7, 132, 149, 212, 241
Richard III, King, 185, 186
Ridler, Anne, 67, 239, 247
Robbins, Rossell Hope, 135
Roberts, Janet (Adam Smith), 149
Roberts, Michael, 149
Robinson, Bill, 17
Rochester, John Wilmot, 2nd Earl of,
63
Rogers, Paul, 163
Rowse, A. L., 4
Rubin, Martin, 125
Russell, Bertrand, 155, 172
Russell, Edith (Finch), 155

Sackville-West, Eddie, 172
St Stephen's Church, Gloucester Road:
burial plot, 171, 228; dedication
Festival, 105; Eliot living in clergy
house, 41; Eliot's position, 40, 41,
123, 159, 233; feast of St Thomas
of Canterbury, 192–4; Mary's
attendance, 40, 105, 107, 121, 190, 201,
233, 256–7; notepaper, 43; requiem,
190; Tenebrae (Night Watch)
service, 71, 93, 159, 201–2, 223; vicar,
107, 229
Sao Shwe Thaik, 78
Sassoon, Siegfried, 120
Schubert: Great C Major Symphony,
156, 213; Trio, 160
Second World War: Allied landings
(1944), 5, 45, 50; Allied troops
in Brussels, 51–4, 53, 55–6, 60–1;
Ardennes offensive, 56; Blitz, 6,
23–4, 27; Brussels liberation, 51;
church attendance, 27; damage and
destruction, 24, 45–6, 58–9, 60, 156;
evacuees, 31; German surrender,
61; internment policy, 24; Mary's
experiences, 5–6, 50–61, 53, 60;
outbreak, 18, 23, 41; Paris after

liberation, 54–5, 61; prisoners of war,
60–1; treatment of wounded, 53–4;
V-1 flying bombs (doodlebugs),
45–6, 51, 56, 58; Wodehouse
broadcasts, 185–6; YMCA convoys
(1944–5), 5–6, 50–1
Selected Prose: T. S. Eliot (ed. John
Hayward), 158, 159
Seyler, Athene, 90
Shamley Green: Eliot's visits, 31, 32,
43, 46–7, 48, 55, 57–8, 62; Mirrlees
household, 31, 240
Shaw, George Bernard (G.B.S.), 129,
135, 137
Sherek, Henry, 99, 167, 178
Siegel, Lee, 111–12
Simenon, Georges, 55, 108, 136, 156, 176
Simpson, Eileen, 84–5
Singh, Sarwan, 96
Sitwell, Edith, 64, 79, 98, 105, 132, 147,
239
Sitwell, Osbert, 105, 147
Smart, John, 64
Smith, Charlotte (Eliot's sister), 211,
261
Smith, George Lawrence, 211
Smith, 'Shardy' (Charlotte, Eliot's
niece), see Talcott
Smith, Theodora (Eliot's niece), 211
'The Social Function of Poetry' lecture
(Eliot), 61
Somerset, Vere, 183, 184
'A Song for Simeon' (Eliot), 213, 214
Speaight, Robert, 19, 125, 146, 161
Spender, Stephen, 74, 79, 104, 223, 239,
261
Stadlen, Peter, 24
Stanley, Jacqueline, 31
Starkie, Enid, 195, 223–4
Stead, William Force, 183
Stokes, Ann, 61
Strachey, Lytton, 120, 179
Streeter, Canon B. H., 183, 184
Strong, Thomas Banks, Bishop, 183
Student Christian Movement (SCM),
2, 6–7, 15, 24, 40, 61

Student Movement House: bomb
damage, 24; location, 6, 7, 17, 23;
Mary's account of (*From the Ends
of the Earth*), 27, 33–5; Mary's career,
5, 6, 7–8, 17, 27, 48, 61, 65; Mary's
relationship with students, 7–8,
10; nativity play, 25, 38; royal visit,
39; students, 7–8, *18, 25*; wartime
restrictions, 23, 24
Suez Crisis (1956), 232–3, 239
Swan, Miss (receptionist at Faber), 42,
43, 244

Talcott, Agnew Allen (husband of
'Shardy', father of Priscilla), 211
Talcott, Priscilla Stearns (Eliot's great-
niece, later Talcott Spahn), 1–2,
210–11
Talcott, 'Shardy' (Charlotte Smith,
Eliot's niece), 211
Tambimuttu, Meary James Thurairajah
(X), 30–1, 78, 79
Temple, William, Archbishop, 41–2
Tennyson, Alfred, Lord, 98, 179, 229
Tennyson Monument, Isle of Wight,
10, 181, *182*
Tereshchenko, *see* Iovetz-Tereshchenko
Thomas of Canterbury, St (Becket),
192–4
Thompson, George, 137
Thorndike, Sybil, 66–7
Tin Tut, U, 78
Townsend, Group Captain Peter, 213
Trevelyan, George Macaulay (G.M.T.,
uncle), 3–4, 125
Trevelyan, Humphrey (brother, later
Baron Trevelyan): career, 3, 232–3,
243, 263, 264; meetings with Eliot,
163, 218
Trevelyan, Mary: appearance, 3, 4, *14,
39*; attitude to homosexuality, 148,
154; attitude to race and colour, 8,
16–17, 75; awareness of Emily Hale's
significance to Eliot, 22, 87, 116,
120, 143, 164, 167, 169, 248; British
Council lecture tour, 174–5; car

(Wolseley), 202–3, 205, 206, 207,
215, 216, 223, 238, 255; career, 1, 5–7,
27–8, 33–5, 65, 72, 174–5, 240–2, 261–5;
character, 1, 3, 4, 5–8, 15, 88, 242, 261,
265; character of Julia in *The Cocktail
Party*, 88, 101, 118, 218, 254; cooking,
4, 123, 124, 126, 143, 147, 156, 187, 221,
223, 225, 265; crossword puzzles,
178, 183, 223; death, 264, 259; end of
relationship with Eliot, 249–50, 253–
4, 255–8, 265; family background,
3–4; final correspondence with
Eliot, 255–8; first meeting with
Eliot, 2, 19–20; flat in Brunswick
Square, 89, 153–4; flat in Chelsea,
153, 154, 155; friendship with Eliot,
1–2, 8–9, 19, 26, 82–3, 87, 140, 265;
gifts to Eliot, 38, 44, 48, 55, 59, 66,
67, 70, 132–3, 134, 136, 189, 195; gin-
drinking, 4, 93, 101, 105, 113, 142, 148,
170, 179, 265; Goats' Club, 240–2,
264; grave, 171; health, 10, 75, 122–3,
133, 155, 172, 175, 181, 196, 217, 238;
honours (OBE, CBE), 221, 264;
journey into liberated Netherlands
and Germany, 58–9, *60*; letters from
Eliot, 8–9, 10–11, 31, 43; literary
advice from Eliot, 49, 65–6; mother,
6, 47, 57–8, 74, 104, 121, 180, 250;
musicianship, 4–5, 19, 133–4; 'next of
kin' to Eliot for medical purposes,
220, 222, 224, 227–8, 231, 234; notes
from Eliot on her car window, 133;
office, 30, 39, 61, 91, 154, 164, 177, 178,
188, 221; Paris visits after liberation,
54–5, 61; piano-playing, 4–5, 86, 89,
117, 133–4, 161, 233, 265; published
works, 5, 7, 27, 33–5, *34*, 49–50, 65–6,
78; reaction to *The Confidential
Clerk*, 187–8; relationship with Eliot,
2, 9–11, 30–1, 47–8, 87–9, 92–3, 94–8,
113–18, 121, 122, 123, 140, 145–6, 150–1,
158, 163–4, 168, 170–1, 186–7, 188–9,
232, 238–9, 265; relationship with
John Hayward, 114, 143, 146, 150, 197,
203; religion, 27, 32, 40–2, 72, 93, 105,

159–60, 206–7; smoking, 2, 4, 127, 137, 139, 190, 210; travels, 5, 7, 15–17, 74, 76, 173, 174–5, 261–4; UNESCO work in Paris, 72, 74, 83; UNESCO work in Burma, 75, 76, 77–8; usefulness to Eliot, 108, 260; wartime work in Belgium with Allied troops, 5–6, 48, 50–4, 53, 55–6, 57–8, 60–1; writing, 4, 78, 174

Trevelyan, Peggy (sister-in-law), 242
Trevelyan family, 3–4
Truman, Harry S., 73
Turpin, Randy, 147
Tynan, Kenneth, 153

UNESCO, 54, 72, 75, 77–8, 83

'The Value and Use of Cathedrals in England Today' lecture (Eliot), 130
van Baaren, Kees, 91
'The Varieties of Metaphysical Poetry' (Eliot's Clark Lectures), 63
Verdenal, Jean, 148, 235

Walcott, Jersey Joe, 162
Wall, Bernard, 42, 43
'The Waste Land' (Eliot): Eliot's readings, 20; *Essays in Criticism* article, 148–9; impression on young people, 18, 30; origins, 36, 37–8, 199;

publication, 19, 23; recordings, 146; Spender's judgement of, 261
Watson, Robert, 242
Watson, Wilfred, 196
Wavell, Lady, 238
Webster, Noah, 2
Welch, Dr James, 30
'What is a Classic?' lecture (Eliot), 58
Whistler, James Abbott McNeill, 189
Wilcox, Ella Wheeler, 110
Wilde, Oscar, 189
Williams, Charles, 105
Williams, Emlyn, 147–8
Willink, Sir Henry, 125–6
Windsor, Duke and Duchess of, 109
Windsor Castle, 100–1, 129–30, 164, 168
Wodehouse, P. G., 185–6
Woolf, Leonard, 41, 217
Woolf, Virginia, 21, 36, 120, 217
Worth, Irene, 100, 101, 233

YMCA: Brussels facilities for released prisoners of war, 60–1; European convoys (1944–45), 5–6, 50; 'hostel' for Allied troops in Belgium, 48, 52, 53; Mary's work, 5–6, 48–56, 60–1; Nijmegen base, 58–9
Yonge, Charlotte, 176–7

Zampa, Luigi, 91

PHOTOGRAPH CREDITS

With the exception of those listed below, all photographs are included with the kind permission of the Estate of Mary Trevelyan:

page 14: Elliott & Fry © National Portrait Gallery, London.
page 34: Courtesy of Faber & Faber.
page 138: Copyright of the Estate of Peter Strausfeld.
page 226: By permission of ESI Media.